Advance Praise for
Bold Move

"**A good read for anyone looking for tangible, science-driven strategies** to help them overcome life's challenges and live a life with purpose."

—Kenneth Cole, founder of the Mental Health Coalition

"Running a fast-growing tech startup can create stress and anxiety, especially when having an underlying mental health issue. Luana has helped guide me on a path out of anxiety, and **this book is an amazing companion** on that journey."

—Paul English, founder of Kayak.com and the Bipolar Social Club

"It's hard to imagine a person who would not benefit from reading this honest and accessible book. Dr. Luana levels the playing field by speaking as both **an expert in the field** and as someone who has danced with suffering and learned to lead. Her attention to illustrating how CBT can lead to **a more fulfilling and valued life** across a broad range of human experiences is **remarkable**, as is her faith in the potential for change within all of us."

—Corinne Cather, PhD, director of Massachusetts General Hospital Center of Excellence for Psychosocial and Systemic Research and associate professor of psychology at Harvard Medical School

"Dr. Luana has **a unique talent** for distilling evidence-based mental health interventions into **everyday life lessons and valuable skills** that any reader can apply to help achieve their personal goals."

—Alex S. Keuroghlian, MD, MPH, associate professor of psychiatry at Harvard Medical School and director of the Division of Education and Training at The Fenway Institute

"Dr. Luana is a refreshing voice in personal growth, walking the journey of building a bold life with you. Her words encourage, **her vulnerability inspires, and her cutting-edge tools work.** *Bold Move* is a must read!"

—Jenni Schaefer, author of *Goodbye Ed, Hello Me: Recover from Your Eating Disorder and Fall in Love with Life*

"Dr. Luana takes evidenced-based approaches to reducing anxiety and makes them **doable, palpable, and compelling** to read. . . . I highly recommend this book to those who suffer from anxiety and/or are avoiding what they know they need to do."

—Steven A. Safren, PhD, ABPP, professor of psychology, University of Miami

"Dr. Luana [invites] us to . . . become our best selves through mobilizing courage, developing (and tolerating) introspection, mastering new skills, and grounding these in deliberative, active alignment with our core values. Her voice is personal, engaging, and seemingly casual, as **she brilliantly interweaves science with clinical expertise.** . . . This is a remarkable book."

—Derri Shtasel, MD, MPH, associate professor, Harvard Medical School

"Dr. Luana's memorable analogies, real-life examples, visuals, and prompts make **building new habits totally attainable (and fun!).** As someone who struggles with anxiety and works adjacent to the mental health industry, I would highly recommend *Bold Move* to anyone seeking a better understanding of their emotions . . . as well as any mental health professionals . . . an insightful, witty, and resonant read!"

—Delanie Fischer, cohost of the *Self-Helpless* podcast and business consultant for mental health professionals

"**Reading *Bold Move* is like having a conversation with your smartest, most relatable friend**—who also happens to be an Ivy League clinical psychologist. Dr. Luana shares practical, relatable tools, backed by science, that will move you toward the life you want to live."

—Torrey A. Creed, PhD, associate professor of psychology in psychiatry, Perelman School of Medicine, University of Pennsylvania

BOLD MOVE

A 3-Step Plan to Transform Anxiety into Power

DR. LUANA MARQUES

HARPERONE
An Imprint of HarperCollins*Publishers*

The names and identifying details of some individuals discussed in this book have been changed to protect their privacy.

 For information, address HarperCollins Publishers, 195 Broadway, New York, NY 10007.

HarperCollins books may be purchased for educational, business, or sales promotional use. For information, please email the Special Markets Department at SPsales@harpercollins.com.

FIRST EDITION

Designed by Ralph Fowler
Brain image © Blamb/Shutterstock
Person walking © Ian Lesogor/Shutterstock
Person thinking © Leremy/Shutterstock
Person with arms up © T and Z/Shutterstock
Buttons © Kindlena/Shutterstock

Library of Congress Cataloging-in-Publication Data has been applied for.

ISBN 978-0-06-327701-4

23 24 25 26 27 LBC 5 4 3 2 1

To my loves David and Diego.

You keep me anchored through
the choppy waters of life.

Contents

PART IV
Align

PART V
Conclusion

Introduction

Am I Enough?

There is a huge irony in my writing a book about being bold, perhaps an irony that only I can appreciate. When I told my friends I was writing a book about tools that would allow people to live boldly, they exclaimed excitedly: "This book must be written because it *defines* you." The irony is that although most of my close friends and colleagues would describe me as capital B **Bold**, I have often felt (and still do feel) scared, anxious, and vulnerable when faced with significant challenges.

As an adult, I know that these fears are partly a product of my childhood in Brazil, where so much of my emotional energy was spent trying to keep my parents together, doing whatever I could to minimize the fighting, end the arguments, and maintain the illusion that the world—*my world*—was safe. Yet I felt as if I had failed big-time: my father left us when I was ten years old, and that was the end of any sense of stability and certainty. In retrospect, my father leaving was a blessing in disguise, but I never met any ten-year-old who gleefully said to herself, "Yeah, my parents are divorced, my mom has to work all the time to feed us, and no matter how hard she tries, at times we end up sharing a single potato for dinner."

And so, as a young girl, what I actually said to myself was, "I am not enough." Not those words exactly, but when I look back on that period of life now as an adult and a clinician, I know that would be the rough psychological translation. I did all I could to try to prove that I was enough. *Should I do the dishes? Study harder? Protect my sister? Watch out for my mom?* The anxious thoughts and feelings were endless. No matter how hard I tried, I often felt so overwhelmed that I would eat my emotions in the form of a big bag of cookies, which ultimately left me feeling like a failure.

To make matters worse, when my mom caught me with said cookies, she would invariably put me on a diet, further proving to me that I was indeed not enough. It was a vicious cycle. In retrospect, I realize she was concerned about my health, much as I am for my own son's health today. But damn, it hurts when someone's way of telling you that they love you is to take away your cookies! At the time, I was hurt and confused. Why was she taking away the only thing that made me feel better in the moment? But, as is always the case, both my mom and I were doing the best we could with the tools we had at the time. Unfortunately, the tool kit we shared was rudimentary. Fortunately for you, the tools I'm about to share are more sophisticated and are supported by hundreds of scientific studies and lessons I've learned through decades of my work.

I suspect my friends see me as bold because I overcame poverty, adversity, and trauma to get to where I am today—an associate professor of psychology at Harvard Medical School (HMS) and the director of the Community Psychiatry Program for Research in Implementation and Dissemination of Evidence-Based Treatments (PRIDE) research lab at the Massachusetts General Hospital (MGH) in Boston. Perhaps my *journey* has been bold, but what my friends don't see is that even today I have feelings of not being enough. So how did I manage to go from poverty to Harvard to becoming a published author?

I credit this seemingly miraculous narrative to three factors: my mom, my grandmother, and science. My mom is a fighter, and to this day she continues to work hard to overcome whatever challenges she may face. As a single mom, she fought tooth and nail to feed us and give us the possibility of a better future. Today, I credit my mom with teaching me that no matter how I feel, the only path forward is *through* my emotions. She showed me that I could do the hard things regardless of the emotions I felt. Later in graduate school, I learned that this kind of behavior—*through*, not *around*—is at the very core of a concept called emotion regulation,[1] which teaches us that experiencing our emotions is better than avoiding them.

The woman I came to think of as my grandmother entered my life when I was twelve, when my mom was dating my stepfather. When I was young, she pushed me out of my comfort zone to ensure that my fears didn't hold me back from pursuing my dreams. Most of the lessons my grandmother taught me can be summarized into two broad concepts: 1) Approach; don't avoid (see part III of this book) and 2) Be the water, not the rock (see the Conclusion).

Equipped with my childhood lessons, I came to the United States to pursue the American dream—first as an exchange student and then for higher education. After my doctoral degree, I immersed myself in what is known as cognitive behavioral therapy (CBT): the gold-standard therapy for mental health challenges.[2] I read every published therapy protocol, studied how to deliver treatments in individual and group sessions, researched treatments for different disorders and diverse populations, and was mentored by the world's leading mental health experts. My early days at HMS/MGH were incredibly valuable and helped me synthesize the science that I now share with you, but they were not sufficient.

It was only when I moved into real-life settings and worked with diverse communities that I truly learned to distill what it takes to become bold. It's one thing to talk about CBT within the walls of the ivory tower (i.e., Harvard) and quite another to teach it to someone when they are facing deportation, prison, poverty, single parenthood, and a variety of real-world situations. And it is yet another thing to apply these concepts to the high-powered executive in the C-suite, whose marriage is about to end while she is leading her team through a major transition. Once my work evolved to address these challenges, I was finally able to integrate the wisdom of my mom and grandmother with evidence-based science, into a method that fits everyone all the time, instead of just some people some of the time.

Bold Move is a set of skills, supported by science and infused with lessons from my life, that I created to help anyone overcome obstacles and live their best life. The three skills shared within this book—*Shift*, *Approach*, and *Align*, will equip you to make bold moves when it matters most. Yet, as you embark on the journey of becoming bold, you will encounter bumps. After all, to live boldly does not mean to live fearlessly or recklessly, but to face life's challenges without being paralyzed by psychological avoidance, the real enemy that most of us face. I invite you to join me in becoming bold and living a "comfortably uncomfortable" life. I am humbled to be where I am today and sincerely hope that by the end of this book, you will have discovered your own recipe for becoming bold.

PART I

The Stuff That Keeps Us Stuck

Chapter One

Anxiety Is Painful but It Is *Not* What Is Keeping You Stuck

Being human is hard. Sometimes it feels like we can't even catch our breath before we're pummeled with a new difficulty to address: impossible quotas at work, unexpected bills, a child struggling in school, a family health crisis, the same fights with our partners. All these things can make us want to just numb out at the end of a hard day. We all have our favorite ways to zone out. But would you say you're satisfied with your life? Are you living your best, most authentic life? Do you even remember what your dreams are? Or does the thought of living a bold, fulfilling life sound impossible—and maybe even exhausting, anxiety-producing, and overwhelming?

In moments of high anxiety, we often feel stuck. We get stuck in unhealthy relationships and in draining jobs. Some mornings we get stuck in bed, trying to find a reason to get up. And some nights we get stuck at home, binge-watching TV shows or scrolling on our phones instead of going out into the world. We all have moments when we feel trapped, and in those moments, we often feel as if we are skating on thin ice and that just a little extra weight will send us crashing into freezing-cold water of unimaginable depths.

In these moments, being bold—living your best, most authentic life—can feel like a far-fetched dream. Who has the time or energy? We may believe boldness is a personality trait possessed by young people—those without piles of stress and responsibilities—or those with greater advantages, fewer problems, and more money to burn. But not us. Or we hear the term *bold*, and we think of people like Martin Luther King Jr., CEOs, or professional athletes—individuals with influence and the courage and confidence we don't have. But what if boldness isn't reserved for a lucky few with advantages, talents, or certain personalities? What if it is meant for us all?

Bold Move: A 3-Step Plan to Transform Anxiety into Power will help you get unstuck so that you can start making moves toward the things you care about—*your* unique bold moves—despite discomfort or obstacles. In moments of stress and anxiety, you can rely on the three skills I present in this book to help you face whatever is preventing you from the life you want: your bold life. A bold life is a life in which you are showing up, fully, as you.

So, if you picked up this book, curious about becoming bold but wearily facing the ongoing challenges of life, you're not alone. That is exactly where I was early in my life before I learned the skills that I will share with you.

Growing up in Governador Valadares, Brazil, in a family where chaos was the only constant, I often felt like there was no way out for me. My parents were and are incredible people, but they had my sister and me young without many resources and were not equipped to emotionally manage themselves and two children. The lack of financial stability combined with drugs and alcohol often resulted in painful shouting matches and, at times, quite violent fights between them. As the oldest child in the family, I did what I could to protect my sister, which often left me scared. Whenever I sensed danger, even when it was not actually present, I would get so anxious that I felt like I had to do something to make myself feel better. So, as a child, I managed by eating my emotions, literally. I devoured box after box of cookies whenever life felt like it was too much. But sometimes snacks weren't enough, and my anxiety manifested physically. On more than one occasion, I was rushed to the hospital, suffering from a terrible "asthma attack." Now, as an adult and a psychologist, I have come to realize that I was having panic attacks, not asthma attacks. But back then, I had no vocabulary to express my fear, and all I felt was that I couldn't breathe. *So, if anyone told the ten-year-old me that I would one day help others become bold, I would have laughed!*

Our lives became even more challenging once my father was out of the picture. Money was scarce, and we had no safety net. Don't get me wrong; we weren't the worst off in the country. But my mom had to keep finding ways to reinvent herself in order to feed us. Picture it: a newly single young mother in an already precarious situation suddenly tasked with feeding, clothing, and educating two daughters entirely on her own. She went from selling hangers and brooms to making industrial uniforms, trying anything and everything to put food on the table. She could have let the stress and anxiety overwhelm her and freeze her in place, but she knew that was not an option. So she took one step forward. And then another. And another. At that time, unlike my mom, all I wanted to do was put on the TV and zone out because life felt too difficult.

Yet, watching my mom thrive despite all odds, I began to understand what it takes to move toward discomfort, to accept its presence, to make it your best friend instead of being paralyzed by it. Though it didn't happen overnight, the skills I learned in my childhood enabled me, a shy child living in an economically challenging situation in South America, to earn a PhD in clinical psychology and to secure a job at Harvard Medical School (HMS) and the Massachusetts General Hospital (MGH), where I currently work.

Although my story might seem like a very specific kind of hero's journey, it was not without its many ups and downs, and at each of these crossroads, I would wonder: *Can I keep going? Can I choose being bold instead of remaining stuck in fear?* I imagine that you might also have found yourself in similar situations, where your brain demands, *Hide under the covers*, and yet life begs you to keep going. No matter what your circumstances may be, this book was written with the intention of helping you move forward, toward the life you want. Some of you might find yourself worrying about how to pay the bills, while others might be dealing with the health issues of a loved one or how to help your child who is struggling in school. Some of you might be considering a career change or contemplating retirement, while others might be facing the end of an important relationship and figuring out how to reinvent yourself in its aftermath. Some might have just landed in a new country in pursuit of a better life, while others are only dreaming of such an opportunity. Challenges—big and small, obvious and nuanced—can leave us feeling weary, afraid, lonely, sad, anxious, overwhelmed, and just plain stuck. If any of this resonates with you, you might be wondering the same things my clients often ask me: *How do I get rid of my anxiety? Why am I so stuck? How do I get out of this rut? Why doesn't this sadness go away? Is it really possible to become bold?*

Hey Doc, Please Make My Anxiety Disappear

This is just what Jake, the CEO of a Fortune 500 company, asked me in our first meeting. If you were to meet him on the street, you would never know that he had grown up with very little, because all you would see is a sharp, handsome white-collar worker with perfect manners, eloquence, a pressed Armani suit, and an air of confidence that you could spot a mile away. In short, to all the world, Jake was crushing it. Yet here he was in my office, describing his crippling feelings of anxiety. He had always been a somewhat anxious person, but lately his anxiety had felt unbearable. As I sat across from him, he leaned forward and, in the same manner one might expect him to deliver a mandate to his employees, said to me: "Doctor Luana, I hear you're the best, so you need to make this anxiety disappear. I can't think straight, and I need to fix this so I can focus on strategic planning for next year."

We started simple. "What is this anxiety like?" I asked him.

"Like I'm about to explode!"

"Explode? Really?"

"Yes! Explode!" His tone surprised me and stood in stark contrast to his polished image. He continued. "I'm surprised I haven't combusted yet. My heart pounds, I feel dizzy, it's hard to focus, the world closes in . . . all at the same time. I feel like I'm about to have a heart attack. But I have had my heart checked a million times, and there is nothing wrong with it."

"How do you manage these nearly combustive moments?" I asked.

"I do whatever it takes to make myself feel better. At work, I cancel meetings or have my COO run them, telling people I have another important meeting with an investor."

Jake looked ashamed and small, all of that hard-won confidence gone without a trace. In a quieter voice he told me, "I lie, but I just don't know what else to do in that moment. When I get home, I'm often so drained by anxiety that I've just stopped exercising altogether. I try not to have that glass of wine, but honestly, I don't last past 8 p.m., and by the second glass, I feel so much better. Then I'll spend hours in front of the computer, working."

He paused. "Well, I tell myself I'm working, but I'm really just staring at the computer, zoned out, drinking to drown my anxiety. Then I eventually fall asleep and wake up even more anxious than the day before. This is too much! I'm telling you, you need to get rid of this anxiety. I can't stand it anymore!"

Jake understood—correctly—that he was at a breaking point, but he misunderstood the reasons why. If I magically took away Jake's anxiety, he believed he would be fine and would be able to engage with his work without a problem. To some extent he is correct: a lot of unpleasant emotions (anxiety, fear, sadness) will paralyze us and keep us stuck. But would Jake be better off if all of his anxiety disappeared? He would likely be able to focus more on work. But would he be concerned enough about his wife's safety to remember to have the car's brakes checked? Or would he have the motivation to put in extra hours to prepare for a big business pitch? Maybe not. Unpleasant emotions are like pain receptors, which are designed to alert us to things that could be harmful or dangerous, like touching a hot stove, and without them we would get burned. So, although painful, anxiety itself can be adaptive and signal something important to us.

Don't Be Fooled by the Fever—Look for the Infection

Jake is not alone. In fact, everyone I have met in my career wants to get unstuck and live a fuller, healthier, and bolder life. Yet, in their attempts to get unstuck, I find that my clients are looking in the wrong places (just like I did before I knew the skills in this book). Often, clients want me to get rid of their anxiety, stress, burnout, sadness, fear, or hopelessness. However, while these emotions are painful, they are most often a symptom and not the root cause of our challenges.

Let me put this differently. Imagine that you developed a high fever, and to address it you took Tylenol. Would your fever come down? Very likely. But how long would it stay down? That would depend on what your body is fighting. If you have a mild cold, Tylenol would help and you might be all set after a few days. However, if you have a bacterial infection, Tylenol would bring the fever down yet not cure the infection. Instead, you might need a different class of medication, such as an antibiotic. The Tylenol would only address a symptom (fever) without curing the underlying problem (infection).

So, when Jake said to me, "Doctor Luana, I hear you're the best, so you need to make this anxiety disappear," I understood that he had a high fever in the form of anxiety, but I also knew from years of research and clinical care that his anxiety was likely not the root cause of his infection.

Anxiety is only one of the fevers that my clients report. Often, I also hear things like the following:

- "If I could just bring my stress down, I would be successful."
- "It's the burnout that's killing me. I just need to be able to schedule things better to feel better."
- "My boss is the real problem. If he just listened to me, I would not be so stuck."
- "I can't seem to do anything productive when I get home. All I want to do is watch TV or scroll through my phone."
- "If my husband hadn't lived at the office, our marriage would not have ended."
- "My online shopping is out of control, but I can't seem to stop. I'm scared to see my credit card statement."

Stress, burnout, difficulty concentrating, marital distress, financial worry—these are real, painful experiences, but what is leading to these problems?

The question remains: What is the root cause of our infection? What I have learned throughout my life, clinical work, and research is that there is one common denominator that tends to get all of us stuck, and that is what I call *psychological avoidance*.

Our Enemy Has a Name: Meet Psychological Avoidance

Psychological avoidance is any response to a perceived threat that brings immediate emotional relief but comes with long-term negative consequences. For the sake of simplicity, I will refer to this concept as "avoidance" in this book (buckle up: you're going to be seeing this term a lot in the pages ahead). Put simply, avoidance gives us fast but temporary relief from discomfort but keeps us stuck in the long run. Imagine that you had an internal thermometer that measures your discomfort in real time, reading from zero (cool, calm, and collected) to one hundred (feeling like you are about to explode from anxiety, fear, or stress). The hotter the temperature gets, the more you want to bring it down—the more you want to *avoid*. After all, who wants to feel uncomfortable?

Throughout my career, I have found it challenging for my clients to understand that avoidance is our figurative infection, because often discomfort itself (e.g., anxiety, stress, sadness, burnout) feels like the primary problem. Remove the discomfort and life would immediately get better—seems straightforward enough. Yet, the problem is not the discomfort itself but *how* we respond to that discomfort.

Psychological avoidance has a real long-term cost because it will always rob you of the chance to live a bold life and prevent you from reaching your goals. Once you start to avoid, you need to keep avoiding again and again to push away the discomfort that, like a villain in a horror movie, just won't stop coming at you. By avoiding, we are teaching our brains that the only way we can manage challenging situations is by running away instead of facing them, which reinforces our need to avoid. We've all experienced discomfort before and will surely experience it again. Each time you avoid, you will feel a bit better, but *feeling* better and *being* better aren't the same thing!

For Jake, it was what he did when he felt anxious that got him stuck, not the anxiety itself. Whenever his heart started to pound, he would get rid of his discomfort by avoiding (i.e., canceling meetings or grabbing a glass of wine). Each time he avoided, he felt some relief. His heartbeat returned to normal, and he could get on with his day.

Jake's actions make sense: Who wants to walk around feeling like they are having a heart attack? But he was stuck in an endless cycle of avoidance—and avoidance is powerful because, by definition, it works! It does make you feel better really fast. In a way, avoidance is a bit of a drug because once you taste it and its effects, you can easily become hooked.

By the time I met Jake, he had found himself at a real crossroads, and many parts of his life were suffering. At work, Jake's COO was frustrated that he was not present, did not engage, and seemed to be checked out, and—worst yet—that she was having to do the work for him. At home, Jake's wife began to be concerned about his drinking, lack of exercise, and disengagement from the children. She urged him to seek help; otherwise, she was not going to stick around. Jake's mother had gotten angry—not understanding his avoidance, she assumed he was not coming to family dinners because he was prioritizing work, which infuriated her. Over time, as it did with Jake, the infection of avoidance will contaminate all domains of our lives.

The Creative Ways We Avoid: The Discomfort of Dating

Dating can be a little scary (let's be honest, it has scared all of us at one time or another), and as such it is a domain of our lives where avoidance often shows up. For me dating was painful because it hit my fear of "not being enough." So what did I do? Yep: I avoided. For a while, I just didn't go on dates, but then my friends intervened and created a dating profile for me on a popular online dating service. Although they were well intentioned, my avoidance was smarter than they were because I just never opened the app. Why look and discover what I knew all along: that no one wanted to go out with me? In the short term, not looking at the app made me feel better, but after months of avoidance it became clear to me that this was not a helpful way to behave if I ever wanted to have a family (which I desperately did). Thankfully, I have a lot of smart psychologist friends who encouraged me to overcome my avoidance (using the skills I will share with you in this book), and eventually I met my now-husband, David.

While my dating avoidance tactic may have been one of the more obvious ones, I have worked with a lot of clients who have had more nuanced ways to minimize their discomfort while dating. For example, Juan was afraid that no one would really love him and did just the opposite of what I did to minimize his discomfort. Instead of completely avoiding dating, he went on a million dates. But wait, how is *that* avoidance? Good question! Juan asked me the same thing when we started working together. Let's dissect Juan's dating patterns to understand whether or not his methods were indeed avoidance.

Juan enjoyed meeting new people, so he would schedule dates with a lot of interesting women. Because the dates were fun, Juan would schedule many in a row, sometimes even two on the same night. One result of his crowded dance card was that he often could not schedule a second date with a woman until weeks later, by which point the woman in question had often moved on. In essence, Juan only went on first dates—a lot of them. Yes, he was dating, but he was so terrified of rejection that he would only go on these first dates. In the aftermath of a date, he would feel momentarily better, but quickly his fears that no one would love him would return, and to feel better he would go on another date to try to ignore his fears. Although this avoidance tactic had worked for him in his twenties, by the time we met in his early thirties he still hadn't maintained a long-term relationship, despite that being something he really wanted. He found himself stuck in the mud of avoidance.

Viviane had just come out, and she told me she was puzzled because she had gone on a lot of dates with other women, yet nothing seemed to stick. When I asked Viviane about these dates, she sheepishly told me that she went on dates only with women she didn't find attractive. At first, I was puzzled. Isn't attraction part of falling in love? Yes, she assured me, but she was terrified that her dates would not find her attractive, so instead of dating women to test her fears, she would purposely sabotage any chance for these dates to lead to anything more. In her mind, she was protecting herself from hurt by going on dates with women she was not attracted to. While this did lessen her discomfort around dating (momentarily), her avoidance tactic would inevitably result in either a relationship that was not satisfying to her or no relationship at all.

Juan, Viviane, and I were all stuck in avoidance, each one of us responding differently to our discomfort around dating. Although *what* each one of us did was different, *why* we were carrying out these actions was the same. We were all trying to minimize our anxiety. And we all paid the price: none of us got the stable, loving relationship we wanted.

Avoidance to You Isn't Always Avoidance to Another

Now, if you're trying to pinpoint the avoidance in your life, you might be questioning whether deleting your dating profile or filling your calendar with dates is avoidance. And it may be, but it also may not be. For example, Mira, a close friend of mine, is young and primarily focused on her career. She loves dating and often goes on amazing dates. In fact, she recently flew to Mexico with someone she had met only a few weeks before and had a great time. But Mira is very clear with the men she meets: her career comes first, and that is what she wants to focus on. Mira is not avoiding dating or being in a committed relationship; she has just decided to prioritize her work life. She often tells me this will change in her thirties, and while time will tell whether it does or not, at least currently it is clear to me that there is no long-term consequence associated with how she is engaging with her dating life.

Let me share with you another example that often plays out in my own home to illustrate how the same action can be avoidance for some but not others. As you learned, from an early age, I managed my stress, anxiety, and fear—especially in moments of high intensity—by eating cookies. For me, when I eat a cookie, I feel slightly better. So, the next time I am stressed, what do I want to do? You guessed it—eat cookies. If you have ever engaged in any emotional eating, you know what I am talking about: anxiety goes up, you start to feel distress, and certain foods come to the rescue.

But listen: if you are eating a cookie while reading this chapter, don't worry. Eating a cookie is not always a form of psychological avoidance, as my husband David is fond of saying. If he could, David would have a cookie every hour on the hour, because he loves sweets. He'll finish his dessert and our son's any day of the week, and yet he never comes down to the kitchen to get a cookie when he is anxious or scared. Cookies for David are not a form of relief for his discomfort; they're just something he loves.

I'm eating a cookie to feel better fast, while David is eating one just because it's something he likes. Yet, eating for emotional comfort is not sufficient to define my behavior as avoidance. There is a second part to this equation that is essential: What is the price tag (or long-term consequence) of engaging in this behavior? For something to be considered avoidance, it *must* be associated with a long-term cost, something that keeps you stuck. For me, eating a cookie to numb my anxiety as a child and now as an adult has led to a lifelong battle with obesity—in fact, I am forty pounds overweight as I write this book. This has never been the case for David, who often fights to keep his weight up.

The reality is that all our avoidance tactics are unique to us, and regardless of how creative, interesting, or seemingly helpful they might be, they always keep us stuck. So, to be able to overcome avoidance, we must first learn what it looks like in ourselves. Think about a time in the past month when you felt uncomfortable. At that time, did you do anything to try to feel better fast? If so, did you:

- Reach for a drink?
- Pull the covers over your head?
- Use drugs?
- Make a lame excuse to stay home instead of going on that date?
- Refuse to speak in class?
- Pass on an opportunity to get a promotion to avoid giving a presentation?
- Walk away from your partner to avoid a difficult conversation?
- Delete a friend's texts instead of responding?
- Let your email pile up because you were too overwhelmed?
- Pull out your phone and mindlessly scroll?
- Purchase something online?

Although our avoidance tactics might come easily to all of us, they are not without a cost.

The Prices We Pay

The prices we pay for avoiding are as unique as we are—relationships crumble, dreams are pushed aside, health declines, work performance dwindles. And, unfortunately, as I see with my clients, the prices are usually high. Meena, paralyzed by the fear of flying, turned down a promotion that would require her to fly regularly. Sawyer spent his entire life avoiding sadness by devoting hours to the latest health trend (ice baths, ultramarathons, intermittent fasting—you name it). Eventually, though, his quest to remove the sadness in his life left little room for a stable job or the deep relationships that he desperately wanted. Rogério, a high-powered executive, was on the verge of a "nervous breakdown" because he was working himself ragged just to avoid the thoughts that crept into his mind each time he slowed down: "I'm too slow," "I won't ever be successful," "I am not enough."

Across all these examples, we are each trying our best to minimize discomfort and anxiety, but these reactions have a real cost. The price we pay is what makes avoidance the real enemy that gets in the way of the life we want.

If Psychological Avoidance Is the Real Enemy, Why Do I Keep Avoiding?

Now, this is the part of the book where you expect me to tell you that all avoidance is inherently bad and to equip you with skills to get rid of it completely: nope. After all, there are many things in life that are helpful (and healthy) to avoid, such as hungry sharks, painfully loud noises, and poisonous snakes. In fact, avoidance is largely a result of our amazing evolutionary brain trying to protect us.

Our brains are complex machines that are comprised of many small regions. These regions communicate with one another through a system of networks.[1] Signals within these networks are responsible for everything we do—eating, breathing, sleeping, remembering, dreaming, thinking, and moving our bodies. But above all, the networks in our brains are programmed to keep us safe, by detecting danger, predicting possible (especially negative) outcomes, and learning what does and does not work in various situations.[2] Sounds like a pretty demanding list of responsibilities, right? And it is.

Since we are focusing on the emergence of our enemy—*psychological avoidance*—in the face of discomfort, let's look specifically at emotion processing. Emotion processing is a complex mental action that involves many different stages and brain regions.[3] The first stage is perception: when your brain senses the presence of a stimulus (potentially a dangerous one) in your environment. For example, the image of your surroundings captured by your eyes sends a signal to the back of the brain, a region called the occipital lobe, to be processed. Similarly, sounds entering your ear are sent to the temporal lobe. These sensory processing areas then send information to brain regions responsible for recognizing and responding to the environment.

One of the main regions responsible for responding to the environment is the amygdala (see figure 1). The amygdala sits deep in the middle of your brain and is heavily involved in emotion processing.[4] The second you are face-to-face with a threat, like a poisonous snake, your amygdala jumps into action and sends signals throughout your body to protect you at all costs. Within milliseconds, and without a conscious thought, the amygdala sends signals that initiate a cascade of biological changes, which feels uncomfortable.

Your heart starts to beat fast to ensure you have enough blood circulating through your body to be able to act. Simultaneously, you begin to sweat, which brings your body temperature down but also makes your skin slippery, which would be helpful if you were fighting an agitated caveman who was attempting to grab you. Blood draws away from any organ that is not immediately necessary

Figure 1: Brain Regions Involved in Avoidance

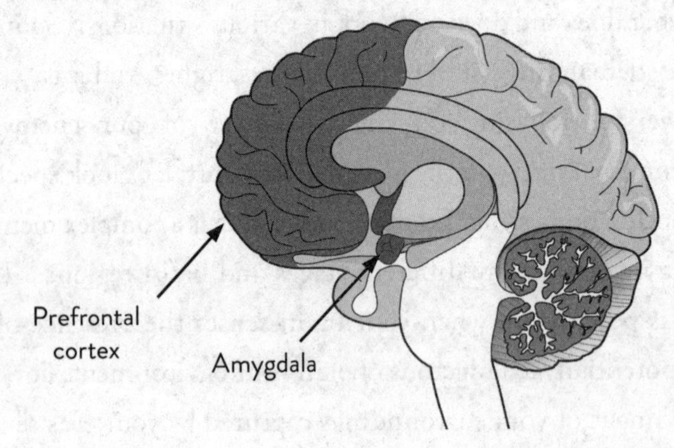

for survival. Blood also drains from your brain to your extremities, leaving many people feeling light-headed or tense. Your stomach will also shut down. After all, no need to digest food when you're trying to do everything you can to survive a brawl with an enraged cave dweller. Unfortunately, you might end up with a stomachache, especially if you just ate, and others might even have diarrhea. Who said stress was fun? Your vision will narrow, focusing on the attacker coming toward you, and as a consequence of this narrowing vision, you might see some light spots.

All these biological changes are intended to increase your likelihood of survival by preparing you to respond: to "fight, flee, or freeze." But they also require a massive amount of energy. So, to ensure that your emotional brain has plenty of energy to keep you alive, the brain tries to conserve energy by inhibiting all other functions it deems unnecessary at that point in time. And one of the brain regions that gets turned off (or at least somewhat offline) is the part called the prefrontal cortex. The prefrontal cortex is the control center of our brains for higher-order thinking, or what psychologists call executive functioning because it is the region of the brain responsible for decision-making, planning, and problem-solving.[5] The prefrontal cortex is a pretty important part of the brain, so you might be wondering why—in a moment of crisis—it's mostly offline. In a life-threatening scenario, calm and rational thinking is less useful than running away.

This primal brain response is very adaptive. For instance, imagine you're crossing the street while texting a friend your apologies for running late to dinner, when suddenly you see an ambulance barreling down the street toward you. Which of the following is likely to be your response?

a. Stopping and musing aloud, "Oh, I see an ambulance is barreling straight toward me. Let's see . . . is it traveling west or east? Hmm. Well, the sun is setting over there, so I guess they're traveling in a sort of north-by-northeast direction. I wonder if the victim is okay. Gosh, I hope so. Maybe they had a heart attack. I hear those are common during daylight saving week. Boy, I really should make an appointment with a cardiologist."

Or . . .

b. Screaming, "HOLY S#%T!" while diving out of the way, headfirst, into a trash can.

Unless you're skimming this book and didn't pay close attention to the options, my guess is you chose B. In a scenario where you're facing a life-or-death situation, the human animal is simply not going to start rationalizing because our prefrontal cortex is mostly offline. You are going to *run*. Instinctually, and very fast. And while a caveman wouldn't know what to make of a modern ambulance, there is a direct link between the frightening experience of texting while crossing the street and our prehistoric ancestors in 10,000 BC encountering a saber-toothed tiger. Whether the threat is a racing ambulance or menacing megafauna, one thing holds true: the amygdala is always going to straight-up amygdalize. The cavemen whose amygdalae weren't quick enough to keep them alive didn't stick around long enough to pass their genes on; we are the descendants of those cavemen with the jumpy amygdalae. And while the resulting jitteriness might sometimes feel like a burden, remember: your brain is only trying to protect you, no matter what.

Your Brain on False Alarms

You might have heard of your body's fight, flight, or freeze response to danger, but why is your amygdala grabbing the steering wheel of your emotions when you get an email from your boss at 10 p.m.? Because the brain is always listening, and when it senses a threat, your emotional brain snaps into action to protect you—even if that threat is just a *perceived threat*. Researchers have shown that even something as small as seeing a picture of someone who looks afraid—a cue for potential danger in the environment—is enough to activate the amygdala and to make rational thinking difficult.[6] We might not like the way a co-worker talks to us or the look on a member of the audience's face when we walk on stage, but I think we can all agree that words and thoughts are not the same as the literal violence posed by an ambulance charging toward you at 80 miles per hour. One is a threat to your life. The other is a false alarm—but damn, it feels real, doesn't it? Especially to the amygdala, which is keen eyed but rather dense in distinguishing real threats from perceived ones.

Let's go back to our dapper CEO to put this into context. When Jake walks through the door at night thinking to himself, "I will never get rid of this anxiety!" and gets caught up in a spiral of negative thoughts, those thoughts don't pose a real threat to his life, but they do cause real discomfort, which his brain perceives as an imminent threat. All of a sudden, his heart is beating faster and faster in order to prepare him to do whatever it takes to protect himself *(run! fight!)*, at which point his brain begins to tell him, "This is bad; you're having a heart attack!" Unpleasant feelings in his body create more negative thoughts in his head, which in turn create more unpleasant feelings in his body. In essence, Jake's symptoms of discomfort (pounding heart, sweat, dizziness, anxiety) are the same regardless of whether he is facing a real threat or a perceived threat. But in the case of a perceived threat, his brain interprets these symptoms as danger, jumps to the conclusion that he might be having a heart attack, and his anxiety thermometer shoots up. Therefore, Jake does what we are all biologically wired to do: he finds a way to move away from the discomfort. In his case, he ends up avoiding by grabbing that bottle of wine for relief.

It is worth pausing here to note that what one person's amygdala perceives as a threat is going to be different for another. For example, while a fast heartbeat for Jake means a heart attack, to me it often means that I am excited. Similarly, if you have a great relationship with your boss, a 10 p.m. email won't trigger a threat response.

However, if you fear your boss, then it almost certainly will. Let me give you another personal example in which my brain's interpretation of a comment prompted a full fight, flight, or freeze response.

About fifteen years ago, early in my academic career, I walked into the office and a colleague of mine, big smile on her face, said: "You look so Latina today!"

I think to myself: *What the hell does she mean?*

The blood rushes in my ears as my primal fight, flight, or freeze response is activated . . .

What does it mean to be Latina?

My heart pounds louder . . .

Am I too fat? Is my butt too big? Do I have too many curves?

I feel dizzy . . .

Am I not American enough? I will never fit in at Harvard . . .

This was back in the days when I had yet to find my sea legs in academia, so to speak, when I was still searching for my professional identity. I didn't feel like I belonged there, and I was easily knocked around by my insecurities. When I think back on this moment, I can feel the same familiar unpleasant feelings bubble up in my chest.

The minutes passed by slowly as I walked down the hallway, my heart pounding out of my chest, my breathing shallow. It all felt too much! While my head swirled in confusion, I knew I needed one thing: to get rid of this anxiety!

Why do I look Latina? How do I fit in? How do I feel better?

Quickly and with the urgency of James Bond defusing a ticking time bomb, I concluded that it must be my floral skirt. That must have been why I looked "so Latina." I must have dressed wrong! So, what did I do? I went home that instant and changed my outfit. Yes, you read that correctly. I, an accomplished academic at one of the most prestigious institutions in the world, just straight-up left work in the middle of the day to change my outfit because of an offhanded and undoubtedly well-intentioned comment from a colleague.

Was I facing a real threat? No, but my brain sure thought so. And in that moment of discomfort, avoiding by rushing home and defiantly changing my outfit seemed like the only solution (you've never seen someone button a boring gray blouse with such conviction!). Coming back to work that day, in my pressed gray suit, I felt oddly powerful, at least momentarily. Though it might seem illogical to you, the reader, I can recall walking back into my office thinking that I had solved the root of the problem!

Now I am more like them! I'm sure I'll fit in now . . .

Although I momentarily felt better, there was a long-term negative consequence to my decision to avoid that day: for the next ten years of my career, I refused to wear anything that could be interpreted as "Latina" to work! Whenever I went home to Brazil, my family and friends would wonder aloud why my clothes were all black, white, and gray (the official inoffensive colors of drab corporate America), and I would just dismiss it. But I knew they were right, and what's more: I like colorful clothing and I'm very proud to be Latina! And yet that day, my fear of not belonging let avoidance win.

When we lack proper training, avoidance is a force far more powerful than any of us can handle. Because, as you learned above, when we're feeling emotional, we're often not capable of thinking rationally. While we might interpret our behavior during such times as calm and logical, it is anything but. Remember this the next time you're in an argument with someone. If you feel blood rushing through your ears and your heart pounding in your chest, chances are your prefrontal cortex is out to lunch. In my case, I wonder how much suffering I could have spared myself if only I had taken a beat to let my prefrontal cortex come back online, before rushing home in the middle of the day to change my outfit and appear "less Latina." If I had paused and given my thinking brain enough time to come online, I might have addressed my feelings and thoughts around the comment (not a threat to my safety!) instead of fighting my discomfort with an outfit change.

Now that you understand a bit about the brain's natural response to threats and false alarms, you have the final ingredient of avoidance: perceived threat. If there is a real threat and you do something to avoid that threat, it is not psychological avoidance. Psychological avoidance is any response to a *perceived threat* that brings immediate emotional relief but comes with long-term negative consequences. When our brains clock a perceived threat, we experience physiological changes (heart pounding, sweating, dizziness) the same way we would with a real threat, and this discomfort happens before we can even determine whether the threat is real.

Because avoidance is unique for all of us, it is important to consider your own avoidance tactic by completing the reflection on the next page.

Because biology largely drives our discomfort, there is no way to completely eradicate it. Your brain will fire the alarms once it senses danger—so it is not the discomfort we are fighting (although I must admit, I hate anxiety myself!); the real infection is psychological avoidance. But before we learn to fight avoidance, I want to share a secret with you in the next chapter. Did you know you already have a superpower that can assist you in your quest for boldness? Let's uncover it!

REFLECTION

Uncovering My Avoidance Tactic

Pause and think about the last time you felt really uncomfortable. Can you picture what that situation looked like? Who was around you? What did you feel in your body? Was your brain predicting that something bad would happen?

Describe the situation below.

____

____

In this situation, what did you do?

____

____

Once you have a clear image of the situation and your response, please answer the following questions:

1. **Did your brain detect perceived danger in this situation?**
   ☐ Yes ☐ No
2. **Before you responded, were you feeling uncomfortable?**
   ☐ Yes ☐ No
3. **Once you reacted, did your discomfort go down fast?**
   ☐ Yes ☐ No
4. **Is this pattern associated with a cost to you (i.e., a high price tag)?** ☐ Yes ☐ No

If you answered *yes* to most of these questions, you have identified the infection: psychological avoidance. Congratulations on taking the first step to living a bold life!

Chapter Two

The Superpower You Never Knew You Had

Every good book needs a villain and a hero, and this one is no exception. You've already met our villain: psychological avoidance. So, you might be wondering, who is the hero? Spoiler alert—you are! You might be thinking to yourself that you don't have the heroic skills required to vanquish your enemy, and this may be true—for now. But that is where I, the Yoda-like character, take you under my wing to teach you what you need to know. While you may not yet have the skills, you do already have one essential weapon with massive power: your brain. If avoidance is the enemy, then your brain, harnessed the right way, is your defense. Your brain 100 percent has the ability to overcome avoidance and enable you to respond boldly when faced with discomfort, but it still needs some training. And that is exactly what the skills in this book are designed to provide.

Everything you will read in this book is grounded in what is known as cognitive behavioral therapy (CBT). CBT is generally considered the gold standard of mental health treatment.[1] It is one of the most heavily studied treatments, with, according to Stefan Hofmann and colleagues, hundreds of studies conducted worldwide.[2] CBT has been shown to effectively treat anxiety, depression, eating disorders, insomnia, anger and aggression, stress, and substance use. Children, adults, and older adults around the world have benefited from CBT. But you do not have to be suffering from a mental health condition to benefit from CBT, because it has also been studied as a way to build resilience.[3]

There are many different flavors of CBT. For example, you may have heard of dialectical behavior therapy (DBT),[4] acceptance and commitment therapy (ACT),[5] cognitive therapy (CT),[6] or cognitive processing therapy (CPT).[7] All of these approaches have different emphases and slightly different strategies, yet they all fall under the CBT umbrella. The skills in this book draw from all of these approaches.

One common denominator across all these approaches is the reliance on a shared foundation known as the *cognitive triad*. The cognitive triad is a way of conceptualizing the relationship between thoughts, emotions, and behaviors in any given situation.[8] Through my research, I have adapted this concept to what I call *the TEB cycle* (see figure on the next page).[9] The TEB cycle shows that what we tell ourselves (thoughts) affects how we feel (emotions) and what we do (behaviors). The cycle can move in any direction—usually very

The Thoughts, Emotions, and Behaviors (TEB) Cycle

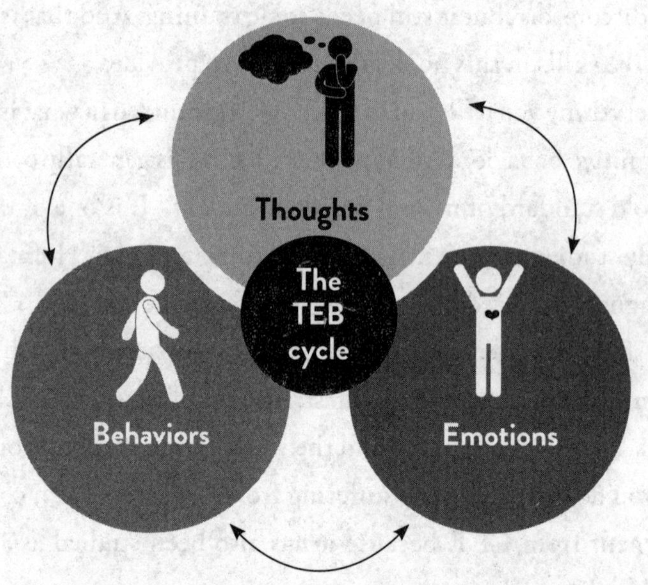

rapidly. The TEB cycle can be a very helpful way to understand how avoidance keeps us stuck but also serves as a technique to get us unstuck.

You don't have to be stuck in avoidance for your brain to spin in the TEB cycle: spinning is just a part of life, especially when your brain senses danger. But in situations that are not part of a long-term avoidance cycle, the spinning tends to resolve itself. For example, just this morning, my son's school called to let me know he had fallen on the playground. My inner experience of this news went as follows (see figure on the next page):

Situation: A call from Diego's school appears on my caller ID.

Thoughts: Is he injured? What happened? Did something really bad happen?

Dr. Luana's Spinning TEB Cycle

Situation: Diego's school phone number appears on my cell

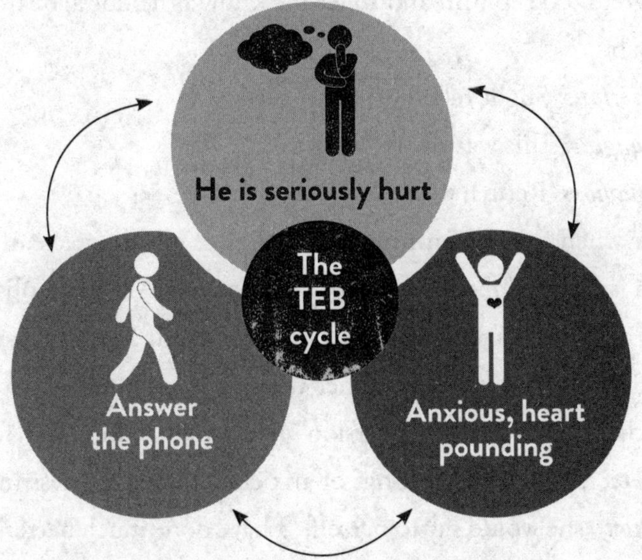

Emotions: My heart pounds faster, I feel anxious and a little short of breath.

Behaviors: I answer the phone and immediately ask, "What happened?" and the kind teacher tells me that Diego fell on the playground and hit his head.

Emotions: Heart pounding out of my chest, fear, and anxiety.

Thoughts: How bad is this? How hurt is he?

Behaviors: I ask the teacher to slowly describe to me in detail what happened. She lets me know that it was a minor injury but that she felt it was best that I come to get him because he is really upset.

Thoughts: What? Get him? Why would I get him if it's only minor? Is she telling me the truth? Is this really only minor?

Emotions: Increased anxiety.

Behaviors: I question her suggestion for me to come and get him because I am not sure this makes sense. After some back and forth, she agrees to keep him and to let me know if he doesn't calm down after a bit.

Emotions: Slight relief.

Thoughts: This was the right call.

Behaviors: Return to work.

But when we are spinning in avoidance, we can get really stuck, which is what happened for my client Fatima. An accomplished interior designer, Fatima would often find herself stuck in a spinning cycle in the final versions of her design. She would say to herself, "My clients will hate this version" *(thought)*, making her feel anxious *(emotion)*. As her feelings of anxiety and helplessness increased *(emotion)*, she would say to herself, "I have done much better designs before; this one is only average" *(thought)*, leading to despair *(emotion)*. As this cycle continued to ping-pong back and forth between thoughts and emotions, Fatima would get more and more uncomfortable, which would eventually lead her to walk away from the design altogether *(behavior)*. After turning away from her work, she would feel a momentary sense of relief, but her brain would quickly say things like, "You will never be a fantastic designer" *(thought)*, which would lead to a deep sense of dread *(emotion)*.

Similar to Jake, the CEO in chapter 1, Fatima's brain would perceive the thought *My clients will hate this version* as a possible threat and would create immediate anxiety. As her emotional thermometer went up, Fatima's anxiety would increase so much that eventually she'd stop her work. Although the relief was helpful, there was a long-term cost for Fatima because her procrastination would often result in her missing deadlines, which infuriated some of her clients.

For Fatima, it had become a chicken-and-egg game of anxiety and avoidance, causing her to procrastinate more and more (see figure below).

Like Fatima, we can easily get stuck in a spinning cycle when our thoughts are unhelpful, our emotions are intense, or our behaviors lean toward avoidance. We get stuck because the more discomfort we feel, the more the amygdala is in control and the less we are able to think the problem through. This is often described as the *amygdala hijack*, because your amygdala is running your life, literally. Now, it is important to remember that the brain is just trying to protect us by avoiding discomfort. There is no one on earth that doesn't get

Fatima's Spinning TEB Cycle

Situation: Working on a client's design

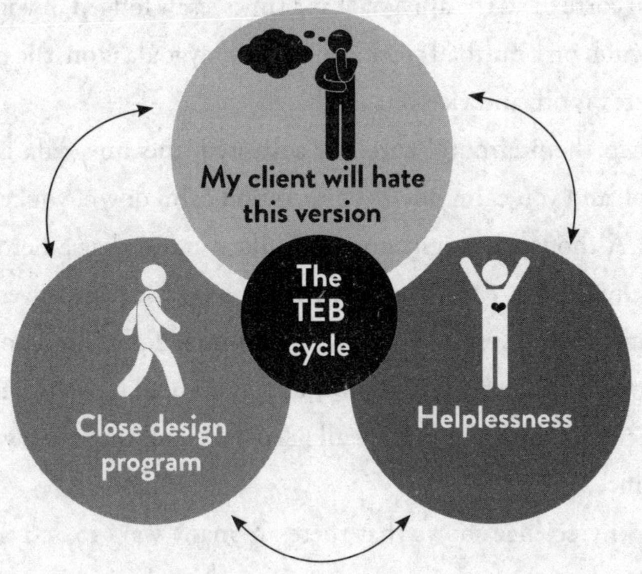

stuck in these spinning TEB cycles from time to time. After all, as you've already learned, our enemy—avoidance—is powerful.

Pausing the Spinning TEB Cycle: Breaking the Avoidance Pattern

Being stuck in a spinning cycle can feel like going on a ride at the fair—unpredictable, unnerving, and a bit nauseating. But you have the power to pause the spinning—by activating your thinking brain, namely the prefrontal cortex, which has the ability to *downregulate* the amygdala response.[10]

To use this power the prefrontal cortex must be activated. When the amygdala is orchestrating a full-on fight, flight, or freeze response, the prefrontal cortex is mostly out to lunch. At the risk of oversimplifying, I like to think of the relationship between the prefrontal cortex and the amygdala as a tiny seesaw lodged in your skull, or a switch on a railroad track: when the amygdala is on, the prefrontal cortex is off, and vice versa.

When the prefrontal cortex is activated, the amygdala is less in control, and you calm down a bit. As you calm down, you're able to pause. Although it might not seem like a move that a hero would get excited about, *pausing is your superpower.* The pause gives you an opportunity to override your preprogrammed fight, flight, or freeze response, evaluate the situation, and make a bold move instead. The pause creates the space that we all need to be able to move away from avoidance.

Luckily, science shows that there are many ways to activate your prefrontal cortex, and one is by writing, including writing down your

TEB cycle.[11] Why? Because to write, we need to use our thinking brain, just like we need it for math, science, and figuring out directions. So, by forcing your brain to shift from emotions to thinking, you are flipping the switch in your brain.

The pause that you create by completing your TEB cycle is your first step to transform anxiety into power. But to get there, you must practice, again and again. Let's do our first practice right now using a situation that fits all of us—reading this book (see the reflection on the next page). By now, you are more than forty pages into the book, and I bet your brain has had a lot to say about it so far, such as *This is interesting, I don't avoid; what is she talking about?*, and *I never knew that my brain reacted the same to a lion as to my fear of asking for a raise.* Depending on your particular thought(s), your emotions will be very different. For example, if your brain is finding the book interesting, you might feel hopeful. Alternatively, if your brain is saying something like, *This book makes no sense; I don't avoid,* you might feel frustrated. Depending on your thoughts and feelings, your behavior might look very different: some of you might have kept reading, others might have been distracted again and again, others might have put the book down. So, let's practice by writing down your responses in the circles in the reflection, trying as best as you can to separate thoughts, emotions, and behaviors.

If you completed the reflection, congratulations! You just finished your first "prefrontal cortex workout." In this book, everything I share with you is skills driven, which means practice is necessary. In my office, I often tell my clients, "What you put in is what you will get out of it." The reality is, you cannot train your brain to become bold—to pause and overcome avoidance—without practice. Just like you can't build muscles without exercising. So, I invite you

REFLECTION

Observing My TEB Cycle

I want you to complete this TEB cycle based on the following situation: reading *Bold Move*. To do so, please write out your specific thoughts, emotions, and behaviors below, ensuring that you are linking your thoughts with specific emotions and behaviors.

Situation: Reading ***Bold Move***

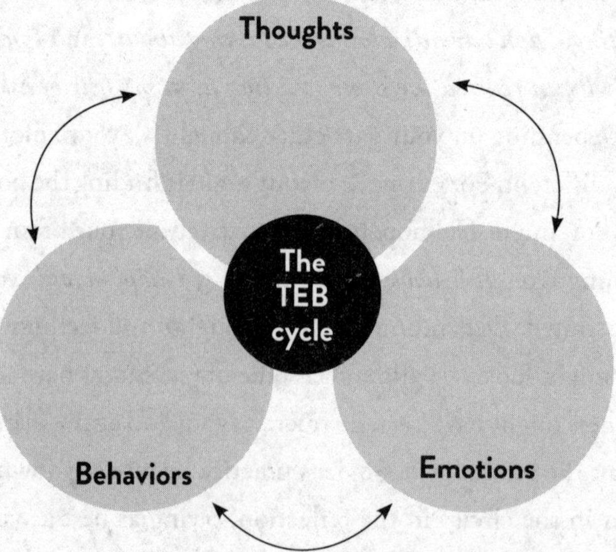

Once you have completed the worksheet, try to observe what you felt doing it. Did writing it out slow down your brain? Did you feel as if you could focus? What happened to your emotions?

____

____

____

to practice completing your TEB cycle often, if not daily, when you are first learning it. I have seen countless clients get immediate relief from their discomfort and gain insight on their avoidance patterns by doing just this practice alone. You will notice that the more you practice, the more you are able to activate your pause button, slowing down your brain and creating the space to be able to choose your response. We can't control our emotions, especially if we are in full fight, flight, or freeze, but we can learn to control our responses by practicing the TEB cycle.

And because practice is necessary, I am going to invite you to do the same exercise again, but this time using a personal situation that created discomfort for you within the past week. Use the reflection on the next page to help you observe your TEB cycle.

Because you are learning a new skill, be kind to yourself: it takes time to be able to get your brain to slow down. But to ensure that you will succeed, here are some guidelines:

- Practice first by completing a TEB cycle for situations that cause mild discomfort. Beginning with lower levels of discomfort is helpful because it means your amygdala is less in control and it will be easier to activate your prefrontal cortex and create a pause.
- Slowly move to situations involving more distress. As your emotional thermometer increases, you will notice that it will be slightly more challenging to slow down your brain but practice will make it happen. This can still help even when you are super upset, but it is going to take more time (and perhaps some degree of patience) to slow your emotional brain.

REFLECTION

Observing My TEB Cycle

To observe your TEB cycle, you must focus on a situation that created discomfort. Then, write out your specific thoughts, emotions, and behaviors in the space below, ensuring that you are linking thoughts, emotions, and behaviors.

Fill Out Your Own TEB Cycle

Situation: ________________________________

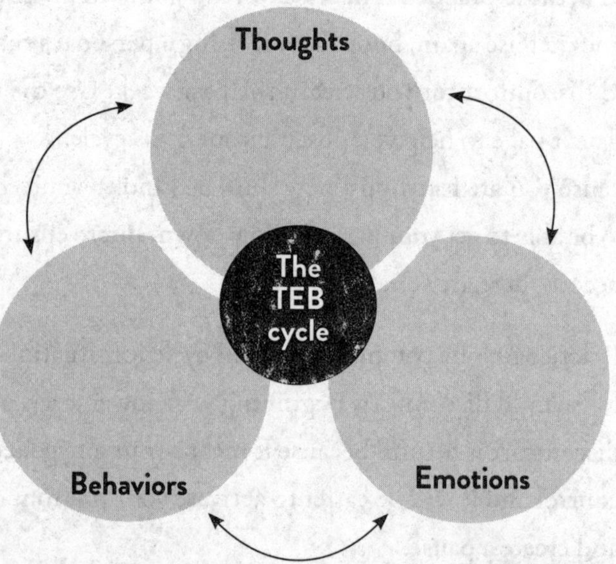

Once you have completed the worksheet, try to observe what you felt doing it. Did writing it out slow down your brain? Did you feel as if you could focus? What happened to your emotions?

____

____

____

- Practice on all situations that lead to all types of emotions (sad, happy, neutral—the spectrum). The reality is, all of them will impact your thoughts and how you react, so it is nice to be able to catch what your brain is doing regardless of the type of emotion.
- As best as you can, try to connect specific thoughts with specific emotions and behaviors. It not only helps to slow the brain down but also to understand what specifically might be contributing to strong emotions.
- And just like at the gym, progress is slow but steady if you keep practicing.

Transforming Anxiety into Power: Shift, Approach, and Align

Now that you know how to activate your superpower—your brain—by pausing through the TEB cycle, it is time to put the pieces of the puzzle together so that we can understand how to transform anxiety into power. In the diagram on the next page, I have illustrated the three possible pathways you might go down in response to your brain sensing danger. No matter who we are, once our brain senses danger, it will turn on our amygdala and we will experience some level of discomfort. Biology drives this process without thinking, so this is not where we can intervene (top of the diagram).

In case of real danger (left side of the diagram), such as a poisonous snake, your brain will be in full fight, flight, or freeze mode, causing you to act. And once you are safe, your discomfort will

Real Danger or a False Alarm?

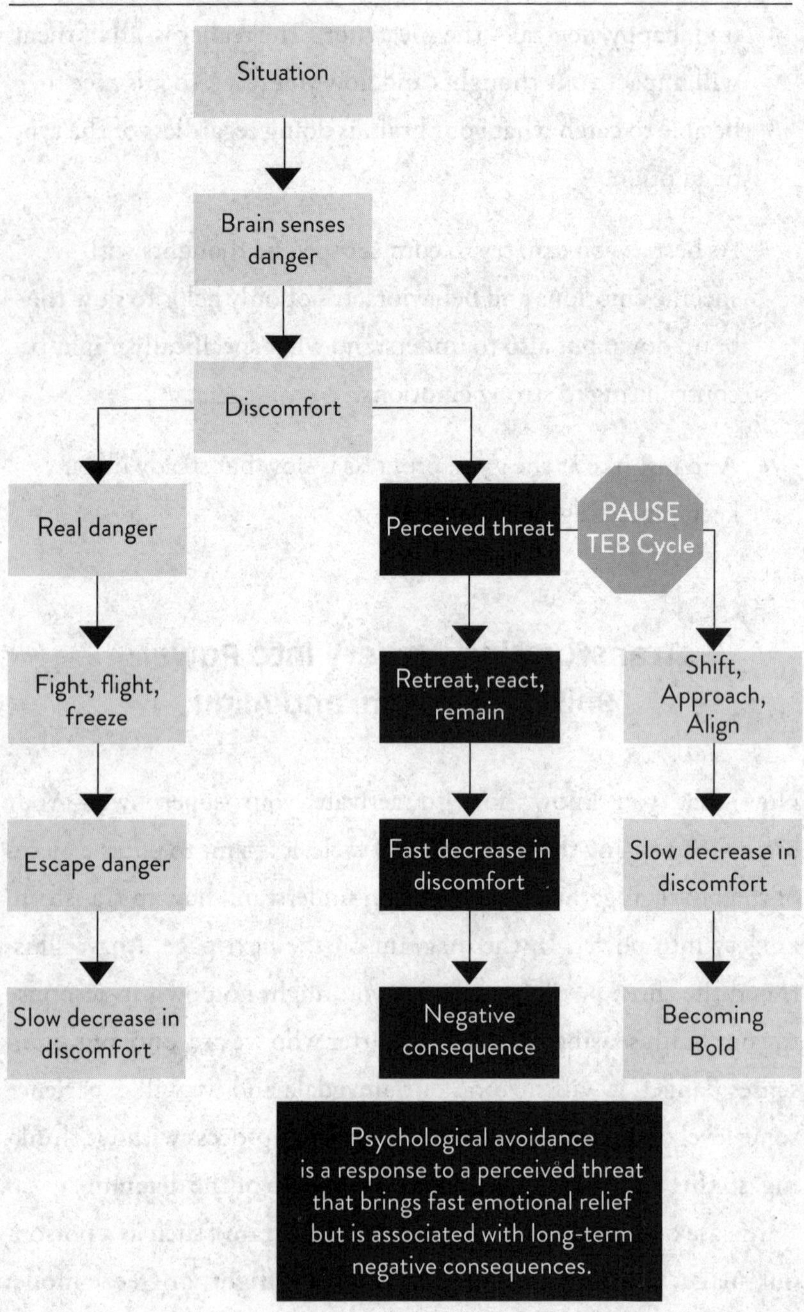

go down slowly. If your child just crossed the street in front of an oncoming car, and they are now safe, it will take a while for your heart to return to baseline. In case of true danger, discomfort comes down slowly.

However, sometimes our brain responds the same way, but to perceived danger (middle pathway of the diagram in black). Because biology is in control here, you will have the same symptoms as fight, flight, or freeze. But because we are dealing with perceived danger, I have labeled our fight, flight, or freeze response as *the 3 Rs of avoidance (i.e., react, retreat, and remain).* Although echoing the same biological cascade, this pathway ends up in avoidance. We will discuss the 3 Rs of avoidance in detail in the subsequent sections of the book, but here is an example to illustrate how each of these responses to perceived threat can end up in avoidance.

Imagine that you just got an email late at night from someone who you have had a lot of conflict with, such as your boss, your loved one, your parent, a close friend, or your child. As you look at the email subject line, it reads, "We need to talk, it is urgent." Immediately, your anxiety increases, and you might respond in one of three possible ways. Some of us are more likely to *react* (i.e., fight) when we sense discomfort. When you react to avoid, you will do whatever it takes to eliminate the potential threat, which really is your anxiety. So, what does it take to bring anxiety down through reactive avoidance? You might quickly compose and send a hasty email back without thinking much about it. When you press send, you feel better (at least I do!), but often feel awful the next morning because very likely you said things that either you didn't mean or you did mean but you said them in a rude or inappropriate way.

Alternatively, you might be stuck in *retreating* (i.e., flight) as a form of avoidance. When you retreat to avoid, you move away from the potential threat. In this case, you might not even open the email; you put your phone down and turn on the TV for distraction. You feel better as you zone out in front of the TV, but unfortunately conflict does not have legs, so it is just there the next morning, which likely leads to even more anxiety.

Finally, some of us *remain* (i.e., freeze) in the face of a potential threat. If you remain, you end up stuck in place with the potential threat. You find yourself stuck, not sure what to do, perhaps just staring at the phone, without action. The freeze response is slightly different biologically than fight or flight, but as a form of avoidance, it does help momentarily.

Regardless of your flavor of avoidance, all three responses (i.e., react, retreat, and remain) function as forms of psychological avoidance because they are responses to a perceived threat that make you feel better momentarily but are associated with a negative long-term consequence.

It is important to remember that these flavors of avoidance are not set in stone and that how you respond to a perceived threat might vary depending on context. For example, I tend to engage in reactive avoidance at work but retreat to avoid in times of interpersonal conflict. Lucia, a stay-at-home mom, often retreats when angry with her husband, but reacts when it comes to her children. It does not matter how you avoid; what matters is that it is keeping you stuck.

But avoidance does not have to always win. There is another path, a bold path (right side of the diagram), where you can learn to transform your anxiety into power. To do that, you will have to first pause through the TEB cycle and create the space so that you can learn not to avoid. At first, it is helpful to write out your TEB cycle to force this pause, but with practice it actually will come automatically to you.

In part II of the book, you will learn a lot more about retreating as a form of avoidance, which often happens when we get stuck thinking about thinking. To overcome thinking as a form of avoidance, you will learn how to *Shift* your perspective to help you get unstuck from black-and-white thoughts. In part III of the book, we will discuss reacting to avoid. To overcome this type of avoidance, you'll learn how to *Approach* discomfort by creating a plan for you to fight your avoidance head-on, thus changing your behavior. Finally, in part IV, you will learn about remaining to avoid, such as staying in a relationship that you know no longer works or in a job that you dislike. You will learn how to *Align* your actions with what matters most to you, your values, so that you can overcome this type of avoidance.

Although the book is written sequentially, the three different bold moves do not need to be followed in a particular order. Which one you decide to use will depend on where you find yourself stuck (e.g., *Shift* is particularly helpful when retreating, while *Approach* is my go-to for overcoming reactive avoidance), but as you become bolder, you might find yourself using all three in the same day, just in different ways. Each of these parts of this book will show you not only how avoiding gets us stuck, but also the science behind that type of avoidance—and, of course, the pathway toward boldness.

The Outcome of Turning On Your Superpowers

Avoidance only wins because we are biologically wired to move away from discomfort; we all hate feeling uncomfortable. Yet, emotions themselves, even negative or challenging ones, are not bad. It is what we *do* when we feel scared, anxious, or upset that tends to keep us stuck. So, the opposite of letting emotions dictate our lives is to learn to regulate emotions—to activate our thinking brain and to act in accordance with what matters most to us. By practicing the skills in this book, you will develop cognitive flexibility, which means that, even when life throws you curveballs, you will be able to handle them.

Is this really possible?

A few years ago, I had the privilege of meeting with Mrs. Barbara Dalio, an incredible woman and philanthropist. One of the domains of Mrs. Dalio's philanthropic focus revolves around helping organizations that work with inner-city youth in Connecticut, who are disengaged or disconnected. We immediately had something in common given that for the past decade all my research has been designed around training paraprofessionals who work with inner-city youth in the skills that I am about to share with you. Mrs. Dalio asked me a question that I often hear from my clients (and maybe one you're currently wondering yourself): *Is this really possible?*

Mrs. Dalio proceeded to question whether or not these youth, who have had a really bad hand dealt to them (in the form of trauma, adversity, neglect, exposure to drugs and alcohol), could really change their brain, rewire it, such that their lives would be different. I could have answered her question with a lot of published research, including my own (which eventually I did!), but here is what I told her: "I would not be sitting here, meeting with you if we could not change our brain. I had my own share of adversity and trauma, and yet the skills that I am talking about got me out of there!"

It was not easy, and some days it is still very tough to overcome my own history of adversity and the stories my brain created as a result, but if I can do this, so can you. As the old Chinese proverb from Lao Tzu says, a journey of a thousand miles begins with a single step. So, are you ready to take your first step to becoming bold?

PART II

Shift

Chapter Three

Brain Chatter: Retreating to Avoid

Imagine you just moved into a new home and discovered you needed a broom to clean up, as well as new hangers to organize your closet. How would you go about acquiring them? I bet you would go to your local megastore, buy the supplies, and never think twice about where they came from or why they cost what they did. In modern life, we give very little thought to the processes behind the things we buy. But I was able to see that firsthand growing up.

Early on, when my mom got a job selling hangers and brooms, I got to witness what happens behind the scenes. What I recall from this time was how well my mom negotiated. You might not think that there's much negotiating to be done in the thrilling world of door-to-door broom and hanger selling, but watching her deal with potential clients was like observing Michael Jordan playing basketball: pure magic. Whenever I accompanied her, I was always struck by how she seemed to enjoy the challenge of talking her way into someone's home and then getting them to willingly part with their money once she'd convinced them they were buying not just any broom but, indeed, the best broom ever made at the best price ever.

Because of this, I was raised with the idea that negotiating is something you are supposed to do. After all, why would any sane person accept less when more is also on the menu? Especially when your ability to feed yourself and your family depends on maximizing your paycheck, customer by customer. Perhaps culture has something to do with this as well. In Brazil, we bargained for everything, from the price of a banana to the cost of a car. So, it was something of a shock to me when I moved to the United States and realized that what was so normal, and almost a source of pride, in Brazil was wholly inappropriate in my adopted country.

I can vividly recall a time when I was a newly arrived exchange student in need of a pair of winter boots. I walked into the nearest Payless, tried on a few sensible (and affordable!) pairs, and upon selecting the ones I wanted, had the apparent gall to ask for fifty cents off the asking price. The cashier looked at me like I was insane, but in my defense, even though my English wasn't perfect, how could I be wrong? The name of the store was literally *Payless*. How was I to know that one didn't negotiate in such a scenario?

This sort of thing happened a lot in my first few months in America. Whenever I would try to negotiate when we were out, my host family would turn bright red, as though I had just made a social faux pas of such epic proportions that they didn't know how they'd ever show their faces in public again. I repeatedly felt like I was living in a comedy of errors, only the joke was on me. Eventually I learned that, in America, the customer is not always right and unless you find yourself at a used car lot, haggling is something of a grotesque curiosity.

So, you might be asking: *What does negotiation (or not) have to do with avoidance?* All of this is to say that the idea of *not* negotiating, especially for things that are related to one's livelihood, such as one's salary, was still strange to me when I entered the workforce in 2006. But I quickly learned that this was a major challenge for most of my colleagues, both men and women alike. This has also been a constant theme with nearly every client I've worked with throughout my career: even the slightest *thought* of having to enter the negotiating battlefield sets off a twelve-alarm fire in their amygdala, to the point where they'd much rather accept less than they can afford than have to be—gasp—momentarily disagreeable with another human being. Sound familiar? It should: this is textbook avoidance. When we move away from negotiating because our brains are saying that we cannot handle it and as a result it would make us feel uncomfortable, we are in fact *avoiding by retreating.* Retreating is when you move away from a situation that your brain has perceived as dangerous (e.g., conflict, negotiating, etc.) with the outcome of making yourself feel better momentarily. Often, what we say to ourselves (e.g., *I don't deserve a raise*) plays a huge role in convincing us that retreating is the only solution, yet there is always a long-term negative consequence.

Before we dive deeper into this flavor of avoidance, here are some additional examples of behaviors that often function as a form of retreating—with the caveat that for some people, this could be a different flavor of avoidance. Keep in mind, for any of these actions to qualify as avoidance there must be a long-term cost.

Retreat

The main characteristic of retreat as an avoidance strategy is moving away from whatever is making you uncomfortable, so that you can have temporary fast relief from discomfort. You can retreat by walking away, but you can also do it by going inward, focusing on thoughts, and distancing from situations in subtle ways. Below are examples of how you can retreat to avoid:

- Looking away during difficult conversations
- Changing the topic of a conversation
- Excessively exercising
- Letting emails pile up
- Putting off small tasks
- Rescheduling unwanted meetings
- Grabbing a glass of wine
- Canceling a date
- Scheduling events to stay away from your home
- Scrolling through social media

The Brain Can Be a Butt

Let's see how thoughts around negotiating got a colleague of mine stuck. I met Janet at a Harvard Women's Leadership course where I was speaking on using science-driven skills to help women get results in high-stakes conversations so as to enhance their ability to communicate as leaders. It turned out that Janet worked at the same institution as I did, and just like me, had been there for many years. We were in different departments but had faced similar challenges, and we immediately fell into an easy and familiar rapport. During one of our breaks, Janet approached me in a polite-but-urgent manner and asked if she could confide in me. We found a quiet corner of the conference center, and she explained to me that for the past three years, she had been waiting for the right moment to ask for a raise but had been almost incapable of forcing herself to do it. Janet is an African American woman, a single mother, and this raise would make a huge difference for her and her three children. She clearly cared a lot about this, and she felt like she was failing at being a provider for her family. She continued to speak, but her voice caught in her throat, and when she looked up, I saw that she had tears in her eyes. I had seen this look of shame and desperation on the faces of many clients in similar situations (and even in my own mother during some of her lowest points). I felt a connection with Janet, but we were due back at the conference any minute, so I invited her to meet me for coffee at the hospital the following week so we could talk more and see if I could help her get unstuck. Janet smiled, a sense of momentary relief washing over her face.

The following week Janet braved one of Boston's early winter snowstorms and, over coffee in my office, shared her story with me. A nurse by training, she had transitioned into an administrative position, managing a large practice at the hospital. She had been with the same department for the past ten years and really enjoyed her co-workers. The team was close, and Janet was seen as a competent and well-liked manager. During this time, Janet's boss had changed many times, and currently she reported to a white man, who she described as kind but intimidating. Janet commented, "I don't know if it is because we're so different, but I'm a bit scared of him."

"How do you mean different?" I asked, not wanting to assume.

She laughed, diffusing the tension, and gestured to herself, "This isn't a spray tan here." She continued, "But there are bigger differences than just the fact that he's white and I'm Black. My background is in nursing. He's a physician. I'm a single mother trying to raise three kids and he's financially well off. It's like we come from totally different worlds," she said.

I could relate, as I'd often felt quite different from a lot of the men and women that I had worked under throughout my career. Coming from a developing country with a different set of cultural norms, and finding myself often in a precarious financial situation, I could understand how these differences are important. Yet from a clinical perspective, I had the sense that these were not the things that were—deep down—actually preventing her from asking for a raise. I'm certain that she believed they were, but when it comes to avoidance tactics, the true motivations are often hidden from us. I decided to dive beyond the narrative that Janet had been telling herself and asked her to walk me through what it's like when she considers asking for a raise.

"I immediately feel anxious, scared, and even worthless at times."

"So even the idea of asking for a raise starts to make you feel really uncomfortable," I said. "Do you have a sense of what you are saying to yourself when you feel those emotions?"

A long pause was followed by a storm of thoughts that came from Janet's mouth:

I am not working hard enough. I should stay late more often.

The quality of my work is not perfect.

The mistake that I made in implementing the new billing system means I am sloppy.

I should get another degree; perhaps it is my education level that is getting me stuck.

I will never get a raise.

I am stuck forever in this job.

I am such a failure—if I was better, I would have been given a raise.

I am worthless.

As tears dropped down Janet's face, I assured her that I had heard many stories similar to hers from my clients and that I could see how distressing these thoughts were to her. I asked her, "When all of those emotions and painful thoughts wash over you, what do you usually do to make yourself feel better?"

"I try to push my thoughts away by checking my phone or scrolling through social media. I try not to focus on them. I momentarily feel better, but the thoughts always come back. I wish I could go ahead and ask for that raise already, but I can't, and it hurts to even think about it."

Janet's thoughts such as *I will never get a raise* were so powerful that they were creating anxiety, tears, and discomfort. As a result, Janet did what she could to try to make herself feel better: she pushed them away through distraction. In the short term, we can all distance ourselves from our pesky thoughts. Yet, this cycle had repeated itself for the past three years and it was causing her significant financial strain, which was making her feel even worse about herself as a provider for her children.

Janet is not alone. According to a survey conducted by Randstad US in 2020, 60 percent of women have never negotiated their pay,[1] and even if they ask for a salary increase, they are significantly less likely to get it compared to men.[2] In fact, a recent meta-analysis of studies conducted across the world found that men initiate negotiations 1.5 times more than women.[3] And the cost is high. In the United States, data shows that women made 84 percent of what men made in 2020.[4] Interestingly, the gender gap in negotiation initiation and pay has been decreasing.[5] I've actually worked with quite a few men who have also had trouble asking for a raise or negotiating their salaries.

At the end of my initial conversation with Janet, she said to me, "Do you ever feel like your brain is just being a butt?"

"I do," I assured Janet. The reality is, I told her, if we were to talk to our friends the way we talk to ourselves, we might not have any friends because they would all walk away!

"But, unfortunately, pushing our thoughts away is just like me saying to you, 'Don't think about a white elephant.' What happens?"

Janet laughed and said, "I can see the white elephant."

This phenomenon is what psychologists call *thought suppression*. Unfortunately, trying to suppress your thoughts only makes you think about them more and more.[6] And when the same pesky, unhelpful thoughts keep coming back, they can *fuel* our avoidance.

Janet was stuck in a TEB spinning cycle. Whenever she would consider doing something like asking for a raise *(situation)*, she would say to herself, "The quality of my work is not perfect" *(thought)*, which made her feel anxious *(emotion)*, and as the cycle continued, she would end up crying and ultimately trying to avoid thinking about her job by grabbing her phone and scanning social media *(behavior)*. The problem is that by trying to avoid her thoughts, she made them come back stronger, which made her feel even worse and led to the long-term consequence of her avoidance tactic.

I never met a person whose brain didn't speak to them in a "less than ideal" way from time to time. Hell, my brain does it daily: *John is really mad at me because I didn't respond to his text three days ago. David will kill me for planning yet another party without consulting him—he will be furious for days. I should know better than to plan a vacation in the middle of a book deadline; I am so impulsive. No matter how hard I try to finish this book, it will never get done. How can Diego have such loud anger outbursts? He can't regulate his emotions—it is all my fault!!!* . . . The list goes on and on and on . . . at times louder, other times very quietly, but the brain is always saying something—at least mine is! And these thoughts . . . they even have *names*.

Knee-jerk thoughts, which happen automatically and yet are very painful, are what psychologists call *cognitive distortions*. To put it simply, cognitive distortions are mental filters that often warp our reality. Because our brain is processing millions of pieces of information at the same time (a lot more on this in the next chapter), sometimes the brain takes some shortcuts in logic, and when it does, we might end up with distorted views of the world, hence the name. There are many types of cognitive distortions.

Common Types of Cognitive Distortions

- **Mind reading:** believing that you can read someone's thoughts so that you know what they are thinking
- **Catastrophizing:** immediately jumping to the worst-case scenario and assuming that you won't be able to tolerate the outcome
- **Emotional reasoning:** using emotions to interpret reality (I feel, therefore it must be true)
- **Personalization:** taking any information that someone says or something that they do and making it about you in such a way that there is something wrong with you
- **Should:** talking to yourself using "should statements" such that you end up seeing things in a negative light
- **Black-and-white thinking:** seeing the world in only two opposing options (all or nothing without any shades of gray)

If you observe Janet's cognitive distortion closely, you will see that she often found herself stuck in personalization. If something went wrong at work, or was not perfect, her brain immediately jumped to *It's my fault.* For Janet, naming these thoughts made them less scary and also reminded her that perhaps, just perhaps, they were not the entire story.

Your turn: use the space in the reflection on the next page to take a stab at identifying and naming your own cognitive distortions.

REFLECTION

Let's Practice Naming Cognitive Distortions

Think about a situation where you felt discomfort, and ask yourself, *What did I say to myself?* Once you have identified the specific thoughts, take a stab at labeling them as distortions. Make sure to refer back to the list on the preceding page to help you give them names. A word of caution about naming your own distortions: Because the categories are not mutually exclusive, sometimes the same thought could be labeled as different types. Don't split hairs—just choose one!

Situation: ____________________________________

Specific thought	Type of cognitive distortion

Trapped in Someone Else's Fairy Tale

When it comes to retreating, avoiding negotiation because of our inner self-talk is not the only way we get stuck. Let's meet my client Sara, whose distorted deeper beliefs about herself were preventing her from being her true self. Sara grew up in a loving middle-class American family that was traditional in every way, centering on religious values, education, and hard work. Her father was in the military early in his career and held strong beliefs about everything from work ethic to gender identity. He was a loving man and would do anything for his family, but his worldview was like hardened cement. Relative to Sara's dad, her mom was the flexible one. She believed that people had the right to pursue their dreams no matter what anyone else believed. She believed that life was too short to worry about what other people thought of you. Despite these apparent differences, Sara's parents had a good marriage based on mutual understanding. They also had been married long enough to know that they couldn't change each other, and their different temperaments made for a nice balance.

Sara was a great student and, though she described herself as an introvert, had a small but strong group of friends. In high school, Sara didn't date at all, and when prom arrived, she decided not to go. The idea of going alone in a long fancy dress was not something that appealed to her. Even though her friends really wanted her there, she just could not talk herself into doing it. From all vantage points, Sara's life was on track when she left for college—or at least it appeared so to the outside world.

Internally, however, Sara had been fighting a war within herself.

From middle school on, she felt different. She didn't care much for the boys in her class, and when she was being completely honest with herself, she noticed that she was more attracted to girls. This confused her. For as long as she could remember, her father adored her and referred to her as his princess. Following the logic, she would often think: *And princesses marry princes.* With her father's perspective framing her own internal landscape, she pushed her feelings aside and focused on her schoolwork and friends. However, the price of keeping this mask on was becoming costly, and she nearly failed her first semester at a prominent Boston-area university. It was at this crisis point that I first met her.

Sara looked sad as she walked into my office, as if she were dragging around a very heavy burden. As we started to talk, Sara asked a lot of questions about my work and about therapy in general and seemed especially concerned about the confidentiality. As soon as I assured Sara that I could keep her confidentiality as long as it was medically and legally appropriate, she began to share her story with me.

I learned about Sara's early interest in girls, her fears related to her sexuality, and how she had been repressing her feelings because of her mother's Catholic beliefs and her own beliefs around her father's desire for her to be his princess in search of Prince Charming. She told me that she identified as a lesbian but had never told anyone before. I considered how difficult this must have been for her, to be eighteen years old and only coming out to a stranger who was essentially sworn to secrecy. I asked Sara to share with me some thoughts that crossed her mind as she imagined coming out and sharing her sexual identity with her parents. In response to that question, Sara looked like she was going to be sick.

She stared at me for a second and said, "I will never be able to come out to my parents," in a way that seemed to indicate that the very notion was completely absurd.

Stating the obvious, I countered, "It sounds like the idea scares you."

She smiled sarcastically. "That's perceptive of you."

I laughed, continuing, "And because of this, you believe that sharing your identity with your parents is impossible. How come?"

"Are you out of your mind?" she asked me. "Do you know what would happen if I were to bring this up at my house?"

I shrugged. "Try me."

"My father would disown me, and my mother would think the devil had done this to me and would want me to go to church with her daily to get the demons out. It would be a disaster."

"Sounds like you imagine losing both parents if you came out to them. I can see why you're scared! After all, who wants to lose the ones that they love the most?"

Sara seemed a bit calmer with my assurance that indeed her fears were valid and that I understood where she was coming from. It is important to note here that I needed Sara to understand that I was *not* saying that her fears were irrational. In fact, some of her specific fears relating to her family's possible reaction to her coming out were likely to be true. What I was suggesting instead was that we needed to consider exactly what she was saying to herself, so we could uncover whether or not her thoughts around the situation were fueling her avoidance and keeping her stuck in place (as opposed to confronting objective real-life consequences). In other words, I wanted to uncover the specific statements that were causing her emotional temperature to rise to the point where her only option was to avoid.

With that established, I then asked her permission to explore any other thoughts that crossed her mind regarding coming out. So, I asked Sara, "Imagine for a moment that you're going home for the holidays and you're about to sit down with your parents and tell them that you're a lesbian. What thoughts immediately pop into your head?"

They'll hate me . . .

My dad will never talk to me again . . .

My brother will be freaked out . . .

My mom will think something is wrong with me . . .

What if they're right? What if something is wrong with me?

I'm ruined, just broken . . .

By this point, there were tears streaming down Sara's face. I looked at my desk's clock: not ten minutes had passed since the beginning of our session, and Sara was already sobbing. I couldn't imagine how she had been holding all of this inside her for the duration of our appointment, let alone her entire life.

"So," I asked her, "what if you are indeed broken? What happens then?"

Sara looked at me in despair. "It means that I'll always be alone, that no one will ever love me."

Damn, I thought. This is why I do what I do! It's a weird thing to enjoy talking with people when they're in crisis, but I imagine it's the same feeling a Formula 1 racer gets when they nail a corner at 150 miles per hour. We continue.

"So, the idea of coming out for you goes from *my parents will hate me* to *I am broken* to *I am unlovable*, is that so?"

"Yes," she said with shame written all over her face.

"Well, no wonder you are saying to yourself that you will never come out! It sounds like the thoughts spiral so fast that the moment you consider sharing something deeply personal and important with your family, you suddenly end up in your imagination alone and unworthy of love. *Of course* that feels unbearable!"

I could tell that she was feeling totally isolated, so I told Sara that she is not, in fact, alone and that I've seen this in many patients before. I told her how thought spirals, just like the one she'd just shared with me, lead to such strong and often unpleasant feelings that we end up moving *away* from the things that matter the most to us, instead of *toward* them. Fearing she would lose her parents, Sara had allowed herself to be unknowable to her parents. The distance she feared was actually being created by her avoidance of telling them the truth.

Peeling the Layers of the Onion

If you were to say to yourself, "My dad will never speak with me again," just like Sara was saying to herself, how would you feel? Anxious? Sad? Upset? I bet it depends on your relationship with your dad. But for a second, imagine that you have a good relationship. How would not speaking with your dad again make you feel? For Sara, that brought on tears, sadness, and fear. However, as I worked further into what she was saying to herself, it turned out that Sara had an even deeper belief that scared her even more: *I am unlovable.* This type of deeper belief that tends to filter our views of the world is what psychologists describe as a *core belief*.[7]

Core beliefs are global views we hold about ourselves, others, and the world that are created early on in life based on our experiences.

Think of them as a broader category that holds all of our cognitive distortions together into one single (and at times very painful) category (see the next page for examples of common core beliefs). Cognitive distortions are like the outer layer of an onion, where core beliefs tend to be at the center. As you peel the onion, you go from more automatic thoughts to deeper entrenched beliefs.

Depending on the environment we grew up in and our life experiences, we will develop different types of core beliefs—some favorable, such as "I am worthy of love," and others unfavorable, such as "I am unlovable."

For me, being brought up by a loving mom, who did everything she could to ensure I could thrive in life, left me saying to myself, *I am worthy of love*; yet the chaos of my upbringing, combined with my father's abandonment and my perceived failure at keeping our family together, left me believing, *I am not enough.* Sara ended up saying to herself, *I am unlovable.* The favorable core beliefs tend to help us strengthen our self-esteem and propel us forward in life, while unfavorable core beliefs get us stuck in avoidance. Not to worry: you will learn to *Shift* your unfavorable beliefs in chapter 5, and with practice you will learn to build more favorable ones.

Once we cement any *core belief*—which at times is not even conscious; it's just the product of how we made sense of the world as a child—we tend to maintain it, and as such, I think of core beliefs as *the hidden lenses through which information gets filtered in our brain.* We will dive deeper into the science behind why our core beliefs filter information in the next chapter, but for now I want you to imagine them as hidden lenses you have been wearing for so long that you no longer notice they are there, even though they are likely causing a lot of avoidance, which is why we are exploring them.

Examples of Unfavorable Core Beliefs

- I am not good enough.
- I am worthless.
- I am unlovable.
- I am damaged.
- I am untrusting of others.
- I don't deserve anything.
- I am uninteresting.
- I am stupid.

Examples of Favorable Core Beliefs

- I am worthy of love.
- I am funny.
- I am accepting.
- I am okay.
- I am friendly.
- I am hopeful.
- I am optimistic.
- I am determined.
- I am appreciative.
- I am healthy.

Take a look at Janet's cognitive distortions on page 61, and ask yourself, what core belief might be getting in the way of her asking for a raise? If you guessed "I am worthless," you are correct. In moments that we are really upset, if we spend time writing down our thoughts, one after the other, without stopping ourselves, we often can go from our more automatic thoughts (e.g., cognitive distortions) to our deeper core beliefs. I had to use this technique myself to be able to identify which core belief was getting me stuck while writing this chapter.

Am I Really Too Busy to Write?

As I sat down to write this chapter this morning, my brain just blanked. I stared at the computer screen, and nothing would come out. Thoughts swirled through my mind:

What do I have to say to the world? Who cares what I think? Is anyone going to even read this?

As a newish author, these thoughts hit a little too close. The resulting wave of anxiety was so overwhelming that I leaped out of my chair and made a cup of tea to try to calm myself down. And when you're a tea hoarder, selecting just the right tea becomes an epic decision in and of itself. A great way to avoid *and* procrastinate at the same time! After my cup of tea, I decided that I absolutely needed to check my email. Not because I was avoiding or anything (wink, wink), but because, *Hey, I'm an author! What if my editor sent me an important email with, like, edit-y stuff?* Of course, this totally disregarded my earlier promise to not check emails until I had written at least one page, but my brain wouldn't quit!

What if there's a book emergency email waiting for me?! Must . . . check . . . email.

So, I checked my mostly empty inbox and felt slightly better as my anxiety level dropped a little. Hey, avoidance rocks!

Then I was back to writing for a minute, aka staring at the computer screen, motionless . . .

You're a hack! You're not even typing!

The anxiety spiked again. Quick! Avoid!

Hey, maybe you're just hungry? Maybe some toast would get the writing fingers going.

Mm. Toast. Mother Nature's salve!

I finally made my way back to my office, and as I glanced at the clock I realized*: Holy crap! I only have thirty minutes left in my morning schedule to write!*

Ah! More anxiety! More negative self-talk! More freaking out!

Finally, the irony struck me. Here I was, writing about how uncomfortable thoughts can lead us to avoid things, while failing to realize that I was doing exactly that! (No offense, toast.)

So, I did what I would encourage any of my clients to do: I wrote down my thoughts as they appeared, to get to the core of the issue, and here's what my brain was saying:

I am tired, my brain is not working today, I won't be able to write.

My clients' stories are not great, people will be bored by this book.

What if I offend someone with the way I describe a story?

What if people think I am a lousy clinician?

What if people find out that I am scared that this book will not be good enough?

What if I fail to finish this in time?

What if I never finish this book?

What if the editor thinks I am stupid?

I will never be successful.

I am such a failure.

I will never be enough.

With tears in my eyes, I said hello to my old core belief "I am not enough." But at least I was able to uncover the enemy that was causing my avoidance. You can't fight an enemy you don't know.

Facing the Enemy

I won't lie to you: taking space to uncover our deeper beliefs is a painful process that requires a lot of vulnerability. I myself ran from this for years. But avoidance will always run faster, so I invite you to take a minute to sit quietly and use the reflection on page 77 to uncover your own hidden filters. There are two ways I have seen my clients know that they have identified their core belief(s): either tears come down their face (at times even with a slight sense of relief) or they want to run in the opposite direction as fast as possible (to avoid!). Give it a try! One word of caution: We all have favorable and unfavorable core beliefs. This reflection focuses on the unfavorable ones because those are the ones getting us stuck. But don't forget to also look at core beliefs that strengthen your self-esteem.

When Is Retreating Not Avoidance?

Before we end this chapter, it is important to understand that not every thought leads to avoidance. At the risk of stating the obvious, fleeing is appropriate in the face of real danger and is not a form of avoidance. Alternatively, let's say you're in a somewhat heated argument with your loved one and you call a time-out to retreat and get some perspective. Asking for time to think, reflect, and address a problem is not avoidance; it is a good coping skill and a powerful tool in the nonviolent communication tool kit! Another tool I find myself using often, which some of you can probably relate to, is to retreat to get some air when Diego is misbehaving. Sometimes a five-year-old does things that drive you to the very edge of your sanity, like the time Diego took an extra-large bag of pancake mix and lovingly dumped it all over our living room couch. I lost my mind. And in times like that, the best strategy I had was to walk away for a moment (or several) and calm down before interacting with him. Moving away from discomfort to cool off so you can successfully reengage is not avoiding because the discomfort doesn't dissipate!

Pulling the Switch to Get Unstuck

For Janet, it was the core belief *I am worthless* that kept her from asking for a raise. Meanwhile, our friend Sara was certain beyond all certainty that if she were to come out, her parents would hate her, which stemmed from the core belief *I am unlovable*. For yours truly, my brain graffiti—*I am not enough*—ended up costing me weeks of avoidance before I was able to get my act together and actually finish this chapter.

Across all examples, what we see is that no matter who you are, your brain can come up with some upsetting grenades to lob your way. Of course, none of this is a conscious effort to be cruel to ourselves, as one cannot simply think a thought before it appears. But no matter how ephemeral or weightless these kinds of negative thoughts may be, they can do real damage to our psyche.

REFLECTION

Uncovering Your Hidden Lenses

Understanding the hidden lenses that might be distorting your view of the world is extremely helpful in overcoming avoidance. Set aside some quiet time to focus on this reflection, grab a pen and paper, and follow these steps to uncover your hidden lenses. Think about a situation in which you felt discomfort, which you wanted to avoid, to walk away from as fast as you could.

1. Describe this situation:

   ____

   ____

2. Now ask yourself, "What was I saying to myself in this situation that got me feeling so uncomfortable?" Write out a few thoughts that you had in this situation.

   ____

   ____

3. Once you've identified them, pick one thought and answer the following questions based on this thought:
   - What does this thought mean to me?
   - What does this thought say about me?
   - If this thought were true, then what?
   - What worries me about this thought being true?
   - Why does that upset me so much?
   - What does this suggest about me?
4. Check the answers above against the list of core beliefs on page 72 to see if you can identify one (or more) core beliefs that might be your hidden filters.

It doesn't matter whether your brain is saying, "I don't deserve a raise," "I am an impostor," "I am unlovable," or "I'm stupid," these types of thoughts can make us anxious, scared, sad, or anything in between. And when emotions become too much to handle, we are wired to avoid.

Instead of fighting these thoughts or ignoring them the way we'd (ideally) ignore a rude person on the street, we end up believing these thoughts, accepting them as God's honest truth, and then we do everything we can to avoid them. It's like we imagine a giant boulder in the middle of the road, and instead of acknowledging this boulder as a mirage, we swerve to avoid it and crash into a tree. I think it's fair to say that this is not the best solution.

Luckily, there is another solution—to *Shift*—but before we learn to *Shift*, we must ask the question that I bet you have been asking yourself: "If distorted thoughts and core beliefs cause us so much pain, why do we keep believing them?" To answer that question, we need to understand one of the brain's primary functions: making predictions.

Chapter Four

The Brain as a Faulty Predictive Machine

"Isn't everyone in the world part of our family?" Diego asks one morning.

"What do you mean, *everyone*?"

"Yes, everyone," he tells me. "I have a million aunts and uncles."

I am surprised, as we have a relatively small family but somehow Diego has decided that he has a very large family. Either he has discovered a hidden part of our family or there is something in his logic that does not make sense to me. How did he get to the idea that "everyone" in the world is our family?

So, I go on a hunt to see how he is making sense of the world. "Tell me, Diego, who is part of our family?"

"Remember," he tells me (like my memory is failing me), "we just came back from Buffalo, and there we have Tia Sarah, Tio Tom, and cousins Noah and Adam, but we also have in Brazil Tia Juliana, Tio Bruno, and cousins Duda and Lucas, and you told me that next week Tia Carina, Tio Cristien, Tia Lud, and Tio Gustavo are arriving . . . and that is not everyone." Diego is on a roll. "There is also Tio John, Tia Alessandra, and Tia Evita and Tio Chris, and I almost forgot Tia Sue . . . and didn't we just visit Tia Cecilia's house in Italy? In Minneapolis we also have Tio Chris and cousins Michael and Anthony . . . See? Everyone is part of our family," he tells me. Diego is proud of himself for explaining his rationale to me and has a smug smile on his face that almost says, "I am smarter than you."

David looks at me and says, "I told you: we are confusing him" . . . at which we both laugh.

Although Diego's logic would not make sense to a fully developed brain like yours, it turns out that his brain was functioning very well based on his developmental age. Let's understand why, as this is at the core of our brain's primary function: *predictions*.

The Brain's Primary Function Is Its Greatest Strength (and Weakness)

As our brain develops, one of the *core functions is to make predictions*.[1] The brain uses two pieces of information to make predictions: 1) sensory information about what is happening around us and 2) our past experiences. Based on those two pieces of information, we guess what will happen next, and then adjust our behavior accordingly.

To be able to predict quickly and efficiently, our brain's processing system learns to create categories.[2] From an early age, we are constantly looking out at the world and forming categories of people, places, things, events, and so on. We sort through millions of pieces of new information every day and sort the data into these categories, and then use the categories to make our guesses of what will happen next.

This is just what was happening to Diego when he believed that everyone in the world was part of our family. In Latin culture we have the custom of calling close friends uncles and aunts (tios and tias) regardless of whether they are biologically related to us or not. So, from Diego's early years, we had introduced our close friends as aunts and uncles. I must confess, I often correct him if he calls someone by their first name alone. Think about this as the equivalent of adding Mr., Mrs., or Ms. in the US: it is a sign of respect—and in Latin cultures, also closeness. So, for Diego to be able to predict who is part of our family or not, he created a category that basically lumped all aunts and uncles together under "family." By doing so, Diego's brain can quickly discern who is in and who is out. Unfortunately in his case, I had inadvertently told him that everyone was in.

Here is another example of the brain creating categories early on in life. One of the first animals Diego learned to identify was a dog. However, for Diego, "dog" was anything with four legs. Chairs, cows, and various farm animals were all "dogs" until Diego learned to sort information into more nuanced categories. Even as adults we use rudimentary categories to understand new information. Have you ever tasted a new food and, when asked by a friend how it tastes, responded, "It tastes like chicken"? Or, you might be familiar with the age-old saying: "If it walks like a duck, swims like a duck, and quacks like a duck, it must be a duck." All of our experiences, big and small, old and new, are sorted into categories. This sorting system allows us to take in information quickly, condense it, and make quick predictions about whether a situation (or four-legged object) is safe or poses a potential threat.

As an adult, you rely on your brain's predictions all the time to decide what to do. For example, if you're driving your car and suddenly see a traffic light switch to yellow, your brain quickly incorporates sensory information (seeing a yellow traffic light) with your prior experiences of watching a traffic light go from green to yellow to red. And, next thing you know, your foot is on the brake to slow down in anticipation of the red light. In a matter of milliseconds, we act based on what we think might happen next. Life is far more efficient when we operate this way, because if we had to stop and stare in complete wonder and incomprehension every minute of the day, with no clue as to what might happen next, we wouldn't get very far. And there would be far more accidents if we couldn't predict that yellow means slow down to a stop!

Could you imagine a world in which we didn't use categories to process information? Every time you saw a new breed of dog, you would have to pause and think to yourself:

Okay, everyone stand back, let me see what we have here . . .

It has four legs.

Definitely furry.

A tail wagging.

Walking on a leash.

Ah! It must be a dog!

This would take up so much of your time, and you would in a very real sense be learning everything again and again as if for the first time. You can see how this inefficient process would make even the simplest decision an epic and arduous task. If the decision was whether or not to run from a furry animal you see in the woods, you might still be working through its characteristics when the bear starts to charge. The brain's ability to process information using categories is more than a time-saver: it has allowed humans to survive and succeed for thousands of years. A quick prediction based on the information we're gathering from our environment, along with categories developed from prior experiences, gives us time to reduce the threat.

So far, we have only talked about concrete categories (e.g., dogs and family). But what happens to our emotional landscape? Essentially the same thing happens. The brain utilizes categories that we formed early in life—the hidden lenses of our core beliefs—to make sense of the world and predict. I often think of this process as two pieces of a puzzle that need to fit together in order for it to make sense. And when these pieces add up, our brain is able to make a prediction (see figure 1). For example, early on in my life, I filtered a lot of my experiences through my lens of *I am not enough,* so that, anytime anything was ambiguous, I would jump to the conclusion that the

Figure 1: How Our Brains Predict

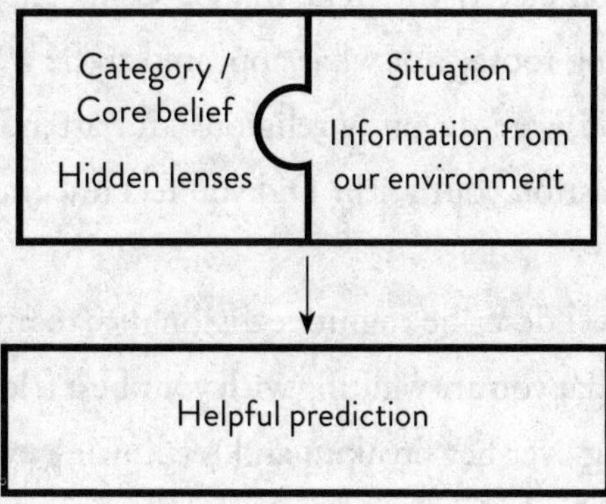

problem was me because I was not enough. This happened a lot in my early dating days. Whenever I was on a first date and the person would give me a look, I would interpret that look as "they are not interested," which is just another pathway to my belief that "I am not enough, so of course they are not interested."

Cows That Meow

Our brains' ability to predict works exceedingly well—as long as what we're sensing around us and our prior experiences add up. If they don't, that's when our brains start to spin. The discomfort we feel when we are confronted with new information that doesn't fit into our current understanding and belief systems about the world is called *cognitive dissonance*.[3] You might not be familiar with this term, but have you experienced this in your life? If you're a human, then I'm guessing so. Have you ever encountered a situation where you came upon new information that challenged your beliefs, and the whole thing just made you feel uneasy? Perhaps you scrolled through a news article that challenged your belief because it was based on a completely different way of seeing the world. Or saw a video featuring footage of what appeared to be a UFO in the sky? Or maybe you were devoutly religious and attended a lecture that made you question your faith? Did you feel uncomfortable? Almost certainly!

Here is how I describe cognitive dissonance to my clients. Imagine for a second that you are walking with your best friend in a rural area. She is sobbing over her breakup and recounting every detail of how her boyfriend broke her heart. You are listening attentively, assuring that you are comforting her, and as such your focus is only on her. There is nothing that can take your attention away from her. Yet, as you pass by a cow (which you hadn't even seen), the cow meows. You read that right: *the cow meows*. What happens to your focus on your friend? Very likely you both would stop talking, look at each other, and ask, "What the heck just happened? Cows don't meow, they moo!" In essence, you would be stopped cold in your tracks, and your brain would be stuck trying to make sense of this surreal world that you just entered. That feeling of being stuck and in discomfort is *cognitive dissonance*. My clients often describe that as *brain lock*.

Let's come back to earth for a second (no, I have never heard a cow meow either). How did you feel when you read the title of this section of the book? Did your brain ask, "Where is she going with this? Cows don't meow!" I bet if you were reading carefully, you had a little moment of dissonance. And that is why I like this example: because it is much easier to understand when things don't add up in the abstract than it is to understand when it is happening inside our own brains. By learning when your brain hits dissonance and understanding the why behind it, you will be equipped to *Shift* (next chapter).

To start to identify what dissonance feels like for you, use the reflection on pages 86 and 87. Keep in mind, you will know that you hit dissonance when your brain locks, meaning it is challenging to think, and you feel discomfort.

If you completed the reflection on page 86 and 87, I bet you sensed relief right away in the first half of this reflection when you confirmed your beliefs. Perhaps you said something to yourself such as, "Exactly!" or "Well, of course!" and instead of wanting to hurl this book at a wall, you kept reading.

However, if you got to the second part, I'm guessing you hit

REFLECTION

Getting to Know My Brain Lock

For this reflection, you will need a pen and paper to record your answers to the questions. First, take a moment to think about something that you believe strongly, such as your political views, dietary ideology, or beliefs about individuals different from you.

Topic: ______________________________

Once you decide on a topic, answer the following question: "What are my views on this topic?" Describe in detail your "truths" related to this particular area.

Now, for the next two minutes, take your phone or laptop out and do a Google search that will bring up stories that support your beliefs. For example, if you are vegan, type in "Eating red meat is bad for you." Alternatively, if you value public education, type in "Why public education is better for children than private education." Fill in your own belief area and search terminology, but make sure to match your truths above. Spend about two minutes reading one of the articles, and then answer the following questions:

- What did you feel as you read it?
- What did you say to yourself?
- What did you want to do as you were reading it?
- Overall, how was your brain experience while you were doing this activity?

Now, let's flip the coin and practice understanding what it feels like when you hit dissonance. You'll basically do the same exercise except that this time you'll search for something that *contradicts* your views of the world. For example, if you happen to be vegan, you will search for an argument that is opposite to your view, such as: "It is important to eat red meat daily." Or, in the case of supporting public education, search for an article that describes the opposite view, such as: "Only private schools can provide excellent education." Make sure to search for the opposite argument within the same topic you described above (e.g., veganism, education). Take two minutes to read one of the articles that shows up, and then answer the same questions.

- What did you feel as you read it?
- What did you say to yourself?
- What did you want to do as you were reading it?
- Overall, how was your brain experience while you were doing this activity?

Integrating your learning: Once you finish both parts of this exercise, take a moment to reflect on what cognitive dissonance felt like:

- How did it impact your TEB (thoughts, emotions, and behaviors) cycle?
- Which of the exercises caused you to feel discomfort?
- What are the signs of dissonance for you?
- What did you want to do while reading the article that contradicts your belief? Did you want to stop reading it? Did you want to quickly counter the argument or disprove it?

dissonance right away. Dissonance probably made you feel uneasy at best, and if you really went for the opposite view, you might have felt as my patient Yolanda describes it: "an internal war between me and myself." Maybe you said something to yourself such as, "There is no way this is actually true" or "What the @*&#?" Perhaps you also felt the urge to quit the activity or close this book entirely.

We can also experience internal sources of cognitive dissonance. This occurs when new information doesn't match our core beliefs. For example, if your core belief is "I am competent" and yet you get a bad review at work, you will feel discomfort: your brain will experience dissonance. Similarly, if you view yourself as reliable, but you show up late to a business presentation, your brain won't like it and you will feel bad.

Roses Are Red, Violets Are Blue, I Like to Confirm What I Know and So Do You

So, what happens when we hit cognitive dissonance? If your brain is doing its job, you might be able to predict what I'm going to share next based on what you've already read. And if you predicted avoidance, you're correct. When we are uncomfortable, we avoid! The brain has a very interesting method of avoiding the discomfort of cognitive dissonance. Whenever our brains have trouble integrating new information with our prior experiences and beliefs, we try to hold on to whatever was true for us up until that moment. Instead of updating the categories we use to make predictions, we try to shove new information into our prior categories (just like Diego affirming that all four-legged objects are dogs and nothing else, or that everyone we meet is part of our family), and in the process, we confirm what we already know. In other words, we engage in something called *confirmation bias*, which makes us feel better (at least momentarily).

Confirmation bias is the process by which our brains search desperately for information that supports our previously held beliefs in an effort to confirm what we already know and avoid the discomfort of updating our beliefs.[4] So when we encounter an opposing view or a piece of information that contradicts a belief, we don't simply change our beliefs in the face of this new piece of evidence.[5] Instead, we keep calm and scroll on, as if to say, "No, thanks! I'm quite happy believing what I already believe I know!"

The brain engages in confirmation bias because it uses far less energy to go along with what is known to be true than it does to pause and question the new information presented. I like to think about it this way: updating your brain is similar to updating your computer's operating system. When the pop-up window appears, telling you that a new software update is ready, you have the option in that moment to click "update now" or "update later." If you click "update now," you will need to stop everything you're doing, save files, search for a power cord, and then wait for your computer to go through the tedious steps of downloading and storing the new software. Not to sound like a pampered modern human, but it's kind of a pain in the ass. So, if you're like me, you almost always click "update later" without a second thought and go back to what you were doing, even if what you were doing was searching on Amazon.

Our brains function in a similar way. When we encounter new information, we have the option to update now or update later. Yes, it's important for the brain to have updated information to do its primary job—making predictions—but the brain also is designed to be efficient and conserve energy.[6] Updating on the fly requires both time and energy. So our brains default to filtering new information into our current system of categories or beliefs. In short, we engage in confirmation bias—even when what we are confirming is painful.

It Hurts, So Why Is It Happening?

Often my clients understand that our brains want to keep the status quo and conserve energy by confirming what we already know. It is sort of easy to match "I am lovable" with knowing my husband loves me, or "I am smart" when I get accepted to a highly prestigious scholarship. It's also not hard to reconcile the core belief "I am reliable" with missing one appointment. Our brain simply rationalizes our action as a mistake or brushes it aside completely. *Yes, I missed the appointment, but I honestly couldn't get there on time given my other commitments. It won't happen again, because, after all, I'm a reliable person.* When it comes to these more favorable views of ourselves, we often can quickly understand what happened and move on. They don't keep us stuck in avoidance. Yet that is not the case with the unfavorable core beliefs. Our brain still works the same way: it tries to confirm those beliefs, but the problem is that the confirmation process is usually painful.

Now, here is the question I often get: *Why is my brain confirming pain? I don't get it! I don't want to think this way, but it keeps happening.* Our brain confirms unfavorable core beliefs to conserve energy. It will do whatever it takes with information coming in to make sure it fits our views of the world, even if it has to bend the information into a pretzel (see figure 2). For example, if you believe that you're a failure and someone congratulates you on a recent promotion, then you might quickly say something like, "Well, everyone gets a promotion after they have been here as long as I have." This thought might not make you feel great, but it feels better than going through the mental energy and gymnastics of asking yourself, *What if I'm really not a failure?* Basically, when the puzzle pieces do not fit each other, your brain pretzels the information to make them fit. "People who get a promotion are usually doing something well," contradicts "I am a failure," but your brain changes "I got a raise" into "I only got a raise because I have worked here for this long." This allows you to maintain the old belief "I am a failure."

Figure 2: How the Brain Makes Faulty Predictions

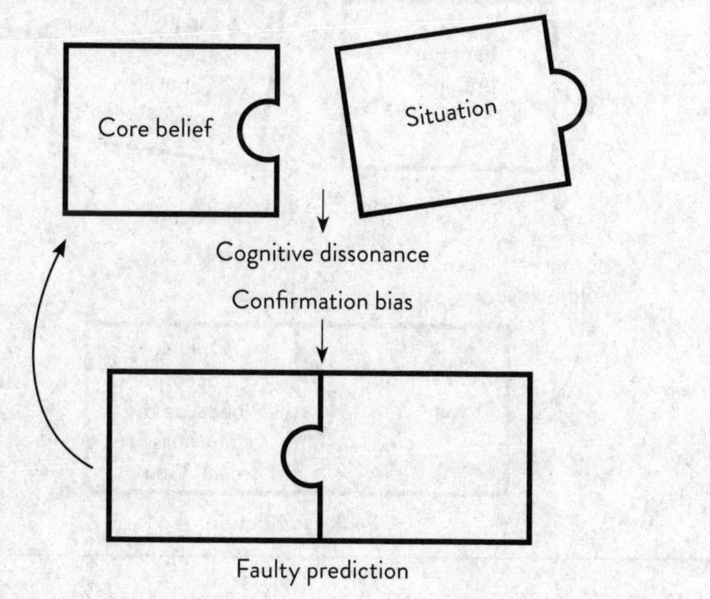

Now let's go back to my brain and its tendency to use the "I'm not enough" category when processing information. Pause for a second and ask yourself: Does being a prolific researcher mean I am not smart? It doesn't! And if you were my client, I would completely agree. Yet, in my brain, it makes sense, even though it hurts. Over time my brain, the product of good old-fashioned human evolution, developed an operating system that sorted all kinds of information into the category of "I am not enough" (see figure 3). In academia, having a paper accepted in a top journal is challenging and often a sign that the authors worked hard, have good science, and likely are smart. Being smart does not fit my puzzle piece, which says that I am not enough. So, for the pieces of my puzzle to fit together, I had to twist

Figure 3: A Look at Dr. Luana's Brain

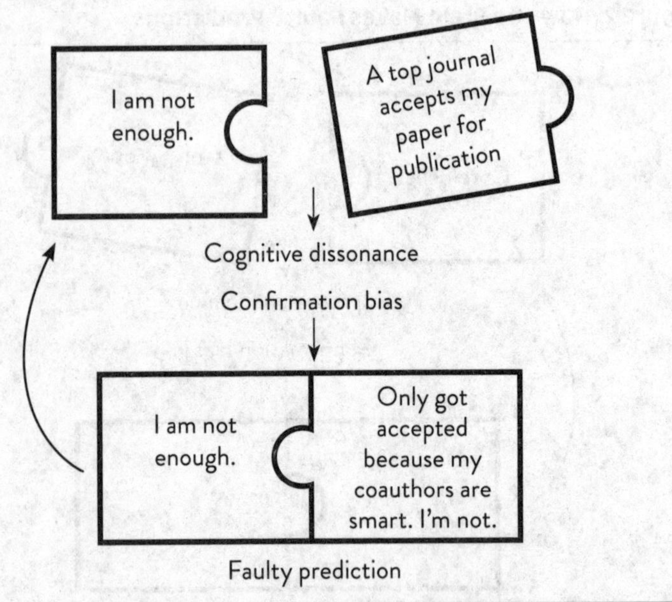

the actual information that I had written the paper, and conclude that it was only accepted because other, smart people were involved. By doing that, I am able to keep my old belief of not being enough alive. Similarly, Sara told herself that she was only asked on a date because they did not know her. After all, her brain concluded, unlovable people don't go on a date. So, to make her own puzzle pieces match, she dismissed anything good about her (see figure 4). Janet's puzzle pieces only fit after she was able to dismiss her co-worker's compliment. After all, her brain said, worthless people are not efficient (see figure 5). We were all avoiding the discomfort of dissonance by confirming what we knew to be true (aka, we avoided the hassle of reworking the entire way we viewed ourselves and the world).

Figure 4: A Look at Sara's Brain

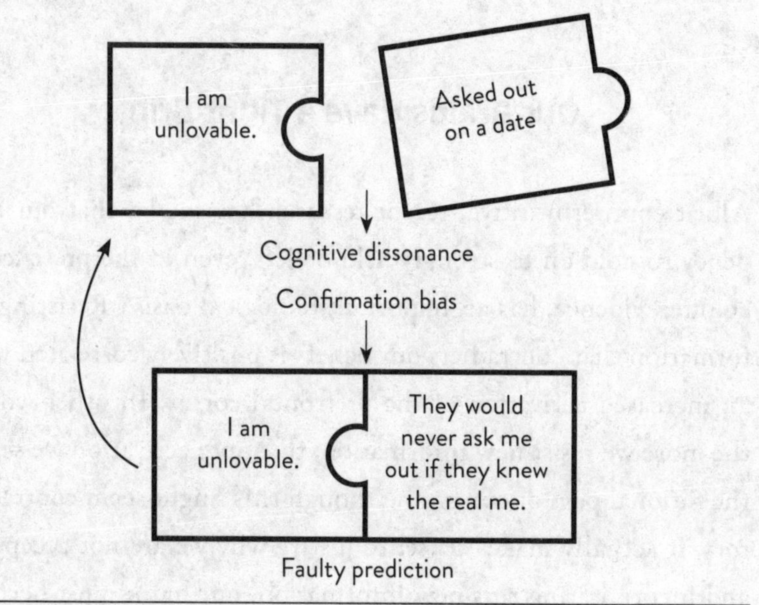

Figure 5: A Look at Janet's Brain

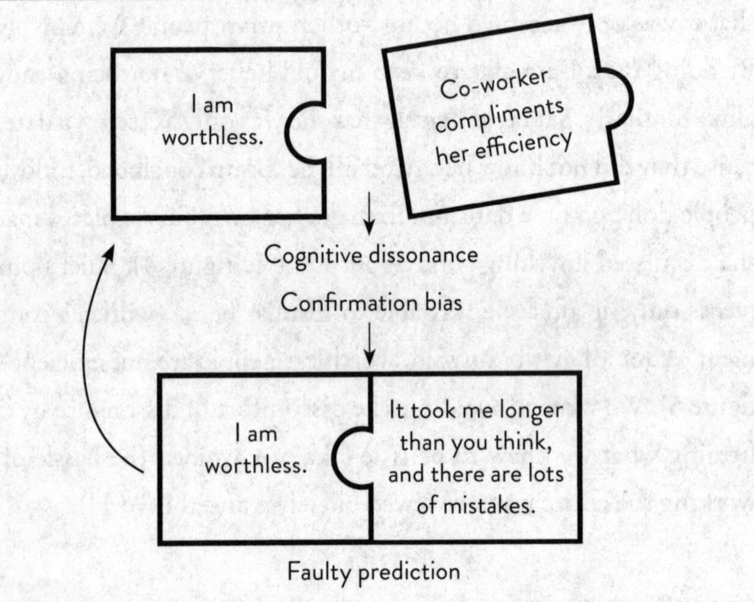

Our Brains Have a Tight Grip

Albeit counterintuitive, recent research has shown that our tendency to hold on to strongly held beliefs, even in the presence of counterevidence, has an important biological basis.[7] Resisting information that contradicts our beliefs is positively correlated with an increased activation of the prefrontal cortex. In other words, the more we resist new information, the more activation we see in the rational part of our brain. Though this might seem contradictory, it actually makes sense: to justify why we are not accepting and incorporating this new information, our brain must become irrationally rational to avoid updating our software and change our minds. In fact, research shows more intelligent people are not less biased,[8] but perhaps more so.

In the short term, creating a rationale to support a prior belief can help us avoid the discomfort of dissonance, but in the long term—say it with me—it keeps us stuck. We end up limiting our ability to see the world clearly because our brain is using outdated software. Sure, we get to remain comfortable enough, but we are far from thriving. It's sort of like using the very first version of Google Maps. Yes, it'll still function, but as new roads and highways are built, using this outdated map with its limited functionality might cause some issues for you.

The Pas de Deux of Cognitive Dissonance and Confirmation Bias

Now you have answers to two of the main questions my clients ask me when it comes to avoiding by retreating. First, *How is my thinking getting me stuck?* And the answer is: when two things don't match, the brain malfunctions! Often people first feel the dissonance in their bodies, maybe a sensation in the pit of their stomachs, and then their brains go off on a scavenger hunt for any information to make sense of the world.

Second, they ask, *Why do I keep saying things to myself that hurt me and make me avoid?* Well, because our brain hates dissonance, it avoids by going into overdrive with confirmation bias about what we already *think we know* about ourselves and the world.

And this is the conundrum of the pas de deux that goes on between cognitive dissonance and confirmation bias. When two things don't compute, we confirm what we already believe, including our fears about the future—which can be very painful.

Renowned Wharton professor Adam Grant described this conundrum in his book *Think Again: The Power of Knowing What You Don't Know*.[9] Grant writes, "Our convictions can lock us in prisons of our own making." He's right. Our own beliefs can lock us into a world of stress, burnout, anxiety, sadness, and hopelessness. But Grant also goes on to say, "The solution is not to decelerate our thinking—it is to accelerate our rethinking." To accelerate our *rethinking*—to overcome our avoidance and get unstuck—we must take on dissonance, dance with it, play with it, hurt with it, and in the end change our beliefs and create cognitive flexibility. Let's learn how in the next chapter: it is time to learn how to *Shift*.

Chapter Five

Shifting to Overcome Avoidance

Our brains are predictive machines that are as amazing in their potential as they are in their ability to cause us pain. Although our brains are only doing their evolutionary jobs, sometimes we end up with outdated lenses that no longer allow us to make accurate predictions about the world. These lenses come in the form of our outdated views of ourselves, others, and the world around us. To maximize our amazing predictive machine, it is imperative that we constantly update the lenses. Of course, none of us have twenty-twenty vision when it comes to our perceptions and beliefs about the world. But the aim here is to improve our vision, not to make it perfect. To do so is to *Shift*. By *Shifting*, you are updating your predictions, taking a wider view of the world, and learning to talk to yourself as you would to your best friend: with kindness, accuracy, and directness. *Shifting* is a skill that must be developed, practiced, and implemented throughout your life. Today, I live a life where I practice *Shifting* daily, in real time, and a lot of times with real success—but don't get me wrong, it was not always this way.

It Is My Fault That He Does Not Love Me!

At fifteen, I was living with my grandmother because she lived in a larger city with a better education system than the small town where we lived. My mom decided this better education system could set me up for a better future. The transition from Governador Valadares to Belo Horizonte had been rough at first, likely because I'd lost my sense of security that I'd usually enjoyed within the comforts of a small town with my mom and sister. But by the end of the year, I had started to adjust and was even enjoying it. Perhaps the joy I had felt at conquering the "big city" is why I agreed to spend a New Year's Eve there with my father, who had been mostly out of the picture since I was ten years old. As a teenager I still desperately wanted to fix whatever was broken—in other words, I still believed that if I were to fix my relationship with him, I would finally overcome my fear of being "not enough" and thus fix myself.

But my father was a no-show on New Year's Eve. Amid tears, sadness, and hopelessness, I sobbed to my grandmother: "If I had been a better child, he would have shown up. He will never love me. I will never have a father. I just can't trust him or anyone. No one will ever show up for me. And now here I am stuck alone, without anyone to spend New Year's Eve with because I told my friends I had other plans. Why did I believe him? I should have known better. It is all my fault."

In her calm, cool, and often collected way, my grandmother asked: "Is there another way to see this situation?"

"No!" I protested. "It is simple: he hates me, doesn't care enough to show up. And it is all my fault. I am the problem."

My grandmother asked again, "Is there another way to see this situation?"

"No! No! And NO!" I told her.

Unfortunately, there is no happy ending to this story. That night, my grandmother was not able to get through to me; there was too much history with my father, too much pain in that moment. As I look back, I see that my brain was in survival mode: my amygdala was predominately in charge, and I was predicting the world through my own beliefs that formed when things fell apart in my childhood: *I am not enough.* Through these lenses, I was unable to even consider another view of the world. Back then, my brain felt like a locked vault; the keys were thrown out, and forever and ever this would be the only way I would ever see the world . . . forever. Did I say *forever*?

The conclusion my brain had drawn generated no dissonance because it just confirmed my core belief. But in doing so, my brain had made a giant pretzel with the information coming in: "My father didn't show" was twisted into "It is all my fault." That day, confirmation bias won: my brain interpreted my father's absence as confirmation that *I wasn't enough.* Yet, there is a catch here. By allowing confirmation bias to guide our conclusions, we are merely confirming beliefs that may no longer fit us or have any basis in reality. That day, I proved that it was indeed my fault that my father was not there because *if I was enough, he would have shown up for me.* (I wish I could give younger me a hug and teach her all that I know today!)

While I hope you have not had the experience of a parent standing you up like this, most of you can likely relate on some level—a friend who disappointed you, a date who didn't show, a boss who did not come through with their promised raise . . .

Let's Look at This Differently

As I write this book, I can fully appreciate the intersection between my grandmother's wisdom and science, and how applying the lessons from this intersection to my own life has allowed me to enjoy a better life, while also helping hundreds of my clients through the work that I do. Yet, at fifteen years old, I had no idea that the simple question my grandmother kept asking me again and again—"Is there another way to see this situation?"—would be legitimized by decades of psychological science.

Today, I know that my grandmother's question is at the core of what psychologists call *cognitive restructuring*, which is the classic cognitive therapy technique that psychologists teach their clients to update their predictions by identifying distorted beliefs and recalibrating them into more balanced views of the world.[1] Cognitive therapy, which relies heavily on this technique, has been demonstrated to be effective to treat all sorts of emotional challenges across a wide range of individuals around the globe—and it has been shown to work for most people.[2] In modern scientific terms, my grandmother was inviting me to question my own brain's predictions and assumptions of the world. She was asking me: *Is the filter you are seeing this situation through the clearest way to interpret this scenario? Is there anything else that you are not considering?*

To *Shift*, you will need to go against the fast and nearly automatic predictions that your brain is currently making when it engages in confirmation bias to consider another way to interpret a situation. Although confirmation bias is fast (and powerful), it only leads to more avoidance in the long term. But when we use the pause we learned to create in chapter 2 to consider other ways to see the situation, we can actually update our lenses and thus our predictions of the world. This pathway will be slow at first and will come with some discomfort because you are forcing your brain to consider another way of thinking. (This very important ability for our brain to pave the way for change is referred to as *neuroplasticity*. And neuroplasticity is awesome!)

Making the Shift

Shifting is a science-driven skill designed to widen our lenses, allowing us to make better predictions in the moment based on the best information we have available to us at that time, while challenging our old assumptions (see figure 1). To change our perspective, we must retrain our brains and actively fight our confirmation biases. To do so, we are going to take three steps: question our automatic predictions, interpret our answers, and update our lenses. As we *Shift*, we will be engaging with cognitive dissonance, and as such, we will experience a little discomfort while practicing this skill. But

Figure 1: A Brain Shift

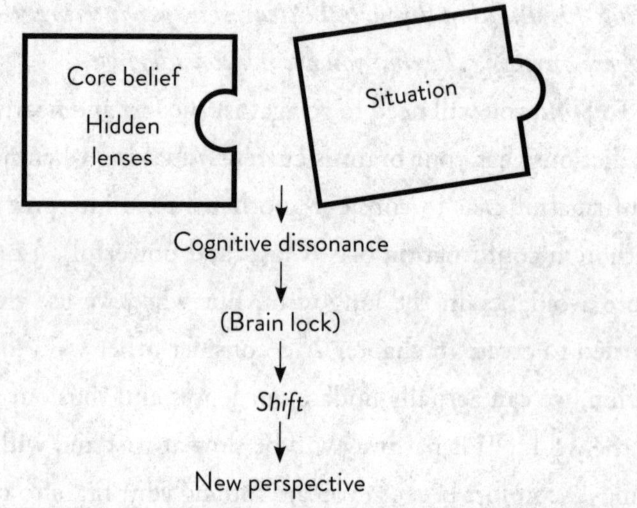

with time this discomfort will lessen and instead we will feel the reward of changing our core beliefs and living a fuller, bolder life.

Janet: I Am Worthless

Enough theory, damn it! Let's apply this *Shift* technique to Janet and see how she was able to get herself unstuck. To review: Janet was an administrative nurse who, by all accounts, was good at her job and worked her ass off. She explained that she had grown up with a strict mother, who had taught her that discipline was the most important path to success. If she worked hard, good things would happen. As such, she was raised to believe that good things happened to good people, and bad things happened to bad people. This became the filter through which Janet's brain processed information. So, when Janet would consider asking her boss for a raise, her brain would put on these glasses without her knowing. Because good things had not happened to her despite her hard ("good") work, she subconsciously believed that she was not worthy of the raise, which led her to see herself as "worthless." During my meetings with Janet, I supported her in completing the following reflection, which led to her *Shift*.

REFLECTION

Janet's Shift

Take a moment to update your brain's predictions by practicing *Shift*. I would recommend that you write out your answers and anchor them on a specific situation so that you can question what you are saying to yourself about that situation. In addition, write your initial prediction and refer back to it so that you can ensure you are asking questions about that prediction.

Situation: Asking for a raise

Prediction: My boss will say no. If I deserved a raise, my boss would have given me one.

1. **Question automatic predictions:**
   a. Is there a different way to see this situation?

      Janet realized she had been working hard and that despite her brain saying otherwise, there were many indicators that she deserved a raise, such as meeting her quotas, delivering several projects on time, and running a large successful team.

   b. What would I say to my best friend in this situation?

(*continued*)

I asked Janet to consider a situation where her best friend was experiencing a similar issue and asked what she would tell her. Janet smiled and told me, "I would tell Pam she has given everything for her job and that she had met all her quotas, so she ought to ask for the raise she so clearly deserves."

2. **Interpret your answers:**
   a. How do these answers change my prediction?
   Janet told me that if she were to continue to believe her current lenses, she would never ask for a raise. But by looking at it through her friend's eyes, she could see how she likely deserved a raise, which made her initial fear and anxiety decrease.
   b. What might I want to do differently?
   If she could believe what her friends have told her, she would ask for a raise.
3. **Updated lenses:**
   a. How will this prediction change my core belief?
   Janet realized that she cannot be "worthless" and still do well at work.
   b. How does updating my lenses make me feel?
   Janet felt relief by considering another way of seeing the world.
   c. What steps can I take to strengthen this prediction pathway?
   Janet decided to keep track daily of any actions she did that went against her belief that she was "worthless" so as to collect information that could contradict her own core belief.

Janet's Outcome

Janet committed to doing this reflection like reps in the gym, striving to really *Shift* how she spoke to herself. At first, it felt unnatural, but eventually she was able to change the narrative that she was worthless. By doing so, Janet was finally able to not only ask for a raise, but also advocate for a promotion, which she received. Janet told me that she no longer felt like a prisoner to her old beliefs and, as such, she was allowing herself for the first time to dream about possibilities of pursuing new career paths. It wasn't easy or without discomfort, but she realized that anxiety was not what was keeping her stuck: it was the avoidance that occurred every time she took the easy way out, leading her back to her prior beliefs and patterns instead of questioning them like any good detective.

But not everything is all rosy. Every so often, she still falls prey to those same old beliefs. Only now they don't hold as much power over her. Here is something important to note: we will never be able to completely quiet our brains with their distorted or less-than-helpful thoughts. The spin will always happen, and our goal here is not to forever eliminate negative or stressful thoughts from our mind, but to do as Janet did: develop a healthier relationship to these thoughts. As you gain proficiency in this skill, you will find that although these thoughts still occur, they happen far less often, and when they do pop up, they don't have the same power they once did to throw you off course and take control over your actions.

Sara's Shift: I Am Unlovable

For Sara, there was one belief that fundamentally filtered her worldview: "I am unlovable." This might strike you as strange: Why would Sara's brain want to confirm something as hurtful as "I am unlovable"? You might be saying to yourself, *Even* my *fucked-up brain doesn't do that!*

Sara and I worked hard for nearly a year to uncover and change her painful core belief. At first, Sara's brain did whatever it could to avoid discussing it. For example, she would change the topic in therapy, but whenever this happened, I would gently steer things back.

In the end, what helped Sara the most was looking at this belief through the lenses of her friends. Being part of a strong and supportive LGBTQ+ community at Harvard, Sara was eventually able to tell me that she would never say to any of her friends at school that they are "unlovable" because they are gay. By considering what she would say to a friend in her situation, Sara was able to slowly free herself from this belief.

After a year, Sara came out to her parents during winter break. As she predicted, it was explosive at first. Her father retreated into his office for days and ignored her. Her mom tried to change Sara's mind, insisting that this was perhaps just a phase. Through tears and fear, Sara held strong and was able to do so because she knew she was, in fact, lovable.

It has been three years since Sara came out, and I recently got an email from her with a photo of her and her family at a pride parade. I will confess, Sara's dad looked very uncomfortable, but as Sara described in the email, he was trying. Sara told me that although there was still a lot of discomfort around her new (to them) identity, things were improving. Like everything else, the big stuff takes time. But Sara was much happier now that she could bring her full self to those she loved the most. As the (useful) cliché goes, we can only control what we can control. By *Shifting*, Sara was able to do just that.

It is important to highlight that Sara wasn't entirely wrong in her prediction of a bad reaction from her parents. When it comes to matters of sexual identity within family structures, people will react in different ways. Data from interviews with 155 LGBTQ+ individuals about their coming out experience found that parents' emotional responses can span a wide range, either lacking, negative, mixed, or positive with accompanying silence, invalidation, ambivalence, and validation, respectively.[3] When parents or loved ones respond negatively to gender and sexuality revelations, there are serious negative consequences, such as higher incidence of depression and lower self-esteem.[4] So sometimes there are hints of truth in even unhelpful predictions.

In Cases of Discrimination, *Shift* Doesn't Cut It

Not every situation can be solved with a new perspective. For example, let me tell you about what Marcus, an African American client of mine, faced firsthand when he got accepted to a prestigious advanced degree at Harvard. He was coming to Harvard from Georgetown Law and had been looking forward to arriving in Boston to start this new chapter of his life. Because he was proactive, he had spoken to the dean of this school within the Harvard system a few times and had decided to come to Boston to meet him in person. Marcus arrived at this prestigious office, announced to the secretary that he was there to meet with the dean, and sat waiting. When the dean came out of his office, Marcus described to me that the dean scanned the room, looked at his executive secretary, and asked, "Where did Marcus go?" In Marcus's words, "the secretary got whiter than a ghost" and pointed to him. The dean, without a thought (so I hope), told Marcus, "Oh, I thought you looked different," which affirmed all of Marcus's beliefs about being Black, being different, not fitting in, and being discriminated against in an institution like Harvard.

As Marcus and I discussed this scenario, my grandmother's questions failed both of us because there doesn't appear to be any other way to interpret this situation beyond prejudice. Yet, for Marcus, this awful and painful experience had triggered his core view of himself—"I am insufficient"—which in turn triggered sadness and led him to consider dropping out of his program.

In situations in which we are dealing with discrimination, sexism, homophobia, or microaggressions, it is important to face the reality of the situation. When we're talking about discrimination, it can be challenging to consider a broader or heterodox perspective on the topic, because injustice and inequality are facts in this world. Yet, cognitive dissonance and confirmation bias can also appear, even in such sensitive topics, and at times this might affirm our own unhelpful core belief. In Marcus's case, he was discriminated against, but because it activated his core belief, it put him at risk of dropping out of the program that he had worked hard to be accepted to.

Today, I love my Latina identity, take pride in my curves, and often talk to my son about the fact that he is "Brazilian, Mexican, and American" and that all of those are part of him. I am trying to teach Diego to integrate his identities in a way that allows him more flexible beliefs about himself and to not get stuck in black-and-white thinking. But I won't lie to you, whenever I am in a white-majority Harvard meeting with mostly high-power, older men, I still have trouble thinking "I am enough." What changed for me is that I now proudly sit at the table!

Don't Sweat the Small Stuff, Just *Shift*

I have been sharing examples in which my clients and I have faced painful deep core beliefs that are causing us significant distress. But *Shifting* is a skill that applies to more than just the "deep" stuff in life. It is actually a way of seeing the world: even when it is just small stuff, *Shifting* will help. For example, my husband, David, was teaching his graduate class last night, when he noticed one student had checked out. His brain immediately said, *I am not engaging well with the students; I need to do better*, which made him slightly anxious while teaching. But David has had his share of coaching on *Shifting* during our marriage, so he asked himself, *What else might be happening here?* and immediately he came up with a few possibilities: 1) it is a night class; perhaps the student is tired, and 2) maybe something happened for them and that is why they seem checked out. David's *Shift* allowed him to keep teaching without his anxiety escalating. In this case, he actually had a nice surprise: the student came to him at break to tell him they were not feeling well so they were going home, and they apologized for being checked out.

Our close friend John tends to get stuck in predictions that would confirm he is "not such a great friend." I bet many of us have had a few thoughts like this, but John has become a pro at *Shifting*. The other day he came over and told me that the fact that I had not returned his text for a week had made him very anxious, afraid that he had upset me. But in a sort of sarcastic way, he joked, "Then I asked myself, *What would Luana say here?*, and the answer was clear: if she was upset, I would know." This helped him to calm down and stop wondering about conflict in our relationship when there was none.

Parenting is another domain where *Shifting* is very helpful because parents (myself included) often jump to the worst-case scenario when it comes to their kids' reactions. For example, our son started kindergarten and came home upset the first day. My brain screamed, *He will hate school. Now we have a problem. Did something bad happen? How do I fix it?* Anxiety knocked on my door, and I opened it, but I answered with my own *Shift* question: "What else can explain why Diego is so upset"? The answer to which was: *This is likely a big transition for him; he needs time to adjust. Perhaps he is tired from waking up earlier than usual. Changing schools and missing all his friends might be scary for him. This will take time.* When it comes to children, we sometimes have no clue what is really happening, so having many competing explanations at a time can really help to calm the catastrophes that our brains can create.

Now it's your turn. Take a moment to practice *Shifting* by completing the reflection on the next page.

REFLECTION

Shifting Our Perspectives

Take a moment to challenge your thinking. I would recommend that you write out your answers and anchor them on a specific situation so that you can examine what you are saying to yourself about that situation. In addition, write your initial prediction and refer back to it so that you can ensure you are asking questions about that prediction.

Situation: ____________________

Prediction: ____________________

1. **Question automatic predictions:**

   a. Is there a different way to see this situation?

   b. What would I say to my best friend in this situation?

2. **Interpret your answers:**

   a. How do these answers change my prediction?

   b. What might I want to do differently?

3. **Updated lenses:**

   a. How will this prediction change my core belief?

   b. How does updating my lenses make me feel?

   c. What steps can I take to strengthen this prediction pathway?

Yoga for the Brain

The great part about developing this kind of cognitive flexibility is that once you become more comfortable changing your perspective, you start to develop the ability to deal with negative thoughts more effectively. By doing so, your brain becomes less rigid and more willing to fight confirmation bias.[5] *Shifting* is the opposite of avoidance. It's like going to the gym. At first you might dread doing a dead lift: it's intimidating, it's a new skill, and it often leaves you sore. But in time, you learn to relish the feeling of accomplishment, and even the feeling of discomfort can have a positive connotation. In the gym and in psychology alike, discomfort often signals growth.

When our brains are flexible, changing our route at will is easier, and this has positive downstream effects in other areas of our lives.[6] Higher cognitive flexibility is related to better reading skills,[7] greater resilience,[8] more creativity,[9] and a better subjective sense of the quality of one's life.[10]

Incremental Shifts

The pain of my father's abandonment is still present when I consider what happened when I was young. Yet through my grandmother's training and starting my brain's own *Shift* process, I no longer see him or the world the same way. In my adult life, I have been able to understand that my father lacked a lot of the skills that I share with you in this book. He lost his father when he was three years old, which meant he never had a model of what parenting as a family could look like. Besides, he had me at twenty-two years old, which means his own brain was not fully developed. In his adult years my father has come to understand the pain that he caused me and has even apologized. He has worked to develop his own skills, remarried, and has a happy new family—all of whom I have a relationship with. It is painful to know that, if my father had had the skills I am sharing with you, perhaps my early childhood would not have been so traumatic, but I am reassured by the fact that all of us can learn to *Shift*, and when we do, life changes.

But it is important to note that *Shifting* is not a magical, bulletproof technique that always works to the fullest extent. We cannot expect to fully eradicate from our brains any trace of cognitive distortions. Throughout my life, *Shifting* my brain has been a constant internal battle, in which I am sometimes able to win by creating a more flexible and balanced way of seeing the world, and at other times I get stuck, avoiding painful thoughts by confirming my own core beliefs. As you commit to practicing *Shifting*, you will notice that it gets easier to arrive at an alternative prediction—assuming you are not in full-fledged survival mode. And that is my word of caution to you here: make sure that when you commit to practicing *Shifting*, you are not working on the most challenging situation in your life. Just like in the gym, we get stronger by practicing good form in order to lift more. Same goes for this technique: we need to practice cognitive flexibility to be able to handle more emotionally loaded situations.

Finally, find your own way to remember to *Shift*. For me, seeing the picture of my grandmother forces me to ask, *Is there another way to see this situation?* Today the question is almost automatic for me. Yet, for Sara, she had to come up with her own *Shift* question to be able to remember. She would say to herself, *How do I talk back to my brain?* At other times, the only *Shift* she could find was to say to herself, *My brain is an asshole, and I am not going to listen.* On the other hand, Julie, the CEO of a Fortune 100 company, told me that after a while she would say to herself, *What would Dr. Luana say in this situation?* I laughed when Julie told me this because I don't have all the answers, but I do like to interrogate my thoughts, so maybe she was onto something.

I want to invite you to hold compassion for yourself as you practice this new skill and to remember that, realistically, it will take time. And if you find yourself getting the hang of *Shifting* but still avoiding, it might be time to learn how to *Approach* or *Align*, which is what we're about to do.

PART III

Approach

Chapter Six

The Pressure Cooker: Reacting to Avoid

One of my most cherished memories of growing up in Brazil is my mother making black beans. A common comfort dish back home, there was nothing better than the smell of garlic mingling with bacon as the beans simmered away. Whenever I heard the pressure cooker whistling as I walked up to our house after school, I knew we were in for a great meal. When I was seven years old, my mom caught me trying to open the pressure cooker while it was simmering and she somehow—with lightning speed and a loud scream—stopped me. I moved away, tears in my eyes, trying to understand why she had yelled at me.

Perhaps because of this incident, I have often used the analogy of a pressure cooker to explain reacting as a form of avoidance to my clients. When we avoid through reacting, it's like we become a pressure cooker without a pressure valve (or if we do have one, we don't trust it will work). When our emotions begin to boil, the temperature and pressure inside us rise so fast and so violently that we figuratively explode. And what do we do when we feel like we are about to explode? We act to eliminate the perceived threat by doing whatever we can to feel better fast. From an emotional standpoint, the explosion immediately—yet temporarily—relieves some of the pressure, but afterward we are always left with an even bigger mess to clean up and plenty of hurt feelings to go along with it. Blowing off steam feels helpful in the moment, but it can turn into a continual reactive avoidance pattern, which ultimately robs us of a bold life.

Reactive Avoidance: My Many Faces

Reactive avoidance has many forms, some harder to detect than others. But I will confess, I know this one well because reactive avoidance is the go-to tactic I have employed my entire life to avoid discomfort. I fight back to feel better. I mean, sure, putting on a conservative pantsuit might not seem like your idea of a fight, but there's a defiance contained within this action that is, deep down, my version of flipping the bird. I will also react with an email (I know, I'm a true Hell's Angel over here). Case in point: About a year ago, my mentor at MGH, a remarkably kind woman named Susan, sat me down and said, "Can we talk about your emails? Specifically, when you're stressed?"

I could see in Susan's face that she was struggling to be constructive, despite the awkward nature of the conversation. I remember the spike in my anxiety, as I waited for her to tell me something awful. *Oh my God, the only person who has my back is about to fire my ass! The traitor!* As these premature thoughts were rushing through my head, I tried to plaster a fake (and probably deranged-looking) smile on my face.

Susan continued, "Luana, you are one of the most productive people I know. You're brilliant, caring, and you know I love working with you."

My heart pounded while I waited for her to say ". . . and yet, I'm tossing you out on the street like a piece of garbage."

But the axe didn't drop. Instead, she proceeded to tell me that she had noticed I might be my own worst enemy. "I've noticed that you seem to respond to emails late at night. Like, very late at night. With urgency. And ferocity. And an almost inappropriate directness. For example, last night you responded to Joe, who had requested to use some of your training material. You didn't only say no; you wrote out a whole laundry list of reasons why there was a problem with his request. I know there is a lot of history there in your relationship with Joe, but was that response at 11 p.m. really needed? And did you really have to wash your dirty laundry in front of so many powerful people who were also cc'd on the email?"

Before she can even finish her argument, I immediately go on the defensive: fighting back to end this excruciating discomfort. I launch into an impassioned explanation! At once! In other words, I'm reacting in response to someone telling me about my reacting! *Oh, so you think my emails feel too direct? Well, let me show you how not reactive I am by responding in a highly reactive manner!*

Of course I didn't know at the time that I was putting my avoidance method into high gear, because I was too busy ranting and raving: "I just wanted to be clear that it is not okay to use my materials and adapt them. Who does he think he is?" I can barely hear myself over the sound of my heart pounding in my chest.

She gives me one of her kind, matronly looks and says: "Luana, I totally get it. You're amazing at what you do, and I know that at times this person has not been fair with you. But between you and me, sometimes you can be a bit . . . impulsive. Too quick to act."

She continues, "It's just not necessary to be responding to emails at 11 p.m. And in some cases, it might be getting in the way of your own success."

I feel myself turning pugnacious for the nth time in this conversation as I hold back hot tears. Susan remains calm and poised, notices my obvious discomfort, and assures me that this is not that big of a deal but that she just wanted me to "give it some thought." As soon as she finishes speaking, I immediately feel some mild relief that this conversation is over. I'm sure my subconscious was telling me, "See? Fighting back always works! When in doubt, put 'em up!"

As I leave her office, I'm left wondering about the things she said. Am I really impulsive when it comes to emailing? Does she have a point? Do I react and respond quickly to avoid my anxiety? I was not sure but also could not dismiss what Susan was saying. I mean, *Sure, I reply quickly*, I remember thinking as I wandered back to my office in a daze. *But that's only to prove to others how competent I am! Am I supposed to let the emails just sit there?* The thought of all those work emails just piling up makes me bonkers! If I get them out of the way, I don't have to feel like I'm sleeping on the job. If caring is a crime, Your Honor, then I'm guilty as charged.

of things that are "important" in their to-do lists, only to avoid the things that really need to get done.[1] As described by Perry, "I am working on this essay as a way of not doing all of those things"—namely, the things he needed to do for his job, like grading papers. What Perry first pointed out was a phenomenon that many people refer to now as *productive procrastination*. Productive procrastinators, Perry says, "can be motivated to do difficult, timely and important tasks, as long as these tasks are a way of not doing something more important."

This is a sneaky type of reactive avoidance because often we are doing something that feels responsible, so how can that be avoidance? But once again we must look at the definition of avoidance: 1) Did my brain perceive threat? 2) Did I get uncomfortable? 3) Did my response provide me with a quick fix? and 4) Is there a negative consequence?

Let's look at an example. My husband, David, is the kind of person who avoids by retreating: if he can go into his brain and try to outthink his anxiety, he'll do it. But just like anyone, including me, he uses more than one avoidance tactic. For example, as I am under the gun in this crazy sprint to finish this book, we are also about to receive twelve houseguests for my birthday (it's a Latin thing). Traditionally when I have guests, I tend to go a little overboard: new sheets, vacuuming the rugs, shopping for groceries so I can make our favorite Brazilian dishes, and so on. However, this time I have a book deadline, so I can't do any of the usual things I do. David, on the other hand, tends to be calmer about these scenarios and he usually doesn't fuss. Yet this time, he's on the move, doing a ton. In the past few days alone, he has painted the deck railing, replaced electrical outlets, bought new covers for our bedroom set, re-arranged the garage, and on and on.

At first, I was impressed by this magnificent display of domestic productivity, but last night at dinner I began to detect a hint of reactive avoidance, or "productive procrastination." David is a professor at Boston University and his academic semester is about to start in three weeks, which means he needs to be prepping for his fall classes. So, at dinner last night I asked the question that had been burning in my brain: "How is the fall prepping coming along?" Now to be fair to David, he is married to "the avoidance guru," so he sheepishly smiled, took a sip of wine, and told me flat out: "Yes, I'm avoiding it, but isn't it nice how much I got done around the house?" We both laughed. It *was* nice, but I also know that he will be paying a price when our guests arrive. Eventually, he will have to prepare for the semester, and he'll be upset if he's stuck doing that instead of enjoying our family gathering. And so, he promised me (and himself) that he would tackle his avoidance ASAP. (As I write this, I can see him teaching Diego to play basketball outside: adorable, yes, but not really helping his upcoming semester. Avoidance strikes again!)

But I don't want to give the wrong idea: productive procrastination is not always a form of reactive avoidance. For it to qualify as such, it must be associated with a cost. For instance, my friend Janaina is the type of person who always has a long to-do list, but she somehow gets everything done and is not anxious about it. For Janaina, this is just how she lives her life. So, if that is you, no worries. What is avoidance for me might not be for you and vice versa.

The Thief of Joy

Have you ever been scrolling through Instagram, Twitter, or another onerous social platform when all of a sudden you bump up against something that is completely opposite from your worldview and it presses your buttons? Take your pick: vaccines, political affiliations, abortion, the latest celebrity scandal. The minute we bump up against something that is oppositional to our views, we feel cognitive dissonance. And guess what: our brains sense danger. And what do we do in those situations? Suddenly, before we even know what we're doing, we're in fight mode, firing from the hip, typing fast, and sending that post out into the world as fast as humanly possible! It's a perfect encapsulation of what it means to *react*. Doesn't that feel better? Of course it does! At least . . . at first.

Passively scrolling on social media inevitably leads to social comparisons. Social comparison, somewhat obviously, is the process of "comparing oneself with others to evaluate or enhance some aspects of the self."[2] We compare how we look, what we've achieved, or how skilled we are at something. We all make social comparisons as a matter of our evolutionary biology, but social media has drastically expedited and magnified our ability to do so.

In particular, making comparisons to others who are "better off" (whether this is actually true or not is irrelevant—what matters is that we *perceive* them as better off) has been shown to be related to increased depressive symptoms[3] and increased feelings of sadness.[4] Social media use has also been connected to negative body image and unhealthy eating behaviors.[5] These negative effects are particularly pronounced in young girls. A study conducted in the United Kingdom found that girls ten to fifteen years old are more likely than boys to have lower well-being as a direct result of their social media usage.[6] When we couple these findings with social media's distorted reality and the complex algorithms designed to deliver content to us, we end up with a potentially toxic relationship to our beloved apps.

While most research on social media comparisons has largely focused on its direct negative emotional impact, such as anxiety and depression, I have seen social media comparison trigger reactive avoidance for some of my clients. That may not seem like too much of a problem initially, but eventually it leads to negative outcomes. It's just a longer and messier route to the same problem. This is where Angad's story comes in.

When I first met Angad, he gave every appearance of having a happy, well-adjusted life. He had just turned twenty, was loving college, had a good group of friends, and was close to his family. Yet Angad shared with me that internally, things were not quite so placid. He had recently created an Instagram account, and complained that he found himself constantly comparing his life to those encountered within his broader social media network: "who looks better," "who travels more," "whose girlfriend is hottest" . . . the list went on and on for young Angad. Angad's description was no different from that of many young college students I have worked with, for whom social media led to comparison. Yet, I was not sure how this was a problem for Angad. I asked him what would happen when he saw a posting where someone else appeared to be doing better than he was.

Angad looked at me with a startling seriousness: "I panic. Like, if I don't do something to match that, I'm a loser."

It can be hard for adults who weren't raised with social media to take such claims seriously. But as a clinician who knows the signs of distress when I see them, I knew Angad wasn't being dramatic. His brain perceived these messages as a threat as real to him as anything else.

I offered to him, "It sounds like when you encounter a post that you find distressing, you get anxious, panic, and that feels awful. Is that right?"

He nodded.

"Okay, so what do you do then?"

"I start posting a lot. See, I have a secret folder on my phone with my best pictures—fun times, cool places, whatever—and I post them as if they were happening right now."

My reaction must have said a lot because he laughed in response. The generational divide between us was now fully established. And yet, the operating system in our brains was the same. Feeling a bit like a dinosaur talking to an astronaut, I asked him to describe the most recent incident during which he felt the need to dig into his secret folder.

"After we came back from spring break last week, a friend was posting all about his vacation in Europe with his new girlfriend. He's an okay-looking guy, but his girlfriend is the supermodel type, just *hot*—" he paused here and looked at me apologetically.

I laughed and encouraged him to continue.

"So, I got anxious, you know, comparing myself to him and decided, 'Hey, I also have pictures with hot girls!' So I posted a bunch from a party last summer."

Following the logic of this behavior, I replied, "It sounds like you solved the problem!"

"Yes, at least for a bit. I can't explain it, but when I post fast, I get this relief, like the panic is going away because I am only focusing on posting. But to be truthful, after a while, I just end up feeling gross. It's not a good headspace to be in." He looked genuinely upset, and I could see the shame and anxiety that this behavior was causing him. No matter the cause, it was clear to me that he was trapped in the avoidance rut with no idea of how to get out.

Although for you, the relationship with social media might lead to a different outcome, for Angad it resulted in reactive avoidance. He would see something such as other guys with attractive girlfriends, which would trigger his brain to perceive danger in the form of "I am a loser," which immediately brought up his discomfort—or, as he called it, panic. To make himself feel better fast, he would post one photo after another after another. Posting photos would temporarily and quickly relieve the panic, but because it is reactive avoidance, it does not keep the panic down for long.

So, does being on social media mean that we are reactively avoiding? Posting rapid-fire on social media is one way we react to soothe our difficult emotions. But when it comes to our engagement with the online world, there are other emotional responses people might have when scrolling. For some, negative feelings can lead to retreating completely: people may avoid social media altogether to minimize the fears around being compared to others (with apologies for the editorializing, this probably isn't a bad strategy, akin to just avoiding fast food). In fact, research shows that one reason individuals create so-called Finstas (fake Instagram accounts) is to escape social scrutiny.[7] Alternatively, some of my clients retreat and avoid things such as writing a college essay by just scrolling for hours on social media. If you find yourself more in the retreating spectrum and you still want to engage with these platforms,

I suggest you work on the skill of *Shifting* (covered in part II of this book) to change your relationship with social media.

Texting to Soothe Anxiety

When it comes to romantic relationships, patterns of avoiding through reacting often show up early. Let's take Filomena as an example. Filomena was adopted from Ecuador at an early age by two loving, yet much older parents. She had no siblings and described herself as always having been mildly anxious. Her mom told me that Filomena always had considerable difficulties being apart from them. From an early age, she would often get upset whenever her mother would leave the house, panicking and wondering whether she'd ever come back. Filomena shared with me that she always feared abandonment (a common fear among adopted children) and attaching to people was hard for her, as she often felt as if the other shoe would drop any minute and she would be left all alone. By the time I met Filomena, she was in college and, by all accounts, had been doing well both academically and socially. But there was one domain of her life that was getting her stuck again and again: forming romantic relationships.

Filomena had started dating in college, at first casually, but she told me that she couldn't do the "casual" thing—it just made her too anxious. So, she tried to get serious with a few guys, but while it felt comfortable for her, the swiftness with which she began calling them her "boyfriend" would make them distance themselves from her just as quickly. She would almost immediately demand exclusivity, which would freak them out, at which point Filomena would just break it off in her own (reactive) manner.

But things were starting to change for her. At the time of our first meeting, she had been dating Ted for a few months and felt that she was starting to fall for him. Distressingly, she felt he was starting to pull away a bit, and the stressful push-pull of her dating life had led her into my office.

Filomena explained to me that out of all the people she had dated in her young life, Ted seemed to be the one with whom she felt the most comfortable: he was reliable, respectful, and always made her feel secure.

"Sounds lovely. So . . . what's the problem?" I asked.

"Well, I have a lot of trouble being away from Ted. I know that we should have our own friends and interests, but I get so scared, you know? He had been telling me that he wanted a little time to himself so he could hang out with his guy friends a bit more, and I wanted to make him happy, so we tried a few times . . . but it was a disaster. I just got really upset and anxious and even when I didn't want to, I would send multiple text messages. The most recent time this happened was last Friday night; I knew he was out with his friends playing pool, but even though I knew where he was and who he was with, I freaked out."

At this point, she pulled out her phone and began reciting their text exchange.

"'Hey,'" she began, "'how are you?' Smiley face emoji. No reply. I try not to text him again because he had asked me to give him some space but two minutes go by and I can't help myself. So, I text, 'Are you guys having fun?' Lots of emojis."

"What are you feeling at this point?" I asked.

"I'm super anxious, wondering why he isn't responding. And I'm worried, too. What if he's not responding because he got in a car accident? A drunk driver or something. I can't help it, but I keep having this image of him dead in a ditch somewhere. Or maybe he's hooking up with some other girl! So I start texting him a ton . . . 'Hey Ted, are you okay? Why aren't you answering me? Are you upset? Did I do something wrong???'" She stopped abruptly, realizing how this behavior must look to an impartial observer. "I know this looks silly, but it made so much sense to me at the time. I needed to know things were okay and each text made me feel a little relief, but when he didn't answer, it just got me more anxious, so I kept texting."

"Did you ever hear from him?"

"Eventually I got a text back from him." She scrolled through her phone and read: "'I'm okay, but this is not cool.'"

She shook her head. "I was crushed! But I also knew that he was right. The problem is, I just don't know how to stop myself in situations like this when I get anxious. I love Ted and I'm afraid I'm going to drive him away if I don't learn to control these urges. It's my own fault, but my phone makes it too easy to act like this."

The reality is, Filomena is not alone when it comes to having access to a phone and how that might have changed how she relates to dating. In fact, in 2019, Pew Research Center reported that five billion people throughout the world had a mobile device.[8] To put that number in some shocking perspective, research suggests that only three to four billion people own a toothbrush.[9] Let that sink in for a minute: more people on this planet own a phone than a toothbrush. And unlike a toothbrush, these devices are constantly pinging, buzzing, and pestering us throughout the day. All our lowly toothbrushes ask of us is two minutes twice a day. (To say nothing of humble dental floss.)

As you probably know from experience, and can see in Filomena's case, sometimes we kinda, sorta use our phones in not-so-helpful ways. I know, a shocking statement.

What? Dr. Luana, are you telling me smartphones don't always encourage us to act in sane or rational ways? How dare you!

I know, controversial stuff. Checking our phones, doom scrolling, and, yes, sending multiple frantic text messages have been shown across multiple research studies to be related to feelings of sadness, anxiety, and stress.[10] As if starting a new relationship wasn't riddled with enough emotions and pitfalls! Now we also have to contend with the emotional sequelae (fancy word alert!) of trying to communicate effectively using our phones (sometimes even using the modern version of hieroglyphics). When we don't hear back from our partner, the anxiety only grows. One particularly relevant study showed that when stressed individuals do not receive responses to their texts to a partner during a fifteen-minute period, they end up with higher blood pressure than individuals who receive even the most mundane messages in reply (like a bland comment about the weather).[11] The pain of waiting for those three dots (the ones that signify that someone is typing) to appear—or, even worse, watching them appear and then fade away—is real.

For Filomena, sending another text was a way to get a hit of relief during this period of waiting. The hope that the next text would get through and she'd soon receive a speedy response let her relax for a moment. But when Ted didn't respond, her anxiety intensified. This is an old pattern of avoidance—short-term gain, long-term loss. Filomena's reactive avoidance had gotten her stuck.

Tick Tick . . . Boom!

For some of my clients, strong emotions don't lead to just blowing a little steam, but to full-blown interpersonal explosions. Explosions or outbursts are yet another way that reactive avoidance shows up, and they tend to occur when the false alarm feels too close or inescapable.[12] Take Oliver, for instance. Oliver walked into my office to address an anger problem, even though he didn't really think he had a problem to begin with. Oliver told me that his daughters had given him a joke gift for Father's Day: a roll of duct tape, upon which they had written the words "In Case of Emergency, Apply to Oliver's Mouth." They suggested that he bring the gift to work and keep it on his desk so that the next time he felt an angry outburst coming on, he could nip it in the bud.

Though the gift was intended as a joke, Oliver wasn't laughing as he told me about the tape. He shared that he actually felt crushed by the fact that those closest to him saw him this way. He said he had always been a self-described hothead but that he never really saw it as much of an issue. Some people run cool; others run hot. He felt he was direct and to the point, and he ultimately wanted to bring out the best in the people who worked for him. "Sure, maybe I don't have the most elegant way of expressing myself, but how is it my problem that my co-workers have such thin skin?"

"Fair question," I conceded, wanting to meet him where he was, "but if it's everyone else's problem, why are you here?" Turns out this visit wasn't Oliver's choice. After a recent blowup at work, Oliver's direct boss—the company's CEO—had mandated that he meet with someone to address his tendency to—ahem—"tell it like it is."

I told him, "Oliver, I totally get where you're coming from. A lot of people tell me I can be too direct sometimes too. A bit too forward. And sometimes it rubs people the wrong way."

"Really?" Oliver didn't seem to believe that the petite, polite New-England-by-way-of-Brazil doctor seated before him could be anything like him.

Oliver seemed a little uncomfortable—which made sense: maybe a guy who was so used to seeking out or instigating conflict was always set to "slightly on edge" as his default. Temperamentally, we didn't seem to have much in common. So, I took a chance to see whether I could get him to chill out a bit and we could begin our session with our rational brains leading the way. Nobody would mistake me for a comedian, but I thought I'd start with a joke. Or at least a funny-ish story. Anything to try to reset his nervous system a bit.

"Funny story," I said to Oliver, hoping he might believe me. "When I first came to the US, I spoke very little English, so I learned about expressions by hearing them. After all, you don't actually see colloquial expressions in a lot of academic books. So, for my first few years in the US, I would always tell my friends that I didn't get this whole '*Shit* around the bush' saying. They would always nod politely and look at me with confusion."

Oliver looked confused too, and I reassured him that his confusion was indeed the correct response.

"So after I'd been saying '*shit* around the bush' for probably ten years, a friend of mine finally said, 'Hey Luana, you do know that the expression is "beat around the bush," right?' I didn't! Naturally, I was embarrassed, yet again. See in Brazil, the bathrooms in gas stations are basically horrifying, so on road trips, the roadside bushes were the much better option, and so I grew up around people literally 'shitting around the bush.'"

Okay, so I'm not the Brazilian Seinfeld (even my comedy references are outdated!), but Oliver laughed and seemed to relax a bit. Mission accomplished. So, I jumped in to try to understand how Oliver saw his own anger. I asked him to tell me about any recent incidents where his anger got the better of him or caused an issue at work.

He told me a story where one of his direct reports included a significant error on a financial report. As he sat there at his desk, he immediately felt furious and, within seconds, found himself storming over to her cubicle to, as he put it, "tell it like it is."

I asked him what a third-party observer would have noticed if they'd been watching him at such a moment.

He paused, as though he wasn't used to thinking of himself in these terms. "Well, I guess I'm talking fast, and I'm probably raising my voice."

"Probably?" I asked.

"Okay, I am raising my voice. And I'm probably going over all the things that were wrong with the report in detail."

"Okay, and then what?"

"I guess I just sorta storm out of there?"

"How do you feel as you're 'telling it like it is.'"

"I guess I feel good in that particular moment. Maybe not good, but competent. In charge. Someone has to have the guts to correct mistakes, otherwise we all look like assholes. Maybe I can even teach whoever I'm talking to a thing or two."

"Alright, so you school your underling on her mistake. What

happens next? How long do you feel good following this exchange?"

"Not very long. I started to feel bad because maybe I was too hard on her. She made a mistake, I chewed her out, and the poor woman looked like she was going to cry. I don't want to be a bully, but it pisses me off when people turn in crap work, because I rely on them to do their job so I can do mine. It's not my job to babysit my employees. I bust my ass all day and the last thing I need is more work on my plate."

I asked him how often something like this happens, and the answer seemed to surprise him: "Pretty much every week." Then he added, "I can't help it. When someone messes up, I have to handle it, you know? That's my job."

"And what would happen if you didn't march down to whichever co-worker's cubicle and tell it like it is?"

"What, like not say anything? That's not an option. I think I would just explode with anger. I just have to do something to deal with it right away!"

I understood what he meant. Every time Oliver noticed an employee's mistake, his brain would perceive "danger," and that false alarm would create intense discomfort—like going from zero to a million on the anxiety scale—so Oliver had to do something to calm down. And what he did was yell, be assertive, tell it like it is. As he engaged with his co-worker, the anger would come down momentarily, but what was the price tag? In Oliver's case, he had been warned by HR several times, and it was getting to the point where his career was at risk.

Oliver's behavior was similar to how many people avoid intense feelings of frustration and irritation. Studies regarding work environments suggest that nearly half of workers who experience anger-inducing situations will express their anger.[13] In particular, individuals who are exposed to high-stress jobs, such as doctors or military personnel, often tend to be quite reactive. During the COVID-19 pandemic, health care personnel reported experiencing elevated anxiety and increased anger.[14] Elevated states of stress also contributed to unhelpful expressions of said anger.[15] Remember, reacting is a biologically driven response to threat (or anything that causes intense emotions that we want to bring down quickly), but that doesn't mean reacting can't cause problems for us.

Now, don't get me wrong: blowing off a little steam now and then can be alright—like calling a close friend to vent about a particularly bad day, or doing an especially grueling workout to burn off excess energy. But reacting is not helpful when it strains our relationships at home and at work.

Reactive Avoidance and You: An Owner's Manual

As I've said many times before, reacting is only avoidance when you are doing it to feel better fast, but in the long term you are paying a high price tag. As you've already begun to see, there are a variety of fun and engaging ways people sabotage themselves. Instead of recounting *all* the stories of reactive avoidance that I've encountered, I present to you a brief list of additional ways that my clients react to avoid (see page 139). Though I share this list with a caveat: it is meant to be merely illustrative, not a definitive checklist, because avoidance is about why you are doing something, not what you are doing. So for some of you, these examples might not reflect reacting.

When Is Reacting Not Avoidance?

It is important to note that sometimes reacting isn't avoidance. Being assertive, defending yourself against aggression, and speaking your mind (respectfully) in a heated conversation are all examples that come to mind of ways in which you are behaving in a reactive way that is justified. Given that the "why" is actual self-preservation against a legitimate conflict, there is an actual threat, not a perceived one.

What It All Boils Down To

Across all the examples in this chapter, reactive avoidance took the form of productivity, comparison, and confrontation. Although the behaviors of each individual in this chapter were vastly different, there was a common function to the reaction: to feel better momentarily by doing something to bring down strong emotions. If you are stuck in reactive avoidance, just like I often am, you can attest that once the explosion passes, you are left to clean up the mess—and that feeling is awful. Before we find a solution, we need to understand the reasons behind this type of avoidance.

React

One common response to discomfort is reactive avoidance, where we act to eliminate whatever our brain perceives to be a potential threat.

Here are examples of ways that one might react:

- Raising your voice or yelling
- Pushing, grabbing, or reaching for someone
- Interrupting or responding quickly
- Confronting someone about a problem or concern in an aggressive manner
- Glaring at people angrily
- Escalating a conversation into an argument
- Responding to an email quickly
- Overworking or overcommitting
- Quitting your job hastily
- Scheduling extra meetings to discuss challenges
- Overscheduling activities
- Submitting work without proofreading
- Completing other small tasks (i.e., productive procrastination)
- Blocking people on social media
- Escalating to higher authorities before trying less edgy approaches

Chapter Seven

There's Science Behind Your Inner Hothead

Superheroes! Full of amazing powers, they can do anything, including glue my five-year-old son to the TV for medically unsafe stretches of time. Diego loves all superheroes so much that he demands we make up a new superhero story every night when we put him to bed. It's to the point where I feel like I'm an unpaid intern at Marvel. However, if there's one superhero that has earned my son's love more than any other, it's Spider-Man. The idea that he can climb up buildings and shoot webs from his wrists is fascinating to Diego, and whenever we allow him to watch thirty minutes of Spidey, he is utterly transfixed. Most of the time, he watches his allotment, we give him a warning that time is nearly up, and he is able to move to the next item on his agenda: bathroom, wash hands, and come to dinner. But when he's tired, David and I are on alert, because trying to turn off the TV rarely ends well. Yesterday, for example, when his Spidey time was up, Diego threw himself on the floor, demanding to watch more Spidey like a tiny dictator of some wealthy but obscure sovereign nation. As I observed him in the midst of a full-blown tantrum, it seemed quite obvious that he felt as if his world was ending and that the only way to communicate this apocalypse was by shrieking as loudly as he could. It's as though he was trying to say, "Damn it, woman, don't you realize what this means?! If I can't watch more Spidey *RIGHT THIS INSTANT*, I'm finished! Kaput! Ruined!"

These outbursts seem completely illogical to any parent, including myself, and though we might try to reason with a child, it's not so easy. Young children can't fully regulate their emotions because the human brain is not fully developed until we're nearly thirty.[1] Naturally, the parts of our brains that are essential to survival develop first, leaving kids like Diego fully prepared to run from danger and utterly ill equipped to handle anything more subtle than a saber-toothed tiger, like my turning off the TV.[2] One essential structure in this survival brain is our old friend the amygdala, the emotional hub of the brain, which, as we have learned, plays a large role in detecting and responding to threats. Since it's more important to be able to sense and respond to threats than to be able to carry out complex computations or communicate poetic thoughts, the thinking part of our brain (the prefrontal cortex) develops later. So, when Diego is screaming into the rug, pleading with an uncaring universe, he is in emotional brain mode and no reasoning can get through (at least not until he exhausts himself with his hysterics).

Before the thinking brain is fully developed and connected to the emotional part of our brain, it's very difficult for us to handle strong emotions. That is why many adolescents and young adults make rash decisions and act impulsively: their internal braking system just hasn't fully developed. Even the space of a few years can make a huge difference, as young adults aged eighteen to twenty-one have more difficulty completing a cognitive task when experiencing strong emotions than do twenty-two- to twenty-five-year-olds.[3] It's bad enough that their emotions are in the driver's seat, but when we consider the developing brain, it's like the brakes have been cut as well! However, time is only one ingredient necessary for the thinking brain to develop. For our braking system to develop, we actually need to learn how to regulate our emotions.

Emotion Regulation

Most of us, at one point or another, will experience moments when our emotions are in control, although this might look different for each one of us. When our emotions are in charge, it is nearly impossible to move forward with calm, cool logic. This ability to take back the wheel and go from an emotional state to a rational one is what researchers and clinicians refer to as emotion regulation.[4]

Emotion regulation skills can be learned at any point in life, including childhood. When we're children, our brains are developing rapidly, and we are constantly learning how to respond to our emotions. The way our caregivers treat us and manage their own emotions, as well as the general emotional climate of those around us, all play a role in determining whether or not we learn how to regulate our emotions.[5] In a utopian world, we would have "perfect parents" and a "perfect household," where parents teach us how to identify what we are feeling and help us learn to ride our emotional highs and lows with grace and mindfulness. In this ideal world, we would all learn that strong emotions are natural and that there is an entire, complex range of emotions, from happy to sad, with every shade in between. We would also learn that emotions themselves, even strong ones, aren't necessarily bad! If we all had this knowledge, we would be able to understand that we can't run away from strong emotions and that in fact it is best to bring them along, in the passenger seat of our cars, without letting them take the wheel of our lives.

But parents are just humans who are doing the best they can, with the skills that they either do or do not have in any given moment. As such, there is no family that can teach their children to "perfectly" handle strong emotions. (Besides, how boring would life be without screaming toddlers and their adorable meltdowns?) And when we don't learn how to regulate our emotions, we end up meeting emotion regulation's evil twin, emotion dysregulation. Emotion dysregulation happens when our emotions become intense and we lack the skills to handle the situation.

Emotion dysregulation has been linked to unhealthy risk-taking, relationship challenges, and negative physical health outcomes.[6] Researchers conducting a large international study with 12,461 participants who had an acute myocardial infarction (i.e., a heart attack) found that 14 percent of individuals reported being angry or emotionally upset one hour before symptoms began.[7] After conducting additional analyses, the research team concluded that being angry or emotionally upset correlates with an increased risk of having a heart attack. Additional research studies have shown that anger is also associated with the increased likelihood of having a stroke.[8] In other words, when our internal pressure cooker explodes from strong emotions, not only do we pay an emotional price but we may also pay a physical one!

For some of us, there are additional barriers we might have faced that can further hinder our ability to learn how to manage emotions. Childhood maltreatment is one example of a "double hit," whereby the child faces increased stressors that cause intense emotions yet lacks an adult role model to demonstrate how to effectively respond to those emotions. A recent review of thirty-five studies found that children who experience maltreatment have fewer emotion regulation skills and are more likely to avoid in response to stressors later in life.[9] When researchers tried to understand the brain processes related to maltreatment and emotion regulation, they found that adolescents who were maltreated as children actually recruit more parts of the prefrontal cortex to regulate their emotions than adolescents who were never maltreated as children.[10] In other words, turning on the thinking brain to regulate emotions is actually a lot more work for children who experience maltreatment. Think of it like running ten miles—a marathon runner is going to be able to complete the run more easily (and with less effort) than someone who only runs when they're late for the bus.

Another more common barrier to developing emotion regulation skills is the experience of what researchers call adverse childhood experiences (ACEs). ACEs are events that happen between birth and seventeen years old that are potentially traumatic, such as household violence, physical or emotional abuse, and living with people who abuse substances or struggle with mental illness.[11] According to the Centers for Disease Control and Prevention, approximately

61 percent of adults have experienced at least one ACE and 16 percent of adults have experienced more than four ACEs.[12] ACEs are linked to chronic health conditions, mental health disorders, and substance use in adolescence and adulthood.[13] For example, studies have shown that individuals who have experienced four or more ACEs are ten times more likely to use illicit drugs,[14] four times more likely to have depression, and thirty times more likely to attempt suicide.[15]

Since you've been learning about the malleable nature of the brain, you might not be surprised that a recent review of scientific literature has shown that ACEs also impact brain development.[16] The review summarizes studies that show that ACEs are related to amygdala hyperactivity and hypertrophy—a fancy word for "enlargement." This finding makes sense because we would expect someone who experienced ACEs to have spent more time in fight, flight, or freeze mode—more time with the amygdala in charge—than people who aren't facing constant threats. If the amygdala is in charge a lot, it's going to get stronger and larger. And while the amygdala is bulking up, the prefrontal cortex is on the sidelines. Neuroscience findings from this review show that individuals with ACEs have less developed prefrontal cortices than individuals who haven't experienced ACEs. I know this is a lot of science, but the bottom line is this: people who experienced ACEs have brains that have developed to react, which in turn limits their ability to regulate strong emotions.

Outbursts to Avoid Feeling

Although enduring maltreatment and ACEs are extreme cases of how our childhood experiences can impact emotion regulation, some of us just never really quite learn how to regulate emotions for a variety of less obvious reasons. Let's take Explosive Oliver for example and consider his tendency to, in scientific terms, lose his shit. Oliver told me that he was raised by a military family and that he himself had spent time in the military. Oliver described his upbringing and his training as having instilled in him a sense that there was always a "right and wrong" to every situation, right down to the ways one did or did not behave, dress, and address one's elders. As such, there was always a strict code of conduct that indicated that one must do things in a certain way, otherwise something bad could happen. That's a healthy attitude for military missions, but it doesn't leave very much room for emotional flexibility for civilians in the real world. In his current role as a supervisor in corporate America, Oliver also wanted things to be in categories. And when they were not, he would blow up.

It is important to note that not everyone raised this way will respond in the same manner, but data suggests that three out of ten military personnel engage in aggressive behavior.[17] Not surprisingly, this kind of explosive response is not limited to individuals with a military background. It's also quite common in people who are exposed to other high-stress situations, such as police officers, frontline doctors, and firefighters, but also—somewhat surprisingly—educators and even culinary professionals. If you can name a job that involves contextually stressful situations with no room for error, there's a good chance that professionals in these industries also may experience this type of explosive response as a form of avoidance.[18] For example, a study conducted in Australia found that professional chefs are more aggressive than the general population.[19] (Consider this next time you're about to send your food back at a restaurant!) Even stress that occurs outside of work or early in life can lead to increases in anger, aggression, and impulsivity.[20] Regardless of the source of stress, outbursts happen when emotions are in the driver's seat, the amygdala is in control, and the thinking brain is nowhere to be found. Similar to what we've learned about fear and anxiety, aggression arises when the prefrontal cortex is not regulating the amygdala's response.[21]

It's worth remembering that our amygdala doesn't kick into overdrive only when some objective degree of a threat is encountered. It's all highly subjective, and as long as there is a perceived threat at play, the fight, flight, or freeze response will activate. As such, one person's fire alarm is another's average Wednesday.

With that in mind, let's return to Oliver and his angry outbursts. One of the biggest things he and I uncovered was the fact that he was never taught how to regulate his emotions when they were in the driver's seat, steering his car off the road.

As a child, Oliver's parents unintentionally taught him that strong emotions are not good and that he needed to keep them inside. In fact, the only time Oliver saw strong emotions at home was when his dad had angry outbursts—just like the ones he was having now—so Oliver learned that the only way to actually show that he was upset or disappointed or frustrated was through full-on anger. Oliver lacked the ability to regulate his emotions and as such there was simply no range of expression in his tool kit. He went from totally fine to DEFCON 1 in a matter of moments! Whenever something was frustrating, no matter whether it was a 1 or a 10, Oliver would begin to feel tense, and his heart would quicken. In these moments, he wouldn't know how to articulate his frustration. This anger over not knowing how to articulate his frustration caused difficult emotions to bubble up, like a child who can't yet speak full sentences.

Not knowing what else to do, Oliver avoided his bubbling emotions by reacting and yelling.

Stressful Situations Don't Always Lead to Anger

Now, not everyone will use anger as a way to avoid strong emotions or stressful situations. Some of us react in a milder way, when our discomfort climbs to orange instead of red. Interestingly, research has shown that we are more likely to react when the threat feels up close and personal (say, a careless driver almost hitting you or your family at a crosswalk) and we wind up holding on to the memory of that threat.[22] So the next time we walk across the street with our family, we're on red alert. Even if reacting isn't your go-to flavor, there may be "momma bear" moments in your life when something threatens something or someone who is close to you, and you react to avoid harm.

There is more than meets the eye when it comes to reactive avoidance. Many other factors can influence our desire to fight back. Two of those reasons are worth covering here: the need to belong and attachment.

The Need to Belong

We all have an evolutionary need to belong to a group or "tribe"[23]—be it at work, at school, on a team, or through social media—but some of us feel this need a lot more strongly than others. Group membership gives us safety,[24] a sense of meaning,[25] and even the ability to self-regulate.[26] Exclusion from groups is a real threat to our well-being. Individuals who are left out of a group suffer from poor time management, work turnover, an elevated heart rate, and less self-control around things like stress eating.[27] So when we feel as though we no longer belong, our fight, flight, or freeze response kicks in and goes a long way toward explaining why many people in our modern era can sometimes twist themselves into knots to remain in good standing with their group.

Because our need to belong is as strongly biologically wired as is our fight, flight, and freeze response, when it is threatened, we often feel like we have to do something, and sometimes that something is reactive avoidance. And I have to confess, I am the queen of that sort of thing. By this stage in my life, I am well aware that I am especially afraid of not belonging due to my childhood fear of not being enough.

When I feel as though I might not belong or am somehow "less than," I feel threatened, and I act quickly. And hey, I immediately feel better! Until I don't. For example, about a decade ago, my biggest goal was to eventually become a director of a research lab at the legendary (in my mind) Massachusetts General Hospital. For those of you who are not academics (read: nerds), this means "you are a rock star and you made it to the top." As such, I was thrilled when an associate director position opened up at the center where I was working. At the time, I was the most senior person on the team, and so I assumed I would just be awarded the position, no questions asked. However, when I approached the new director to discuss it, she told me that "only individuals who hold a medical degree" were being considered for the position. I was crushed; even though I had a PhD,

I was out of the running! In that moment, I not only saw my dreams slip away from me, but I also felt as if I didn't belong (in this institution, in this career, on this team). My thoughts began to spiral: If I'm not a medical doctor (MD), I'll never direct a research lab! I don't belong and I never will!

Although there were a million ways I could have handled the situation—including discussing it further with my superiors—I avoided. And I did so in a super reactive way. Literally minutes after that brief interaction with the director of the lab, I practically ran back into my office and decided that I was going to apply to another job and leave this position. If I was never going to be a leader and belong at Mass General, I better go somewhere else, and fast. While from your perspective this might seem a bit rash, at the time I didn't think this was avoidance at all. In fact, I thought I was being super proactive! It all seemed quite logical.

As such, I immediately started to research job openings in psychology, wrote out cover letters, and even went as far as asking a few trusted colleagues for letters of recommendation. As long as I was doing something, I felt slightly better (avoidance is powerful!). Yet, after a weekend of preparing to apply to dozens of academic jobs all across the country, I still didn't feel fully better.

That is when David called me out. He gently asked me why I was so upset with my boss, and it wasn't until I began explaining the situation that I realized I just felt threatened, like I didn't belong at all because of my degree (or lack thereof). David asked me if I really intended to move to a new city, or if there was another way to address this problem. In talking things out rationally (hello, prefrontal cortex!), I realized that I was once again in avoid mode. I had reacted to her "MDs only" comment by getting ready to apply to jobs that I didn't even want.

While preparing to apply for these jobs helped me feel better, the relief was only momentary. And this relief was not without its consequences, for just like the pressure cooker that blows its lid, leaving a huge mess in its wake, I then had to go and explain to my colleagues that I was in fact not leaving MGH after all (embarrassing!). As you can see, fighting avoidance is hard, even for "fancy academics" like me (okay, only fancy because of my great red glasses!). But trust me, it can be done, and I will help you plot out a roadmap in the next chapter. But before we get there, let's consider another reason why we might find ourselves stuck in reactive avoidance: attachment anxiety. To do that, let me share a bit more about my client Filomena.

Oh No, Don't Go! Attachment Anxiety

For Filomena, the explanation behind her reactive avoidance is slightly different. She was not reacting from anger or from a feeling of not belonging. She was instead reacting in direct response to her worst fear: abandonment. You may recall that Filomena was adopted at a young age and, like many adoptees, she experienced relationship insecurity and anxiety.[28] The only way Filomena felt secure in her relationship with Ted was when she was physically close to him. Otherwise, she would feel inescapable anxiety, which made her feel insecure, which led her to text again and again to try to feel close to Ted, if only for a moment. Have you ever been in a relationship where you or your loved one felt that way? Where security came only with physical proximity? Perhaps you didn't text all the time, but instead you asked for reassurance in the form of questions like:

Do you love me?

Are we okay?

Are you mad at me?

This is what would happen to Filomena as well, and since she was unable to tolerate the ensuing discomfort, she would then seek reassurance from Ted that their relationship was okay. *Reassurance seeking* is the term psychologists use to describe the pattern someone gets stuck in of asking questions to get validation. Because reassurance seeking is a mild form of avoiding emotions, people often can't catch it because of the subtle way it shows up.[29] Each time Filomena asked Ted about his love for her, and he reassured her that he did love her, she felt a bit better.

Yet, the sweet relief of reassurance isn't the only motivator here. Filomena's behavior is also influenced by the way she has learned to relate (or "attach") to people.[30] The notion of "attachment styles" has become rather popular in recent years, and most people likely have heard of the four distinct attachment styles: anxious, avoidant, disorganized, and secure. In attachment theory, Filomena's insistence on getting a response is described as *protest behavior.* Protest behavior is any action that is taken to reconnect with a partner or get their attention.[31] I often think of protest behavior as a reactive form of avoidance because every client I've worked with who has a similar situation to Filomena describes this desire in a way that feels viscerally urgent. It's almost the psychological equivalent of "the squeaky wheel gets the oil," only instead of oil, they get a brief hit of emotional relief. They react by protesting and it relieves anxiety momentarily, but as you can see for Filomena, it was causing significant conflict in her romantic relationship.

And our friend Filomena is not alone: results across 132 studies suggest that individuals with an insecure attachment style, like Filomena, often experience less satisfaction in their relationships.[32] Have you ever noticed a similar urge in your relationships? Perhaps an urgent desire to frequently affirm and reaffirm your connection to your partner? You might not send a flurry of texts, but instead might ghost your partner or give them the silent treatment. Maybe you try to make a parent or friend feel jealous.

As her clinician, I could understand where Filomena was coming from, but as a human, I deeply empathized with Filomena because I also was very anxious as a young child. I remember being twelve years old and begging my mom to let me stay home from school one day because I was convinced that, if I left, I would come back hours later only to learn that my mom had left me behind. These challenging experiences form us, and sometimes it's up to our adult selves to create a new path forward. It's easy to think of these situations as unfair, and perhaps they are, but it's more useful to look at them as an opportunity to break old habits that no longer serve us so we can forge a healthier mode of being—so we can become bold. And that is just what we will learn how to do in the next chapter.

Learning at Any Age

The good news for all of us is that we can continue to strengthen our emotion regulation skills throughout our lives. We now know that the brain continues to change throughout its lifespan[33] and emotion regulation is a skill that it is never too late to learn. Researchers have shown that there is no difference between younger adults and older adults when it comes to their potential to learn to regulate emotions.[34] So, for the Old Dogs out there, it's not too late to learn new tricks. It's also not too late for anyone who has experienced adverse childhood experiences (ACEs) or has been living in avoid mode. We might all have a different starting point, and for some it might be easier than for others, but we all can learn to better regulate our emotions. Think of it like getting in shape: it might be harder to get in amazing shape at fifty than it is at twenty, but with the right training and dedication, it's never too late to become Quadzilla. In addition, my own research has shown that developing emotion regulation is possible even in the most challenging circumstances.

From 2014 to 2019, our team at Massachusetts General Hospital (Community Psychiatry Program for Research in Implementation & Dissemination of Evidence-Based Treatments, or PRIDE) partnered with a community-based organization named Roca, Inc. Roca was founded to support young men at high risk for reoffending and unemployment, who were unable or unwilling to engage in any other programming. Roca excelled in their understanding of their service population. They knew that the high-risk young men they served needed skills to regulate their emotions, but the program was having trouble finding a science-based curriculum that could be implemented on the streets. Therefore, Roca teamed up with us to cocreate an emotion regulation skill-based curriculum that could be delivered by youth workers.[35]

Throughout our five-year partnership, we iteratively tested and refined the curriculum to fit the needs of Roca and the young people they served, which primarily included young men involved in the criminal justice system.[36] Together, we created a final product that was well liked, doable, and effective. Evaluation of 980 young men receiving services from Roca between 2014 and 2017 found that young men who had at least one experience learning or using emotion regulation skills had a 66 percent lower risk of dropping out of programming and were 65 percent more likely to secure a job than young men who did not use any of these skills.[37] Let me put these data in context for you: for every day that a Roca young man is at programming, he is not in the streets and he is not back to prison. As you can imagine, we were thrilled by these data, but we were equally encouraged by the transformational stories the young men shared with us. One shared,

> [The skills] have definitely taught me how to channel my anger . . . [and] focus on my responses because usually I am very impulsive. . . . I always . . . find myself in a way where I have to pump the brake so to speak, really get ahold of my thoughts and my actions . . . also my feelings.

And we didn't only hear from the young men. The youth workers in the organization also witnessed the life-changing impact of developing emotion regulation skills.

> Today . . . my participant who has incredible anger problems, he destroys property, that's what he does . . . So he had a fight with his girl, she kicked him out, he was still there yelling and he calls me, he's like, "I'm riding the wave, I'm riding the wave" [a phrase linked to an emotion regulation skill]. And then he left and obviously he's still [going to] have a lot of emotional

> problems with that, but no physical action was taken. He didn't bust up anything in her house, he didn't break any windows.... I didn't think I was ever going to get him to stop doing that. So for me that's like, "Alright, yes, this stuff is working."

So, as you can see, even young people coming out of jail, who have had their share of adversity, can learn the skills necessary to pump the brakes when their emotions try to take control. Ultimately, the skills we shared with Roca rely on the same science as the skills I'm teaching you in these pages.

If you're like me and react to avoid—whether it's texting someone without thinking or posting on social media as a knee-jerk response—it is crucial to understand that we are just doing it to try to feel better. In these moments, our emotions are driving wildly in an attempt to avoid feeling discomfort. As we've seen in this chapter, the style of driving and the reasons behind it vary widely, but reacting as avoidance is still the common denominator. Now that we understand the science, let's learn how to pump the brakes and turn on the thinking brain. The trick to combatting reactive avoidance is to *Approach*, but in a science-driven way. After all, boldness doesn't come from "just doing it" any more than learning to play piano comes as a result of "just banging the keys at random with my elbows." It is a skill we must develop, and that will be our next focus.

Chapter Eight

A Move That Changes the Game

A driver cuts you off on the highway at a dangerous speed. An anonymous internet commenter insults you. Your child accidentally sets fire to the couch. You spend an hour navigating your cell phone provider's phone tree, only to get dropped. If there's one thing each of these scenarios has in common, it's that they are all likely to set off an average human's anger to one degree or another. What happens next is largely a result of said human's ability to regulate their emotions. As you learned at the end of the previous chapter, emotion regulation is a skill that anyone—from the local librarian to a fighter pilot—can learn. In fact, you've already learned one skill that can be used to regulate your emotions: *Shifting.*

Shifting changes our emotions by changing what we are saying to ourselves in the midst of challenging moments. It's the ability to take a new perspective, such as considering what a friend might say, to overcome challenges. However, there is another way to regulate emotions, especially the fiery, reactive ones that we've been focusing on. To learn to regulate emotions, we are going to rely on the principles of cognitive behavioral therapy (CBT)[1] and dialectical behavior therapy (DBT), [2] science's sexiest power couple.

The technique is quite counterintuitive: we *Approach* the difficult feelings instead of avoiding them by doing the opposite of what our emotions are telling us to do, a technique that is called *opposite action*. When you reach some level of fluency with this technique, you will be able to stay cooler in tough or triggering situations and stop reacting in unhelpful ways. All it takes is a little practice.

Overcoming Reactive Avoidance by Learning Your Triggers

One of my favorite games to play, aside from "cookies are vitamins," is thinking of challenging emotions as little buttons all over the body, like a DJ mixer with tricolor lights. Some of these lights are blue, some are green, some are yellow, a few are orange, and others are red.

Blue buttons are situations that we experience as low levels of emotion, when our thinking brains are online and active. If a situation leads to one of my green buttons being pushed, I might feel a fleeting sensation such as a wry smile or a flash of annoyance, but most of the time I won't do anything. Once my yellow buttons are pushed, I'm starting to feel pretty uncomfortable. Orange buttons might elicit

Emotion Buttons

When our red buttons are pushed, we end up losing our ability to think critically, which can often cause us to react. What triggers a red versus a green button is unique to everyone. Below are some examples of common triggers for different buttons. But keep in mind that this is unique to you, so make sure to come up with your own examples.

Blue	Green	Yellow	Orange	Red
"I am cool, calm, and collected."	"That wasn't ideal, but I am okay."	"This is hard, but I can handle it."	"I'm heating up."	"I'm ready to explode."
Hanging out with friends	Doing housework	Talking to a friend who is upset with you	Speaking at a conference	Your child being disrespectful
Reading or watching TV	Waiting in line	Visiting family members who are complicated	Getting passed over for promotion	Getting fired from work

a comment from me, and I might even raise my voice, but I'm still unlikely to dive headfirst into reactive avoidance. But press a red button, and we've got problems! Picture a toddler just stomping on a red button repeatedly: your emotions flare up (the music blares) and alarms go off in your body. So, you must act (or should I say *react*) to get that toddler out of there and turn down your emotional temperature. This is reactive avoidance in a nutshell.

But when you don't know which buttons do what on your

personal DJ mixer of emotions, it's hard to change how you act. So, it's important to first identify what types of scenarios hit our green buttons and which scenarios hit our red buttons (see reflection below). After all, if you don't know which button is causing

REFLECTION

Identifying Your Hot Buttons

The first step in learning to *Approach* is to make a list of the situations that tend to trigger reactive avoidance for you. This reflection is designed to help you slow down the process between a triggering event and your response, and as such, I would suggest that you focus only in the past week. If you can catch your reactive patterns here, you are better equipped to implement a solution.

Situation

Describe a situation that pressed one of your buttons.

____

____

____

Emotions

Name the emotions you felt during this time.

____

____

____

negative feedback, you can't really fix the problem. To do so, you must create an inventory of situations that function as your reactive triggers. These are the types of situations that people colloquially refer to as things that "push our buttons."

Intensity

Name the intensity of your emotions: blue, green, yellow, orange, or red.

____

____

____

Current actions to manage emotions

What do you do when you feel this emotion?

____

____

____

Is this avoidance? (yes or no)

____

____

____

Remember, for an action to be reactive avoidance, you must have engaged in it because you felt discomfort, and the response itself was designed to make you feel better fast. But you notice that this reaction tends to keep you stuck.

Angad's Hot Buttons

If you recall, Angad often compared himself with others, especially on social media, and when he felt anxious, scared, or fearful, he would post several photos to try to prove to himself (and others) that he was cool. However, his actions were purely reactive and never made him really feel better, and so he found himself feeling embarrassed and a little icky afterward. To help Angad understand his reactive avoidance, we worked on first identifying his personal hot buttons.

But before we began, he asked me one important question that I often receive from my clients: "Won't tracking my hot buttons make me feel worse?" At first, when you pause to write out your hot buttons, you might feel a slight increase in discomfort, but only because you are no longer avoiding (remember avoidance works fast!). But I encourage you to try to just observe these feelings instead of immediately being hooked by them. Additionally, by writing your hot buttons out on paper, you are activating your thinking brain, which means your emotional brain won't have as much sway. While writing you can actually experience the lovely effect of bringing your emotional temperature down. So, feel confident that tracking is a hell of a lot better than remaining stuck in avoidance, and it will absolutely create a path out of your reactive avoidance pattern.

After two weeks of tracking his hot buttons, Angad had come up with several different scenarios that caused him so much discomfort that he would engage in reactive avoidance to feel better, but all were also associated with a negative price tag for him (see table on the next page). In addition to social media, Angad learned that any conversations

Angad's Hot Buttons

Situation	Emotions	Intensity	Action	Avoidance?
Friend posted on Instagram about a trip that I missed	Regret	Yellow	Posted pictures of my vacations	Yes
Was talking to a friend and realized I had nothing interesting to say	Annoyance Sadness	Yellow	Shared a story about a vacation to Spain last year	Yes
Noticed that my latest Instagram didn't get many likes	Sadness Shame	Yellow	Edited the caption to make the post more interesting	Yes
Lost 10 followers on Instagram	Fear	Red	Followed 100 random strangers to try to boost my numbers	Yes

where friends talked at length about their accomplishments would activate his emotional brain and he would want to react to cool off. During such episodes, he found that he would either do something impulsive, such as posting on Instagram, or would begin boasting in conversations, trying to prove that his life was fun and interesting enough to make any sane human sick with envy. At first, these actions might seem harmless, but over time Angad felt like he needed to maintain an "active" social media or else he would be bedridden with feelings of inadequacy.

Angad is stuck because he is avoiding his emotions. Every time his emotional temperature goes up, he does something to fight the discomfort. But it is not the action itself that keeps him stuck; rather, he is stuck because of the reason he is doing the specific action, which is to avoid his own emotions. If Angad were able to feel his emotions, by not reacting fast when they happen, he could develop a new relationship with them.

Lessons Learned

As you saw with Angad, tracking leads to insight and the ability to really catch where, when, and why reactive avoidance is taking over. Here's how it worked out for our other cast of characters.

Filomena realized that in any situation where she perceived abandonment, she would try to cling to the relationship like a drowning person to ship wreckage, which is what happens when one has an anxious attachment style.[3] Ted's being away from her threatened her sense of security, so much so that she would unleash a stream of nonstop texts to lower her emotional temperature as fast as possible. But beyond Ted, she would also behave this way with her family and closest friends. Filomena learned that by tightly holding on to those that she loved, she was actually creating worse relationships.

Lastly, Oliver found that whenever he was in a situation where the rules (whether social, personal, or professional) were not followed, he would feel great discomfort to the point of exploding. So, when one of his team members, Martha, made a mistake, he became anxious. To deal with his own anxiety, he essentially bullied her, creating momentary relief followed by immediate shame and regret, and ultimately landing him in my office. And it wasn't just at work. He would find himself in similar situations at home. Oliver shared with me that every time his family members broke some unspoken rule, like eating dinner later than expected, he would find himself raising his voice (even while acknowledging the insignificance of eating dinner half an hour later). The altercation would typically result in dinner being restored to its regular time, but would also make Oliver feel upset and small for yelling at his wife. This sort of thing also happened with his daughters, hence the joking-but-not-really-joking duct tape gift. His family viewed him as the "hothead dad," and everyone felt as if they needed to either walk on eggshells around him or risk another outburst. They could joke about it, but the impact this behavior had on his family was unmistakably detrimental.

As you can see, the process of identifying hot buttons allows each person to learn something about themselves. The insight gained through tracking is more than an intellectual endeavor; it is actually a strong motivator for behavior change because as the adage goes: you can't change what you can't measure. If you've ever worn any kind of watch or bracelet that tracks your steps, you might already be familiar with this concept. Just knowing how much (or little) you have moved can motivate you toward actionable steps (no pun intended). And this isn't just my wonderfully insightful opinion. A recent review of studies found that adults who self-monitored their sedentary behavior became more active.[4] We can also use the motivating magic of self-monitoring to help us prepare to *Approach*.

From Tracking to Approaching

Once you know your specific hot buttons, you basically know the land mines that set off that reactive explosion. With this new understanding of what makes us tick (and go boom), we must then learn to regulate those emotions by using opposite action.

What is opposite action? Opposite action is defined as "acting opposite to an emotion's action urge."[5] In other words, if discomfort gives us the urge to avoid, opposite action is anything we do to approach that discomfort and engage our thinking brain. Opposite action is a powerful emotion regulation technique that is often used in dialectical behavior therapy (DBT). DBT was created by Marsha Linehan, PhD, to help people manage their responses to strong emotions in a more productive way and to break the patterns of behaviors that get us stuck. Although DBT was originally developed to treat individuals diagnosed with borderline personality disorder, the treatment has been shown to effectively treat a wide range of problems including eating disorders,[6] anger and aggression,[7] and substance use.[8] In addition to addressing an array of emotion regulation problems, DBT works for a wide range of individuals from adolescents[9] to older adults.[10] DBT includes many different skills, but we are going to focus specifically on opposite action.

By engaging in opposite action, we are equipping the prefrontal cortex to downregulate our emotions. In essence, strong emotions want to drive your behavior, and they do so through reactive avoidance. Instead of letting your emotions take the driver's seat, you can create a plan of moving in the opposite direction whenever you find yourself confronted with your triggers. To do this, we create a plan to *Approach* discomfort. By *Approaching* discomfort, your brain learns that no matter what you're experiencing, no matter how painful, it is most likely a false alarm.[11]

The purpose of opposite action is not to avoid powerful emotions. This is never the goal, whether we're talking about CBT or meditation. Thoughts and emotions are just byproducts of our biology. Without them, being a functioning human and experiencing all the textures of life would be quite difficult. In fact, emotions, no matter what they are or how strong they feel, have a purpose, but when they are driving our behaviors and actions, they often lead to avoidance. As such, our job here is to get back in the driver's seat. We are not in control of the emotions we feel, but by being mindful and utilizing opposite action, we do have a say in how we respond to them.

But I Have Tried, Dr. Luana

Oliver's anger would urge him to raise his voice at Martha (reactive avoidance). The opposite action would be anything that can keep him from doing that. For example, Oliver might consider sharing his feelings with Martha (instead of attacking her). As I described opposite action to Oliver, he asked a question that many of my clients have asked: "Don't you think I have tried to not yell at Martha?"

The reality is, most of the time my clients have tried "opposite action." And I'm no stranger to this either! I can't tell you how many times I tried to not react with one of my rapid-fire emails after Susan brought it to my attention. So, in this sense, Oliver was not wrong. I'm sure he had tried not yelling at Martha many times. But what

Oliver was failing to understand was that there is a difference between the "just do it" approach to fighting avoidance, in which you just try to white-knuckle yourself away from whatever your strong emotions are trying to make you do, and actually training your brain to not engage in reactive avoidance through a planned action. The difference is that through a planned action, you're doing something intentionally and with skill versus doing it because of a fight, flight, or freeze instinct. And to gain this skill, you don't start practicing *Approach* in scenarios when your red-hot buttons are pressed. You need to strengthen your brain's ability to act (instead of react) little by little.

It's like when I finally joined the bandwagon of buying a Peloton. On that first day, I did an extremely difficult hour-long class because, damn it, I was going to *Approach* my health and lose that pandemic belly! Opposite action to no exercise = Peloton! The result? I was barely able to walk for days afterward and ended up avoiding the Peloton like the plague. Somehow, I decided that after two years of zero exercise, it was well within my ability to immediately jump into the deep end, but my all-or-nothing approach didn't work! In my case, it was merely a physical limitation, but for many of my clients, they try to stop avoiding their discomfort by exceeding their emotional limitations. To prevent this, we can rely on science to practice opposite action as a skill, instead of as a knee-jerk reaction.

Setting Up for Early Wins

Although practicing the opposite action might sound rather simplistic, it can be quite challenging. We are going against our very biology, after all. Like Oliver, you probably attempted a version of this skill one time or another but never found success. So, the decision on where to start is crucial to learning this skill successfully. To do so, I want to encourage you to identify hot button situations in which you could have *early and easy wins*. Basically, this is the opposite of what I did with my Peloton: I went all in and ended up with the complete opposite of an exercise routine; I avoided that damn bike because of how sore I was. So what would be the easy win? Starting small, doing it consistently, and building strength.

How does this translate to your own practice? *NEVER practice on RED situations first.* Our brains can easily snap into fight, flight, or freeze mode on red button situations, and without prior practice, you won't have enough of your thinking brain online to really be able to ride the emotional wave that comes. Choosing something to practice on in the orange range sets you up for the possibility of success, but keep in mind that this is a skill, so you will need training. And as with any training protocol, sometimes you will nail it and other times you'll fall on your ass. The trick is to keep going.

Practicing Opposite Action

Angad and His Social Media Reactions

Angad agreed to practice opposite action by changing up his social media habits. First, he committed to spending only thirty minutes on Instagram each day. I literally had him set a timer when he opened the app. When the thirty minutes was up, he was finished. Next, when he felt the urge to post, he was going to rewire his brain by calling a friend instead. This is a powerful technique when it comes to creating lasting behavior change: replacing old habits with new ones. Last, when it came to discussing triggering topics with friends, his opposite action was to listen and *not* fight back (react) by telling stories about his successes or prior vacations. Whenever he would fight feelings of insecurity by trying to outdo his friends, he was letting his emotions drive the car. We were trying to get his prefrontal cortex back in the driver's seat. Ideally, we agreed he would practice these steps first with close friends, who he knew were less likely to boast about their lives (and not judge him if he told them about his struggles) before he progressed to more challenging situations. If he could not tolerate the situation, the plan was to make an excuse and politely exit the situation (a trip to the bathroom) until he could collect himself.

"But wait: If I leave the situation, isn't that avoidance?" he asked.

I would agree with his assessment, but in this situation, we were using it intentionally as a smaller tool in a larger arsenal designed to make positive change.

"What I don't want to see, Angad, is a situation where your emotional temperature becomes too hot to the point where you can't engage in your opposite action plan. So, sometimes we do a slight amount of calculated avoidance to get to a point where we can rid ourselves of the avoidance all the way."

After several weeks of practicing and not reacting, Angad had started to learn to tame his social media impulsivity. One day, he excitedly told me that a friend had posted a photo of himself on vacation in New York City and yet Angad did not post in response. It was not easy, and he admitted to drafting multiple posts, but he never actually posted any of them. How? He stuck to the plan! He had been practicing his opposite plan in a clever way, too. Angad told me that whenever he felt like posting something out of desperation, he instead opened his photo folder and proceeded to edit and organize them without posting any. This process of reviewing his own photos cooled his emotions off and by the time he finished going through his photo albums, he no longer felt the need to post something. By the way, this was not my idea—it was Angad's! I commended him for it, as it allowed him to release some of the internal pressure, but it prevented him from reactively posting. I have seen this with most of my clients, where after practicing opposite action with me based on the plan we come up with together, they end up creating their own plan, which often not only is more effective but further empowers them. It's times like these that tell me my clients are really making change in their lives.

Filomena's Opposite Action

Filomena had tried her hardest not to text Ted when she was feeling the worst of her separation anxiety, but as you know, that didn't work. So, what could she do instead? Well, we created a list of ways she could handle separation from others without seeking reassurance. We started by creating shorter, planned separations, during which she would find something to do that did not involve her phone. In the first experiments, Filomena and Ted would schedule times when he would go out with friends for a few hours while she would go to the gym (opposite action—without her phone!). As we increased the amount of time they spent apart, she had to really focus on tolerating her discomfort by planning the opposite action beforehand. And once Filomena and Ted reunited, we made a rule that she was not allowed to grill him about every last detail. But because we didn't want to create any new forms of avoidance around the relationship, Ted agreed to share what he wanted and she could ask questions, but the moment it turned into her seeking reassurance about the relationship, Ted would note this and the discussion was over. This technique works well for couples, but only if both are on board. I often say to clients: I will answer any question you have once, but if you start to ask again and again in different ways, you are likely just avoiding by having me reassure you, which never helps. So, I taught this trick to Filomena and Ted, and they were able to implement it successfully.

Unfortunately, by the time we started to implement the opposite action plan for Filomena, her relationship with Ted was already fraying and, before long, Ted broke up with her. Filomena mentioned to me that she felt as if the damage to the relationship had been done and no matter how much she tried, Ted still felt wary around her. Filomena was devastated at first, often crying in my office and saying things like, "If I had just known this stuff earlier, I could have saved the relationship."

We talked a lot about the fact that our brains always want to make sense of things and come up with one conclusion or another to minimize dissonance, so it made sense that she wanted to blame herself. And she wasn't wrong: I agreed with her that not knowing her avoidance pattern certainly made the relationship challenging. Yet I often remind my clients who find themselves in the midst of romantic turmoil that it really takes two to tango, and in this case, Ted inevitably had a role in the breakup as well.

Filomena continued to work on opposite action when her fear of abandonment would arrive, including with her parents. And so it was with some delight that I recently received an email from Filomena, in which she wrote that she is now happily married with a newborn. From what she shared with me, her dating life was challenging for a while, but she was finally able to break her own avoidance pattern and came out the other side truly happy and (finally) comfortable in a romantic relationship.

Oliver's Opposite Action Plan

As for fiery Oliver, most of his reactions were triggered by feelings of anger, and he would go from zero to sixty in seconds before exploding. When it comes to anger, DBT teaches a clear plan of opposite action involving a few different methods. One method is the simplest: you can just avoid the person you are angry with until the anger passes. In other words, as soon as Oliver felt anger toward Martha for making a mistake at work, his opposite action would be to stay away from her—instead of engaging in a pointless and hurtful verbal attack—until he was no longer in amygdala hijack. Sometimes this is too hard for the client, and instead they could take a time-out, where they substitute "go shriek at so-and-so" with "take a walk around the block." Whatever it is, I would recommend that you have a plan in place before you find yourself on the brink of exploding into anger. Believe it or not, it's actually quite hard to formulate a rational plan when you're seconds away from tearing someone's head off. It also depends on how triggered the client is feeling. For Oliver, waiting even three minutes to address a subordinate's error could feel like a lifetime, but when it came to anger he felt toward his own family, waiting three times as long felt easier.

Finally, DBT also suggests that you can choose the most extreme opposite action, which in this case would be to go out of your way to be kind or to try to understand the person you're angry with. Oliver looked at me like I had three heads when I suggested this.

"You want me to be kind when I am angry?"

"Yes!"

"How would that even work? It's impossible!"

"Well, let's take your wife. I know you love her very much even when you're angry at her, so what is one kind thing you could say or do toward her in those moments?"

Oliver looked at me skeptically.

"Oliver, don't strain yourself here. I'm just asking you to say something kind about your wife."

"Well, she's an excellent cook, for one."

"Okay, then perhaps if you're feeling upset about eating later than usual, maybe instead of raising your voice and getting sarcastic, you could say something nice to her about her cooking."

"But isn't that fake?"

"Not if you mean it. What do you like about her food?"

He went on to describe in great detail all the amazing meals she prepares, and as he did, he relaxed. I pointed this out to him and explained that when we engage in new behaviors, they activate other emotions. When we smile at someone, or praise someone, our physiology actually changes.[12] When we engage with kindness, we feel happier.[13] When we engage in violent acts, we feel angry.[14] When you consider that anger is really just a pattern of thoughts that hook us into acting on them, it's easy to see how if we just bring mindfulness to our anger and take control away from our emotions, the actual feeling of anger is rather short-lived. The only way to stay angry is by thinking about how angry you are and then responding to it with angry and unhinged behavior. It's fine to live that way if that is your choice, but I doubt that anyone reading this wants to go around being yanked in whatever direction their thoughts and feelings dictate. It's one thing for a dog to go wild barking at a squirrel or a passing dog, but quite another for any of us to spend years of our lives making our loved ones miserable.

After months of implementing his opposite action plan of making the effort to compliment his wife whenever he felt anger at home, Oliver was ready to tackle his reactivity at work. He took the duct tape that his daughters had given him but crossed out their original message and instead wrote "BE KIND" in capital letters. He put the duct tape by his office door, so he had to see it whenever he marched off into the rest of the office. He did this after a few incidents in which he had completely ignored his plan and reacted impulsively and unpleasantly toward his team. Oliver also practiced starting his conversations at the office with one kind thing he could think of about that person, even when he was angry. Oliver had finally realized that when he was on red alert, he could not be kind, and so at these moments, his opposite action was to first avoid the person for a short while until he cooled down a bit. I would eventually coach someone like Oliver to help him reduce these red alert moments, but baby steps are important when it comes to anger management issues.

Although most of my clients, like Oliver, tend to think of me as the "avoidance police," I am not so black and white when it comes to these things. The reality is, sometimes we need to give the amygdala time to cool off before we can regain access to our rational brains. So what did Oliver do during his time-outs? He practiced another emotion regulation skill that I love, which is often thought of as rebooting your system. Whenever Oliver was having a red alert, he agreed to hold an ice cube in the palm of his hand. Yes, you read that right, an ice cube. See, science teaches us that exposure to cold actually slows down our heart rate,[15] which is a key part of our fight, flight, or freeze response. So for the price of a single ice cube, you get a nifty tool to bring your emotions down fast before you react.

By the time I finished my work with Oliver, he told me his daughters had noticed his efforts and complimented him on his progress. Even Martha, the employee with whom he had previously had a lot of conflict at work, had noticed how much better he was doing. For his part, he had also apologized and told her about the efforts he was making to change. When in doubt, a little vulnerability goes a long way. Admitting we have been wrong and that we are working on changing takes guts, but it's hard to think of a better way to open yourself up to kindness from others. Martha and Oliver have been able to work closely now and instead of Oliver's flying off the handle at her every little mistake, he has started to mentor Martha and to teach her his process as another way to prevent his emotional outbursts. Oliver has learned through his own trial and error that mentoring really helps him, because when he is in that frame of mind, he can use more of his rational brain instead of turning into a rage monster.

Additional Examples of Opposite Actions

When I am first working with someone on their opposite action plan, I often see that my clients get stuck on cooking up the "perfect" opposite action, as if finding the one perfect action would eradicate all their avoidance. But let's call this out for what it is: searching for a perfect opposite action while your life is happening all around you is just another form of avoidance. Why? *Because the action you take when you practice opposite action is essentially irrelevant.* So, as you practice, I want you to be creative and try different things while keeping this in mind: your goal is to experience your emotions, not to run away from them. Making these changes might take time, but the result is worth it. Before long, you will find yourself *Approaching* when the going gets tough, not avoiding. Remember: these are patterns that you've fallen into; getting out of them will feel unnatural, but freeing yourself from involuntary self-sabotage will be a tremendous reward.

Because you are learning a skill, here are some suggestions adapted from dialectical behavior therapy to get you started. You can use some of these strategies to create your own opposite action plan (see reflection on the next page).

Examples of Opposite Action

Emotion	Reactive Avoidance Behavior	Opposite Action
Anger	Yell	Refrain from talking during an upsetting conversation
Embarrassment	Isolate	Stay around people and start a conversation
Shame	Numb out by bingeing Netflix	Take a walk or do something active

REFLECTION

Creating Your Opposite Action Plan

When emotions are in control, we can't plan. As such, it is important that you come up with your own opposite action plan beforehand. Use the spaces below to create your own plan. Keep in mind: it's best to choose a place to start where you are not in the red. Setting up for an early win will help you keep going.

Hot button

Reactive avoidance behavior

Opposite action

Changing the Game: Increasing Your Ability to Regulate Emotions

One important note to remember: as you challenge yourself to improve your ability to *Approach*, you might find that sometimes things become *more* uncomfortable, not less so. But becoming good at navigating this sort of thing involves learning to live a "comfortably uncomfortable" life. Think of it like exercise. Once you can comfortably deadlift one hundred pounds, you don't remain there forever. No, you add weight, because the only way we continue to improve is by challenging our body (and in this case, our mind). The trick is to find just the right amount of challenge. Too easy, and we lack the stimulus for growth. Too hard, and our form breaks down or we get injured. As the saying goes: optimal stress + optimal rest = optimal progress. This is what I teach my clients, and this is what I hope this chapter will help you do as well.

Addressing Roadblocks

One important point to note: no matter how much you try, there will still be situations in which your buttons get pushed so hard and you will react. In those situations, don't feel discouraged. Instead, ask yourself a few questions. First, did I know that this situation could be a hot button? If no, add it to your hot button list. But if yes, ask yourself, did I plan an opposite action plan? Finally, consider what you could do if this were to happen again.

Long-Term Benefits of Practicing Opposite Action

Although learning opposite action can be challenging at first, there are a lot of long-term benefits. You've already seen a few from the client stories I shared. Angad developed a healthier relationship with social media. Although Filomena lost her boyfriend, continual practice helped her enter a happy marriage. And lastly, Oliver improved his relationship with his co-worker Martha. Each one of these stories reflects the real change experienced by someone. And I know you too can experience the transformational power of *Approaching.*

Let's Continue Our Journey

Approaching is a skill designed to help us identify our reactive avoidance, to *Approach* by going toward the discomfort. How? By creating a clear opposite action plan, we can learn to regulate our emotions and live happier lives. It is my favorite skill but not the only one in this book. To build resilience over time, it is necessary to always move toward the things that matter the most to us. That is why we are going to dive into our final skill in this book, *Aligning.*

PART IV

Align

Chapter Nine

Should I Stay or Should I Go? Remaining to Avoid

After fifteen years living in downtown Boston, I knew every street, public alley, and bizarre shortcut in that glorious, ancient (for America, anyway) city. But when I moved to the suburbs, I was totally lost. It's a strange feeling to start from scratch on something as simple as knowing your way around, and yet there I was, utterly disoriented and incapable of giving a stranger even the most basic instructions on how to get somewhere. But thankfully our cars are equipped with a GPS. It's incredible to me that we now have this on our phones, and even our wrists if you're the owner of a fancy smartwatch. It's a wonderful tool—that is, if all goes smoothly.

However, a few weeks after moving to the suburbs, I found myself at a crossroads—literally and figuratively. I was at a major intersection, on my way to Boston for a meeting. I was running late, so I was already a little edgy. The GPS informed me that there was a major accident on I-90 East heading into the city, so it sent me on a detour. As I sat at the traffic light, I noticed a line of cars behind me—I guess their GPSs had recalibrated too—and it was starting to become clear that this route was going to have a lot of traffic as well. As I anxiously waited for the light to turn green, my GPS suddenly went offline! All I was left with was the dread in my stomach and the blank screen's useless message: "Recalculating . . . recalculating . . . recalculating."

By then, my heart was pounding and my thoughts racing: I knew I only had a minute or so to decide which direction to go before the light turned green. The problem was, I had not been paying attention—only blindly following my GPS—so I had no clue which direction Boston was. Left? Right? Straight? I honestly didn't know what to do. In the seconds that passed, my brain just froze. Finally, I made a quick mental calculation: the GPS has to come back online eventually (even though the screen was frozen), so perhaps I could just stay put for a bit. *Sure, I would be holding up traffic, but this would just take a second*, I told myself. *How bad could it be to hold up a line of cars during rush hour?* Although I was trying to calm myself down, my anxiety just continued to going up.

With the seconds ticking by, I had only one wish: I wished that I had a compass with me. (There was actually one on my iPhone all along but it turns out I was the last person on the planet to find out about this.) You might be wondering why I'm talking about compasses. But I think the compass is one of the boldest devices known to mankind. But before I make my pitch, let me briefly highlight the core difference between a GPS and a compass, and why I wished I had a compass that day instead.

The Perils of Using a GPS

In addition to the kind of predicament I just described, GPS can also lead you astray if you accidentally enter an address in the wrong town. Sure, the GPS will get you to the destination, but you won't end up where you wanted to be. This unfortunate shortcoming of the GPS was one of the reasons some new clients would be late for our first session in my downtown Boston office. They would key in: "Cambridge Street," and often the GPS would default to: "Cambridge Street, *Cambridge*, MA" instead of "Cambridge Street, *Boston,* MA." Usually by the time they realized they were going in the wrong direction, they were already across the river in Cambridge and would be thirty minutes late for a forty-five-minute session. After this happened about five times, I started to email new clients to give them a helpful reminder.

A compass, on the other hand, is a navigation instrument that is designed to help you determine your direction relative to Earth's magnetic poles. Because the compass does not think for you, you need to always be watching where you are going (off a cliff, into a tree, down a chasm). The compass is designed to *guide you through your journey*. So you can see how on that unfortunate day, a compass could have been more useful in that it at least would have gotten me moving in the general direction of Boston. Sure, it would have taken longer as I worked my way east, but it would have been leagues better than a frozen GPS.

Remaining to Avoid

I share my unfortunate tale of traffic paralysis with you because it illustrates beautifully how many of us get stuck in life when we are operating following an external GPS. This, to me, is what it looks like to remain as a form of avoidance, where we just stay stuck in place with the perceived threat, just frozen. We know the status quo is not working for us, and yet we are too paralyzed to do anything about it. Someone who struggles with remaining usually gets stuck doing the same thing over and over despite feeling drained. Below are some examples of the ways in which I have seen my clients get stuck in remaining to avoid.

Remain

At times, especially when you perceive a threat, your body stays stuck in place and you remain frozen. When you freeze in place, your brain feels stuck, like you can't think or feel much, and there is no action you can even imagine taking. Here are examples of ways you might remain:

- Stop contributing to a conversation
- Stay in an unhealthy relationship, platonic or romantic
- Be unable to answer when asked a question by a superior
- Stay in the same job even though it is making you unhappy
- Sit for long periods of time without getting anything done
- Check out and stare into space
- Put off making career decisions
- Stay in an unhealthy living situation

Because remaining involves inaction and staying put despite discomfort, it can at times be hard to pinpoint. Yet I have never met a person who was remaining and didn't know that they were a bit stuck. Usually, they just don't know what to do. Remaining is the "deer in the headlights" type of response, and it can show up in many domains of life. To identify ways in which you remain, complete the reflection below.

REFLECTION

Remaining to Avoid

Take a moment to consider your current life circumstances. Are there situations where you find yourself lingering even though your current situation isn't ideal? Do your find your current situation frustrating or draining yet feel the idea of change to be paralyzing? Usually, we remain within certain areas of our lives. For example:

- **Have you ever found yourself in a romantic relationship you knew was no longer working for you, but you just didn't know whether or how you should end it?**
- **Have you been in a job that was no longer satisfying but staying in the position seemed more reasonable than pursuing the unknown?**
- **Have you ever found yourself complaining about the same thing to your friends, over and over again, without doing anything differently?**

(*continued*)

- **Have you ever wanted to reinvent yourself—perhaps the kids have gone off to school and you want a new career—but you just don't know where to start?**

After reflecting on the questions above, take a moment to write about a situation where you find yourself remaining stuck in place.

____

____

____

Because avoidance robs us of a bold life, imagine for a second that you could overcome your paralysis. How would your life be different?

____

____

____

Your Internal Compass

Completing the above reflection helps us identify areas of our lives that we are navigating using a GPS. Living life while blindly following a GPS will inevitably leave us stranded and stuck (after all, even the best technology sometimes fails us). But it does not have to be that way, because it turns out that all of us always have access to an internal compass: *our values*.

Values are incredibly powerful navigation tools for life. When I think about what exactly a value is, I am reminded of the work of Dr. Steven Hayes, the developer of acceptance and commitment therapy (ACT),[1] who is a clinical psychologist and the author of forty-seven books (and counting). ACT was designed to help individuals pursue a meaningful life while accepting the pain that inevitably goes with it. The core practices of ACT include diffusion (a technique designed to separate or detach from one's thoughts or emotions), acceptance (facing thoughts and feelings as they are), contact with the present moment, observing one's self, committed action, and—the most relevant to this chapter—values.[2] A few years ago, while at an academic conference, I heard Dr. Hayes describe values as "the quality of being and doing that you would *live by* if it was just a secret between you and yourself." In other words, *values are intrinsic internal compasses that guide our decisions, attitudes, and behaviors, and they are unique to us*. For example, you might care the most about humility, whereas someone else might care the most about achievement.

If you search online, you'll find hundreds of different lists of values. Surprisingly (or maybe unsurprisingly, given the quirkiness of humans), the world hasn't agreed on one definitive list of values, although Shalom H. Schwartz and his intercontinental research team have identified nineteen values that are common across nearly thirty countries.[3] To give you an idea of the common values that I often see while working with clients, I've created an initial list on the following page.

Take a moment to reflect on this list. Is there anything that jumps out to you? A value that is more important to you than the other ones? A value that you don't care about as much? A value that you feel is missing? Whenever you find yourself stuck, is there a value that you could use as your inner compass to get you unstuck?

At the end of the day, whether you resonate with each value listed or not is okay (and even expected because our values are personalized to us). It's also okay if there were multiple values that stood out to you. See, we rarely have only *one* value. Usually, we find many different values important, even if they aren't closely related to each other. The trick in using your internal compass to navigate life is to choose which value is most important in each specific moment.

Yet identifying your values alone will not change your life. For many of us, our values exist like a painting inside a home: they are nice to look at and reflect upon, but they don't play an active daily role. We sort of know our values (or at least have a gut feeling about what they could be), but we don't actually refer to them often. When we ignore our values, we are back to the GPS life, whereby we let an external source (culture, society, friends, family) tell us how to move forward, all the while never really being clear on why we are doing what we're doing—and that is how we all get lost.

Common Values

Achievement
Adventure
Ambition
Authenticity
Beauty
Belonging
Charisma
Commitment
Community
Compassion
Courage
Creativity
Curiosity
Decisiveness
Dependability
Directness
Discipline
Diversity
Equality
Excellence
Fairness
Faith
Fame
Family
Financial freedom
Forgiveness
Friendship
Frugality
Generosity
Gratitude
Growth
Health
Honesty
Humility
Humor
Impact
Inclusiveness
Individuality
Justice
Kindness
Love
Loyalty
Open-mindedness
Optimism
Passion
Patience
Perseverance
Playfulness
Pragmatism
Presence
Productivity
Recognition
Risk-taking
Security
Self-expression
Self-respect
Simplicity
Sustainability
Teamwork
Tradition
Vulnerability
Wealth
Wisdom

How I Lost My Way

Early on in my career, I had a clear value by which I guided most of my actions, both personally and professionally: ambition. To me, ambition meant working hard to be successful, and I believed that by being ambitious I could prevent any chance of ever falling back into poverty. When you're raised in such challenging conditions as I was, all you can think of is getting the hell out of that situation once and for all. It may not be the most spiritually enlightened stance, but depending on how far toward the bottom you're starting out, money really can buy happiness. Even more than that, I realized that if I could make it professionally, I could eventually be in a position to support my family. So ambition drove me and was one of the main forces that got me all the way to the United States.

Ambition is a legitimate value, and research shows that when we make moves in life that reflect our values, our feelings of stress, anxiety, and depression decrease.[4] And that is exactly what I experienced as a graduate student and in the early days of my academic career. I would actually get a high from doing the hard work, and the more ambitious I got, the better it felt. Though I'm not a runner, it probably wasn't that dissimilar to the famous runner's high that endurance runners are always going on about. From the perch of my ambition, I would set clear goals such as "get into a PhD program" or "work at the most prestigious department of psychiatry in the US," and many others. So, in a very real sense, ambition kept me focused on my goals, and in those early days of my career this was not at all avoidance. I really was living in line with my values—at that time.

Yet, somewhere during my career this changed. At what point did my actions go from being "in line with my values" to avoidance? It's hard to say exactly when this occurred, but it was most certainly during the middle years of my career. I stopped paying attention to the *why* (my *value*) of what I was doing, and just focused on the *what* (aka the *goals*) that I felt I needed to achieve. I was so focused on what people were telling me ought to be my next goal that I was almost entirely living up to their idea of success, not my own. I kept climbing their ladder, but I was no longer headed toward my dreams.

In other words, I was off course—trying to navigate life without checking in on my values. The problem with ignoring our internal compass is that we usually end up moving in a direction that doesn't reflect what we care about most. And journeying along a path that is not aligned with your values is usually uncomfortable. For example, if you care about honesty, and yet you find yourself telling a lie, you will feel uncomfortable. Similarly, if you care deeply about creativity, but you find yourself in a job that resorts to doing things the way they've always been done, you will be unsatisfied. If health is a core value of yours and yet you are overeating and not exercising, you will feel awful.

When we feel the familiar pang of discomfort, we remain. We often just keep doing what we've always done, because it feels like the only thing we can do—and at times we just push ourselves even harder, as if more of the same would make it better (guilty!). We tell ourselves that it will get better, but it doesn't seem to. This is the essence of *remaining as a form of avoidance*—we stay the course even if that means moving further and further from the life we want. We don't run away or fight back; we just stay in our current patterns. Of course, staying the path feels better momentarily because remaining is avoidance and, as we've seen, avoidance works in the short term. If we end up blind to our true north, our emotional and physical health pays a price. This can happen to anyone, and as I continued chasing goals without considering what mattered most, it happened to me.

Holy Shit: Am I Having a Stroke?

I knew there was an emotional cost to what I was doing, and usually I was face-to-face with this cost in the wee hours of the night in those lonely, quiet moments where I would, for once, allow myself a little glimpse behind the curtain of this goal-driven treadmill of a career. Often, I found myself lying in bed, unable to sleep, anxious, staring at the ceiling as thoughts pounded on the shores of my brain:

What am I doing?

Will I always feel this anxious if I keep going?

There is no other way; I must stay in this career!

If I just write another grant, I will feel better.

Why am I doing this?

For whom am I doing this?

Why am I so miserable when I have achieved so much?

I don't have the right to feel miserable given how fortunate I am.

If I quit this job, who will I become?

But long-term stress has a way of showing up in your body too. According to the American Psychological Association, stress directly affects the musculoskeletal system, cardiovascular system, respiratory system, endocrine system, gastrointestinal system, nervous system, and reproductive system.[5] At the risk of being alarmist, it's worth noting that stress can lead to death. Studies conducted in England have shown that even *low* levels of distress are related to a 20 percent increased risk of mortality.[6]

In early 2021, the physical effects of stress finally hit me. I was home, working on a research grant, when all of a sudden I started to lose sensation in part of my face. My first thought was: *Okay, I am just a little stressed, this is a simple physiological reaction, calm down, there is nothing going on, this is just anxiety*, but after a few minutes I had lost all feeling in half of my face and panic began to set in. *Oh my God . . . I'm having a stroke!* A few tears dripped down my face as I tried not to lose it, and I kept saying to myself, *Is this anxiety or am I really having a stroke?* With the last bit of my thinking brain that was available to me, I called my doctor's office and reached a nurse. I described the symptoms: numbness on the right side of my face, a little tingling in my legs and arms, a heartbeat of 150 (while seated at my desk). Despite her attempt to temper her voice, the nurse on the line seemed alarmed and my brain immediately went to . . .

Oh my God, I am *having a stroke! I'll lose everything I worked so hard for, this is the end!*

Tears were now streaming down my face as I struggled to speak with the nurse, who urged me to get to the office as fast as I could. My brain was spinning, and all I could do was get David to drive me. As we drove, my thoughts swirled and I saw my entire life pass in front of me.

I was quickly evaluated by my primary care doctor, who determined that I could be having a stroke. But it was not clear, so they ordered a brain scan. By that evening, I was in a satellite hospital stuck in the giant MRI machine, and I vividly recall saying to myself: *I have hit emotional bankruptcy and there is no coming back from it.*

The next twenty-four hours went by in a blur, with my brain predicting the worst-case scenario, while I tried to keep it together in front of my son. In the end, it was determined that I hadn't had a stroke, and no one knew what actually had happened—perhaps a severe migraine is what the neurologist told me. But regardless of what happened physically that day, emotionally this was my tipping point, where I could no longer ignore that my goal-driven treadmill of a life chasing ambition was no longer working for me and that I was the one paying a very high price.

The Cost of Ignoring Our Values

The crippling anxiety, stress, and fear I experienced that day is exactly what my clients experience. It's almost as though I can see the stress piling up as soon as they start to compromise their own values. And usually, they feel it too: their sleep is off, they feel a little more irritable or even angry after work, their stress is constant, and worst of all they can't really pinpoint why this is all happening. This feeling that something is amiss is the price of navigating without a compass, a price that is often hidden until we hit a wall, at which point we can no longer continue on as we have been.

A common manifestation of the cost of remaining to avoid is burnout. The Network on the Coordination and Harmonisation of European Occupational Cohorts recently conducted an extensive review of the literature to develop a single definition of burnout that was approved by experts from twenty-nine countries: "Burnout is a state of *emotional exhaustion* due to prolonged exposure to work-related problems."[7] But burnout is not only related to work. You can also experience burnout after prolonged life-related stressors (e.g., caregiving). According to the World Health Organization, common symptoms of burnout include feeling drained or fatigued, having feelings of negativity toward work or mentally distancing oneself from work, and experiencing a reduction in productivity.[8]

The irony is that whenever we experience burnout (because of remaining), some of us (including myself) just keep going, doing what we've always done, and hoping for a different outcome. We keep avoiding! We escape even the potential of being uncomfortable by choosing to face the devil we know rather than stare into the void of the unknown that accompanies any drastic life change. I want you to ask yourself: *Has there been a time in my life that I just kept doing what I always did even when it hurt?* And if you have, you are not alone: we have all been there. Companies with thousands of employees around the world have conducted surveys to measure rates of burnout, with McKinsey & Company noting that 49 percent of individuals report feeling at least somewhat burned out[9] and Deloitte noting that 77 percent of individuals report having experienced burnout in their current position.[10]

Usually by the time we hit burnout, we have been avoiding for a while. We've gotten into the habit of ignoring what matters most to us, and we end up feeling worse and worse. The worse we feel, the harder it is to get back on track, and when we encounter an obstacle of some kind, moving forward feels impossible.

Making a Choice (Without a Compass) Is Painful

The obstacles we face often come in the form of a turning point or fork in the road where values collide and a decision needs to be made. For example, it's 9 a.m., you are due for a meeting with your team, but your kid wants a hug and a kiss and all your attention. Do you end up late for your meeting to attend to your kid, or do you disappoint your kid and focus on work? Family and work collide often for many of us, and when they do, we sometimes make a decision that is designed only to make us feel better fast in that moment (aka avoid).

In the same sense that we can't travel east and west simultaneously, we can't do two things at once. No matter what we do in life, when it comes to work, family, and health, when you focus on one, you are not doing another. Our time and attention and energy represent the pieces of a zero-sum game, and once we spend some of that limited currency, it is gone forever. Just as I can't buy a sandwich *and* a pizza with the same ten-dollar bill at the same time, one must make choices when deciding what to chase down in life. And when we are stressed, anxious, and stuck in a long pattern of avoidance, we often make decisions based on how we feel in the moment, our emotions, and perhaps not on what might be best for us long term. After all, we all want to feel better soon.

This is just how my client Ricardo lived day to day. Ricardo describes himself as a true family man. When I met him, he beamed as he talked about his two children and his wife, their early days as a family, and the cherished family vacations. Ricardo immediately took out his phone to proudly show me pictures of his children, who were seven and five at the time. Family was the most important thing to Ricardo—his true north, he told me. This family-centric monologue puzzled me because when Ricardo sought me out, he had just been served divorce papers by his wife. I asked him to explain the apparent contradiction.

Ricardo sighed and went on to describe the Friday afternoon before we met, which he told me was a clear example of why he was stuck. He was running late at work, and was anxiously checking the time, as 4:30 p.m. was the cutoff for school pickup. Since his wife had asked for the divorce, they were still sharing the household and were dividing responsibilities for the kids 50/50.

It is important to note that Ricardo was a VP at a financial company. He loved his high-profile job and the chance to excel in a difficult field. On that Friday afternoon in question, Ricardo was in the midst of negotiating a potentially huge deal with a new client. He had been working to bring this client—let's call him Mark—to his firm for a couple of years, and Mark had finally decided to move all his investments to Ricardo's firm. This would represent a huge win for the company, not to mention an incredible bonus at the end of the year, which Ricardo now needed due to the impending divorce.

Ricardo was ready to get out of the office to go pick up his kids, feeling on top of the world, when his office phone rang. It was Mark. Ricardo's heart sank immediately. What if Mark was having second thoughts that needed to be massaged? If he didn't answer that call, he could potentially lose Mark's business. But if he did answer it, he would be late to pick up his children. In a quick calculation, Ricardo picked up the phone as he sent a quick text to his wife to ask her if she could pick up the kids. This was a huge ask at the time, as their relationship had become quite strained, and even small conflicts tended to boil over into full-blown arguments. Ricardo knew that in prioritizing work, he would be taking a risk vis-à-vis his wife, but this was such a big potential new client that he felt like there was no other choice: he needed to put work first; that was the fire burning hot in front of him. But as he greeted Mark, all he could focus on was the feeling of dread he had.

"So what happened next?" I asked Ricardo.

"Well, as it turned out, my wife"—he looked sad as he said the word—"was also in a meeting at work and didn't see my messages, so the kids were stranded at school. Thankfully not alone, because their teachers stayed with them for an extra twenty minutes, but man, they were furious with me when I got them."

Ricardo's eyes welled with tears.

"It's not like I was consciously choosing work over my family! Sometimes these things just happen, and I end up always choosing what feels most pressing in the moment. Honestly, I think that's why my wife is leaving me. She says that I'm not a true partner, someone she can rely on. And after eight years, she says she's had enough. I don't think I can change her mind, but I need to figure out how to behave differently, because I know that while I only have my family's best interests at heart, they don't see it that way, and that kills me."

For Ricardo, this decision between success at work and dependability for his family had been particularly painful because he often found himself choosing success at work and compromising his family life. When Ricardo's wife finally asked for the divorce, he was crushed because in his heart he deeply loved her and fully understood why she was upset. In fact, he shared her frustrations with his own behavior! He wanted to change but didn't know how to stop avoiding by doing what he had always done.

I often find myself stuck just like Ricardo, and perhaps some of you reading this feel the same. Every day I wake up and say to myself, *I will exercise this morning!* Then, before I know it, Diego is up, gives me a hug and a gorgeous smile, and asks: "*Mamãe, vamos brincar?*" ("Mom, let's play?") At this point, my heart melts and all I want is to spend every second of the rest of my life with him and any and all hope of spending my morning on a stair-climber or picking up a barbell goes out the window. I prioritize him at that moment (and all such moments), and it feels good . . . momentarily! But it also has an unpleasant whiff of avoidance to it because this choice always has me stuck in place, doing what I usually do, with forty pounds to lose and feeling physically tired and achy, none of which will get easier to fix as time goes on.

Luckily, we don't have to wait until a breaking point to identify areas of our lives where values are colliding. These areas are usually ripe with avoidance. So, take a moment to complete the reflection on the following page and uncover where in your life you might be hitting a crossroad.

Is Remaining Always Avoidance?

When I am teaching the idea that sometimes we stay in situations as a form of avoidance, one question I often get from trainees is: *Are you telling me that the person stuck in a domestic violence situation is*

REFLECTION

Identifying Crossroads Where Values Collide

Experiencing the stress of colliding values is not something unique to Ricardo and me—we all deal with this all the time. It is not the collision that is the problem: the problem is when we feel the tension of making a choice, but instead of being intentional about our choice, we avoid. Looking back at your values that you identified earlier in this chapter, reflect on a recent situation where two of those values collided, and think about the following questions:

When my values collided, what did I do?

____

____

How did I feel after I took this action?

____

____

Is this something that I do over and over again?

____

____

What is the short-term consequence of my action?

____

____

Long term, does choosing a specific action related to one of these values keep me stuck?

____

____

avoiding? Domestic violence is a serious and multifaceted situation. I know this not only as an expert who has treated many trauma survivors over the past two decades, but also from witnessing my mom go through it for years. When it comes to situations that can be life and death, there is only one certainty: safety comes first. So, if you are reading this book and find yourself in this situation, I strongly urge you to find a provider or a close friend and to ensure you care for your safety above all else. Although I imagine that the way out is difficult, I saw how my mom changed after she was in a safe place. Don't get me wrong, it was challenging. But it led to a better life for all of us.

Here is another example of someone who is remaining in place but not avoiding. Kate, a client of mine, called me the other day to check in and talk about whether or not she was avoiding. Kate had been in a very abusive and unhappy work environment when we met and was frozen in place. She had gained a hundred pounds over the years, and she was feeling terrible. While Kate and I worked together, she was able to get a new job. She had been happy there for a while, but here she was a year into that job and things weren't going well. Similar to the first job, she had decided to stick it out but was wondering: *Am I avoiding?* So, I asked Kate why she had decided to stay, and here is what she told me:

"Despite this not being an ideal job, if I stay for another six months, I will get a significant bonus, which I need to help our family get out of debt. So, I decided I will stay for that time, do the best I can at the job, and when that date approaches, I will look for another job."

"How did you feel when you made that decision?" I asked Kate.

"I still don't like the job, but making the decision made it easier to handle the daily grind of it all. I guess I feel like there is a plan now and I have to execute it. I guess I feel comfortably uncomfortable!"

That is when both Kate and I understood that she was not avoiding; she was just weighing her options until she could get to a better situation. Life is hard, and at times there are no good options right away. So just because you stay put, that does not necessarily mean you are avoiding. If you're wondering whether your specific situation and behavior constitute psychological avoidance, I would encourage you to refer back to the diagram shared on page 46.

When We Dance with the Devil We Know, We Are Still Dancing with the Devil

When we live our lives focused on only one goal, without checking in on how it is serving us, we risk turning our lives into an endless cycle of stress and burnout, just like you saw in my life during my time on the academic hamster wheel. Despite the fact that the trajectory I was on no longer fit my desires for my life, I kept going. So, going back to the old saying, I think it is a lot safer to face the devil you know because there is some degree of certainty in fighting a known evil. So, in the day to day, when we are dancing with the known devil, it might be hard, but we know how to act and what to expect. Yet, it's still the devil. And the minute that devil becomes a collaborator in keeping you stuck, you will start to see negative long-term consequences. I had to nearly have a stroke to wake up and call the devil by his other name: *avoidance*.

Overworking despite the price tag is only one way we end up remaining as avoidance. Sometimes we get stuck because our values collide. Ricardo cared about his family but often failed to show up for them, usually because he was focusing on work. Or maybe you're like me and put family first but to the detriment of your own health. If remaining to avoid ends up hurting us more in the long term, why do we keep doing it? Let's dive into the science behind this flavor of avoidance in the next chapter.

Chapter Ten

But Why Do I Stay?

If we have an internal compass—our values—why don't we use it instead of avoiding? It seems logical that we would navigate the world and make decisions based on what matters most to us. However, we sometimes get stuck in our old habits to avoid the possibility of discomfort. Based on my experience working with hundreds of clients around the world, there are three common substitute guides we rely on instead: emotions, goals, and other people. To understand how these problematic guides end up leading us through life, let me start by telling you a short personal story.

When I first came to the United States, I found it particularly challenging to understand what people meant when they would ask me "What are you thinking?" whenever I would get quiet during a conversation. The idea of focusing on what I was saying to myself, not on how I *felt*, seemed strange to me. Growing up in a Latin country, emotions *are* us: they define the culture, the individual, and how we respond to everything. We lead with our hearts. If you're wondering what this looks like, just watch Brazilian fans during the World Cup: tears, strong emotions, screaming . . . that is just what we do. (Though I will admit, it's not like Brazilians have a monopoly on crying during soccer matches. I'm looking at you, Italy.)

As an exchange student, I recall taking a debate class in my first semester (what a disaster!) and still remember making arguments that *felt* very logical in my brain: "I *feel* strongly that women and men should be paid equally!" I still believe that women and men should be paid equally, but arguing for pay equity based on feelings alone wasn't very convincing, and it left out plenty of nuance on a rather complicated topic. I am laughing at myself as I share this with you because, as an adult, I probably say a million times a day to my clients and my son: "Emotions are valid, but they are not facts." But as an eighteen-year-old exchange student, I would have *never* agreed that my feelings were not facts. I felt them, therefore they must be true. During that time, the teacher kindly kept asking me to make a *logical* argument using data, but weren't my feelings good enough data points for a debate? Short answer? No. Imagine how many political arguments over the past few years would have been nipped in the bud if both participants had been required to leave emotion at the door and rely solely on logic, empiricism, and data? Imagine how many Thanksgivings would have been saved!

Although this scenario in the debate class is funny today, it was very frustrating at the time. Learning English was my ticket out of Brazil, and as such, something that I really cared a lot about. Yet, I recall countless times in my first semester in the US when my brain would just fail me. Even when I knew the words and the sentence was nearly formed in my brain, I still could not articulate it, even if my life depended on it. In the debate class, I vividly recall standing in front of the class about to debate a very cute Russian guy. The teacher put us each behind a podium, and I organized the note cards I had written the night before, which my host-mom had so kindly worked on with me. That morning I had been feeling confident, telling myself that with my host family's help with English I could win this debate. Yet once we began, the world closed in on me.

To say that my heart was pounding is an understatement: it felt a lot more like those old cartoons where someone's heart is beating out of their chest. I imagined that everyone could see how anxious I was and the entire cascade of fight, flight, or freeze reactions took place. It was like my emotions had kidnapped my thinking brain, and nothing logical could come out of it. So what did I do? You can probably guess: I remained in place, stuck saying nothing, just avoiding. I stared at my peers, trying not to make eye contact with the handsome boy! It wasn't until I sat down in my chair at the end of the debate that I finally felt some relief. My professor took pity on me and gave me a passing grade (to be fair, it was a pass/fail class, so this wasn't high praise).

As a scientist today, I understand what was happening in my brain: my amygdala had kicked my prefrontal cortex out and had taken my brain hostage. As such, it may well have been impossible to make a logical argument during that time. But back then, I didn't know the science behind any of this. All I knew was "emotions feel bad" and therefore I needed to calm myself down by avoiding.

Emotions Gone Wild

Emotions are powerful, and usually the fastest way to reduce the intensity of our emotions is to avoid. This type of knee-jerk behavior is what psychologists often refer to as *emotion-driven behavior.* Emotion-driven behaviors are behaviors that directly reflect our current emotional state.[1] In other words, when a person is upset or under stress, they may do something they will later regret to try to feel better fast.

When we are acting based on emotion, we are not engaging our thinking brain,[2] which can lead us to drink more than we planned, eat excessively, neglect our responsibilities, and even be unfaithful to our loved ones.[3] Some of these actions might not seem that problematic in the moment, but they can have long-term consequences. Patterns of impulsive and reactive behavior can lead to chronic substance use problems, weight gain, job loss, divorce, financial strain, and delinquency. All these situations are examples of what happens when we navigate through our lives based on emotions. And the catch-22 is that these consequences cause even more of the intense emotions that we were trying to reduce in the first place!

When Ricardo found himself stressed at work, he would often stay later, take a phone call on his way out of the office, or do one last thing before leaving. He would remain in his office to avoid. These behaviors gave him temporary relief. But then he would be late for dinner with his family, causing another argument with his wife and disappointing his children. In these moments he was guided by his emotions. He put work first not because he consciously wanted to, but because he felt it was the only way to manage his discomfort in the moment, and this led to his divorce.

I often struggle with emotion-driven behaviors myself. As I shared with you, I have tended to prioritize time with Diego, which is lovely, but honestly I do it based on how it makes me feel in that moment: his sweet eyes, smiles, kisses, and hugs every morning make me feel so loved that I choose to spend time with him, even though I know that taking some of that time to go to the gym would be better for me in the long run. But I have to confess, it is challenging. I often find myself falling prey to my emotions in that moment. Then I wind up upset with myself later in the day when my back hurts or my pants don't fit. At such moments my brain scolds me: *Hypocrite! Whatever happened to practicing what you preach?*

In these moments, Ricardo and I are *acting based on how we feel, not what we value.* And that is why emotion-driven behaviors are problematic when it comes to living a life in line with our values: these behaviors rob us of the opportunity to move toward what matters most to us. This is why I often refer to emotion-driven behavior as the fire extinguisher approach. Sure, we *might* be successful in putting out the closest fire, but we might also miss the broader opportunity to save what matters most.

Are All Emotions Bad?

Absolutely not! Our emotions have important functions. If you've seen the popular Pixar film *Inside Out*, you probably already know what I'm talking about. You can't have a limited set of emotions and still live a rich and fulfilling life. Living a human existence means being open to all our emotions. Moreover, emotions contain information about our environment that helps us keep safe from harm. Out in the wilderness, if we are face-to-face with a lion, our fear propels us to get the heck out of there. At home, the disgust you feel when sniff-testing the milk in your fridge protects you from drinking rancid milk and getting a horrible stomachache.

Emotions don't just benefit us; they can help others too. The emotional expression of others also contains details about our environment that help us make our next move. For example, if you see a random child crying, you will do something to soothe that child. If you walk into a meeting late and your office bestie passes you a wide-eyed glance of warning, you might proceed with caution and do your best to sneak a seat without catching your boss's eye. If you are interrupted by loud knocking at your door and indistinguishable yelling indicative of anger, you may think twice about answering.

These are only a few examples of the nearly countless tidbits of information that emotions can carry, but let's now return to the maxim that emotions are valid but are not facts. While experiencing strong emotions is part of being human—and even if they carry some valuable information—they usually don't carry *all* the information. For example, if we see someone rush into the room wide-eyed and panting, our heart might quicken and muscles tighten out of fear before we know whether the person is running from something scary, excited to share good news, or merely tired from finishing a four-mile run. So, while it makes sense that we should try to use our thinking brain whenever possible, that is not always how we respond to life, especially when we experience strong emotions. Emotions themselves are not good or bad; problems arise when we choose our actions based only on emotions as a means of avoiding experiencing discomfort.

F*ck Your Goals

Emotions (although very helpful and necessary) can certainly prevent us from living our best life, but they are not the only reason we end up disregarding our values. Clinically, one of the reasons I see most people being stuck is the confusion between values and goals. Goals are what we plan to do, while values are intrinsic motivators that guide our actions. Many cultures throughout the world value goal achievement,[4] and we often teach our kids to pursue goals—get onto the soccer team, study hard to get into a great college, work overtime to get a raise—but many times these goals are not anchored on personal values. For example, I told myself that I was driven by ambition, but I was actually living a life focused on only my next goal. For a while, this worked out for me. But the reality is, it eventually got me stuck pursuing goals, one after the other, while ignoring the emotional cost.

My experience paying the price of blindly following goals is well supported by research. For example, in 2017, *Psychiatry Research* (a renowned academic journal) published a study showing that people who link their goals to their sense of self-worth and pursue their goals at all costs are more likely to experience symptoms of depression.[5] Why? Well, I would imagine that the individuals in this study kept pushing through life toward the *what* while neglecting the *why*. Sure, getting to a goal is always satisfying, but how long does that satisfaction last if it is not aligned with what you care about? Have you ever gotten a promotion that you had been wanting for a long time, only to ask yourself, *What's next?* instead of being able to treasure the moment? This empty feeling is the result of navigating through life using goals—or using a GPS that is focused more on the destination than the journey.

You might be asking yourself, *Why do I keep relentlessly pursuing my goals even when I know they are no longer what I really want?* I've asked myself this same question many times. One reason we keep pursuing goals is to *avoid* any possible negative outcomes.[6] The path we're already on feels safer than the unknown. For me, climbing the academic ladder was familiar—difficult, yes, but a known challenge. Branching off on my own to pursue another career was risky because I hadn't done it before.

So I pushed aside my values and tried to focus on the next goal. The double-edged sword was that, in order to keep achieving my goals, I needed to deal with the discomfort that came from continuing to pursue goals that weren't fulfilling. We might realize this only when it's too late, such as I did only when my health started to waver. In those moments, I felt—and you likely have felt this at times too—that there wasn't another way.

East Meets West

The third common guide we follow is other people's values instead of our own, especially when we face real obstacles (e.g., moving to a new country, making a career change, marrying into a family). Often these obstacles are challenging because they lead to conflict between personal and group values, which inevitably leads to interpersonal challenges. To show you what I mean, let's meet Stephanie.

Stephanie was a young first-generation Chinese woman who I worked with a few years ago. Stephanie's actual birth name was 梓涵 (Zǐhán), but outside her home she preferred to be called Stephanie, though this was actually a secret she kept from her parents, who did not approve of any "Americanization," as Stephanie explained.

Stephanie was born in mainland China, and her family moved to Boston when she was a baby. Stephanie's parents spoke very little English, so Mandarin was the only language spoken at home. On the other hand, Stephanie's English was perfect, and she described being very proud of it when we first met. She talked about her parents as loving people who wanted her to pursue the opportunities America would provide (though *not* the actual American dream, because they sincerely did not want her to be an American in any meaningful way). They were also very strict when it came to their Chinese cultural beliefs. For example, they insisted that Stephanie celebrate all major Chinese holidays.

As a child, Stephanie had complied with her parents' demands and even enjoyed the elaborate holiday traditions, but by the time she was a college student in her twenties (living at home and commuting) she was rebelling, preferring instead to spend time with her "American friends." I use quotation marks here to show how Stephanie talked about this in our sessions: her parents did not approve of her non-Chinese friends, and they crudely separated people into categories. This often made Stephanie feel badly about wanting to hang out with her college friends, as though she were betraying her family. And yet, that is what she wanted to do. When I asked

Stephanie why she had decided to come to talk to me, she said one of her professors, who happened to be a close friend of mine, had urged her to seek some help because she was isolating and her school performance was being impacted.

At our first meeting, Stephanie told me that she had recently been feeling a lot of anger. She didn't know where it was coming from but was certain that if I could help her "get rid of it" she'd be happy once again. In response, I returned to my beloved symptom/infection analogy and told her that we would not be wasting our time addressing her anger during our time together. What we *would* seek to accomplish in therapy, I told her, was finding a way to solve the root cause of her anger.

I asked Stephanie to give me a sense of what life at home was like. She told me about the many admirable values her parents had instilled in her and how those values had led her to study hard, honor her Chinese culture, and put family above all else, which had instilled in her a more collectivist view of the world, versus the individualism found in the US.[7] For a young person who had come from a precarious background, she had achieved quite a bit, and yet in addition to her gratitude, she felt that her upbringing and life at home had also been rather constricting.

"It's like when I'm home I must be as Chinese as possible, and that is all I can be."

I asked her to elaborate. She paused for a moment, as if she were about to betray her family.

"Okay, for instance, even trivial things like the TV shows I watch have to be Chinese. My parents don't want me watching American TV, so I'm only allowed to watch shows that are in Mandarin. I want to be able to watch the same shows as my friends, but it's not allowed at home, and even though it might seem small, it makes me feel like an outsider at school."

"What happens at school?" I asked.

"When I'm on campus, I wear makeup, change my hair, whatever. I just act and appear as I want to. It's like I can be more American, or at least, more American to whatever degree I choose. But then my parents started getting on my case about it and made me 'tone it down,' which was incredibly frustrating."

From here, she switched into Mandarin without realizing it and detailed an entire argument between herself and her parents. For the next five minutes, I sat patiently waiting, not understanding a single word. (I launch into Portuguese when I'm upset, I could relate.)

Eventually, Stephanie looked up at me and realized that I had no clue what she was saying and we both laughed. But I told her I got the gist of it all. Some things go beyond language, and one of those things is the way our families can occasionally drive us insane, no matter how much we love them.

"It sounds like you're finding yourself stuck between two distinct cultural values, and you don't fully fit into either of them. As a consequence, your schoolwork and happiness are suffering."

"Exactly! I feel like there's no good answer to this. If I choose one, I sacrifice my happiness, and if I choose the other, I turn my back on my heritage."

Living and working in an international college town like Boston, I've seen many patients like Stephanie, whose cultural values from back home (wherever home may be) collide with the new cultural values they're experiencing in the US, and this tension creates quite a few interpersonal challenges. In fact, the research community, never shy about making up new words, has a term for this: *acculturative stress*.[8] How families respond to the acculturation process has a direct impact on the level of stress experienced. One study (of Asian American college students, as a matter of coincidence) found that acculturative family conflict is directly related to increased stress.[9]

Cultural values colliding is something I know well. When I first came to the US, I wanted more than anything to be an American (you'll recall my horror when my colleague told me I "looked so Latina"). For many years, I would take offense whenever people I encountered heard my accent or took one look at me and shifted to Spanish. Not only was it the wrong language, but I just wanted to be accepted as an American! Whenever this happened—and it happened often—my brain would start spinning and all I wanted to do was scream, *"Can't you see I'm American?!"*

My own acculturation process took years, but there is one funny story I recall early in my Boston days that represents the point in time where I began to feel confident enough to begin integrating my Brazilian identity back into my newfound American identity. I was trying so hard to be an American, but one bright sunny winter afternoon in my first year at MGH, we were discussing cultural identity and, as you probably guessed, I was not ready for this conversation, nor did I want to be a part of it. This was in the spring of 2005, and back then I had almost no real insight into my own ethnic identity. So as the director of our training program went around the room asking people about their ethnic identity, I began to get very anxious. By the time she got to me, all I could manage to do was blurt out, "I'm Latina!" My great friend Dr. Molly Colvin, an amazing neuropsychologist, also one of the most in-touch people I know, looked at me and said, "Damn, Luana. You must be having a really bad day. You *never* identify yourself as Latina!" And she was right! I knew that at that point, I needed to address my own acculturation journey. I was just not sure how to manage my own acculturation, which is how I came to understand patients like Stephanie.

So in our own way, both Stephanie and I were dealing with culture clash, and this conflict was taking us further away from what mattered to each of us. Because of this, we would often defer to culture to dictate our actions, without ever asking *why* or looking into our own intrinsic values. Bringing things back to avoidance, let's consider an important question: What made Stephanie's behavior a form of avoidance? Well, when culture impeded on her personal values, Stephanie let the norms of her Chinese culture dictated by her parents set the course for her actions. (For me, it was American culture, dictated by my own desire to belong.) Did our actions make us feel better in the moment? Yes, but they moved us away from living a life based on our values because we were operating on automatic pilot, following a cultural value that might no longer be *our* value. Culture, another person's compass, can be a factor that prevents us from living a life in line with our values.

Let Values Be Your Guide

The opposite of living a life driven by emotions, goals, or other people is a values-driven life. A values-driven life is one in which your values function as the internal compass guiding you *toward* and helping you define your goals in life. To live a values-driven life is at times much more challenging than being led by our emotions, goals, or other people because it means we have to face our avoidance, identify it, and often recalibrate our lives toward what matters most to us. To do so, you will have to make decisions that in the moment might lead to more discomfort but will yield more long-term fulfillment. For example, choosing the gym in the morning will always collide with my time with Diego and, to be honest, it is less immediately rewarding than his kisses, but by choosing to *Align* my daily actions with my value of health, I am much more likely to have a longer and better life and overall more time with Diego long term. In fact, more than one hundred studies that looked at acceptance and commitment therapy (ACT; the therapy I briefly introduced in the last chapter) have documented the positive impact of values-driven behaviors.[10] People who have learned how to live a values-driven life have less anxiety, depression, substance use, and even physical pain. Although a values-driven life can be challenging in the moment, when viewed in the long term, it leads to a more fulfilling life. To live a bold life, it is crucial to align values with actions, and that is what we will do in the next chapter.

Chapter Eleven

Calibrating Your Inner Compass

As we approach the final chapter of *Bold Move*, I have a confession to make. For the first several years of my career, I never talked to my clients about their values, even though I often thought a lot about mine. I was trained in what the psychological field today calls the "second wave" of cognitive behavioral therapy,[1] which meant I focused most on my clients' thoughts and actions, often creating clear plans to teach their brains to stop reacting to false alarms (see parts II and III of this book). And despite the fact that there are plenty of research studies to support this methodology[2] (to say nothing of the fact that many of my clients improved), after a while I began to feel that something else was missing. It was almost like I had taught them to improve their health through exercise while completely ignoring their diet and sleep.

Speaking of which (and at risk of destroying the above analogy), I did spend a fair amount of time talking to my patients about what they ate, how much they exercised, and how much they slept, because taking care of your physical health helps improve your mental health.[3] In a study published in *The Lancet Psychiatry*, frequently ranked as one of the top three journals in mental health, a survey of 1.2 million adults in the United States found that people who exercised regularly experienced 43 percent *fewer* poor mental health days.[4] The researchers conducted additional analyses to find the sweet spot for mental health benefit: thirty to sixty minutes of exercise, three to five times per week. Even just getting out for a morning walk in the sunshine has tremendous benefits. What a life hack!

In addition to ensuring my clients engaged in regular eating, sleeping, and exercising, I also paid close attention to their ability to be present and mindful, helping them learn to pay attention in the moment in a nonjudgmental way.[5] Beginning in 1998, I had become attracted to mindfulness research, and for years I attended every workshop taught by Jon Kabat-Zinn. I'm glad I focused on this domain because today we know scientifically how important mindfulness and meditation can be for our emotional health. A review and analysis of 142 randomized control trials (i.e., experiments that randomly assigned patients to receive either a mindfulness-based intervention or another treatment) found that mindfulness-based interventions were just as effective as other evidence-based mental health treatments.[6] These results may be unsurprising to anyone who has attempted to multitask. When our attention is split between two activities, we might think we are getting more done, but in reality, our performance quality decreases.[7] The place we've been seeing this more and more is in the classroom. Students who text, browse the web, or check social media during class have lower test performance and GPAs.[8]

So while I supported my clients by helping them *Shift* their thinking, *Approach* instead of avoid, practice healthy habits, and observe the present moment, I knew that something was missing. It was after making this realization that I decided to dive more deeply into acceptance and commitment therapy (ACT).[9] (As a reminder, ACT is an evidence-based treatment[10] that focuses on pursuing a meaningful life while accepting the pain and discomfort that inevitably goes with it.) Specifically, I was really interested in this idea of how values might complement the work I had been doing with clients.

And what I found is that when I incorporated values in my work with clients, they started to end therapy sooner. Success! After all, I've always viewed my primary job to be working myself out of a job again and again. Not only were my clients' symptoms improving, but with a values-driven plan they were better equipped to navigate future challenges. And that is my wish for you, too, after reading this chapter.

If our values serve as our internal compass, then the goal is to live a life where values and actions are aligned as often as possible. Not only will this decrease the stress we feel, but it will also increase the meaning in our lives. When I teach the steps to *Align* to my clients, I find it useful to borrow lightly from tennis. Instead of "Game, Set, Match," we call it "*Name, Set, Match.*" In the game of life, you are going to start by *Naming* your values, because you can't move forward without a clear compass. Then, you will *Set* a bold vision for your inner compass. This provides inspiration, allows your brain to get out of its rut, and provides a vision for where you want to go based on your values. Finally, you are going to *Match* your values with clear daily actions.

That Mass of Muscle Between Your Ears Needs a Workout Too

Naming, *Setting*, and *Matching* all require effort and practice. If we were actually playing tennis (instead of learning skills for emotional health), you might already know where to start. We have learned a million ways to exercise our bodies and have endless guidelines instructing what type of exercise to do, how much of it to do, and how often to do it. (Along with this, plenty of good information intersects with awful information.) The world teaches us that to get stronger, stay fitter, and prevent frailty, we must move our bodies and move them with intention. Yet, our modern culture has divorced physical and emotional health from each other.

Somehow, our culture has ignored that *the brain is just another organ*. And that, as such, it also needs "exercising." Sure, you can't do push-ups with your brain, but by working on the skills in this book, you are building *cognitive flexibility*. But just because we're talking about the realm of ideas and concepts, that doesn't mean you will just "get" this overnight. You must consider this in the same context that you would consider any other skill, whether it's building up a powerful back squat or learning a language. But I get it: waiting sucks. And I, like perhaps some of you, have tried skipping the line.

In 2000 when I got to graduate school, my great friend Berglind talked to me about yoga and how it was helpful to her. She encouraged me to join her for a beginners' yoga class. I loved it; it was (and is, after twenty-two years) very grounding for me. But at the end of that first class, I went up to the teacher and said, "What do I have to do to get to the next level? Can I do it by the end of the semester?" In other words: *"I want enlightenment, an iron core, and a gymnast's mobility NOW!"*

The kind and gentle teacher looked at me and said, "This is a journey, not a destination." I hated hearing this kind of trite mantra, as I still thought of life as goals to be mercilessly achieved. To hell with this journey nonsense! But I kept going to yoga and chipping away at it, and I am glad I did, because it was the only way I got through graduate school. And by the end of the semester, although I had not learned the secret to levitating, I had definitely made real progress, to the point where I actually felt comfortable trying things like handstands (something that terrified me at first).

I share this with you to encourage you to embrace values work not only through the course of this book, but also as you travel through the journey of your life. I hope this can become something you return to anytime you reach a major crossroads or transition in your life. It may be trite nonsense best uttered in a yoga studio, but the journey really is the thing. Or, if you prefer, choose progress over outcomes. So, let's progress—it's game time.

Name Your Values

Naming your values is the first step in living a life where values are aligned with your daily actions. Although a simple list is an easy way to identify your values, there is an even more powerful and scientifically valid way: *writing about what matters the most to you*.[11] The two value identification exercises that follow are the most typical exercises used in ACT.[12] They're often referred to as "the sweet and sour" exercises, and I have adapted them based on my clinical expertise to ensure you are able to work through them in this chapter.[13] One is designed to help you identify your core values through an exercise that allows you to examine a moment of joy (i.e., the *sweet* exercise), while the other is designed to look behind a painful moment (i.e., the *sour* exercise) to identify why that hurt occurred. They both help us get to the values that we care most deeply about. Because these exercises are two sides of the same coin, you don't necessarily need to do both to figure out your core values. To decide which one you want to work on, just see if one seems to call your attention more. If in doubt, start with the sweet moment first and see where that leaves you.

How Sweet It Is to Live by Your Values

Because the delicious moments of life often have our values hidden within them, let's start by focusing on a specific situation that has been going well for you in the past two months (see reflection on the following page). If life has been particularly challenging and nothing comes to mind, skip to the next reflection, which focuses on identifying values in the pain points of life.

REFLECTION

Experiencing Sweetness

Think about one specific moment where you felt sweetness within the past two months. It might have been fleeting, or it might have lasted an entire day. It doesn't matter. Visualize this moment as if this is a movie playing out in front of you, and try to capture its essence. Don't censor your brain or try to interpret this moment with needless concepts. Just try to throw yourself back to that moment as much as possible, using all of your senses to land there. Once that movie is created in your mind, I want you to take a piece of paper and write about that moment for ten minutes. To make sure you keep yourself accountable, set a timer. Just free-form journaling here, nothing fancy. Write whatever comes to mind about this awesome time in your life. If you find yourself stuck, here are some questions to help you write about this moment:

What were you doing?

Who were you with?

What were you feeling?

How did it feel afterward?

How would you describe that moment to friends?

I encourage you to really spend time writing out this narrative as we will use it to help you identify some of your core values in the next exercise.

Ricardo's Sweet Moment

Let's go back to Ricardo to see how he identified his values through this exercise. Despite the pain of Ricardo's pending divorce, this exercise really resonated with him, and he worked on it to better understand his values. Ricardo focused on his family and described a vacation moment when he recalled feeling alive and present with his children, Gabriel and Julia, and his wife, Maria. Here is an excerpt from his many pages:

> I am holding Gabriel and Julia's hands as we walk down the beach in Miami. It is a hot day, sunny, and the beach is crowded. I look over to Maria and she has a broad smile. I feel complete, as if were life to end here, I had achieved most of what I wanted. As the sun hits my face, I have a sense of being alive, like nothing else mattered in the world than this moment. As my feet touch the sand, I felt as if the world was moving slowly. . . . As I hear Gabriel's laughter at a half-joke I crack, I am reminded of how precious these moments are and how I love being with them.

Ricardo went on to describe in more detail a conversation he'd had with Maria that day, how much she valued their vacation time, and how he'd been able to focus on his family that morning and be the father and husband he wanted to be, without being distracted by work.

After Ricardo read it aloud to me, we worked on a few reflective questions to really identify what values were important for him in this domain.

Here are some of the questions we examined:

What do I care about in this domain?

What does this moment suggest about the life I want to live?

What qualities does this moment bring out that illustrate the life I want to live?

Ricardo really cared about *belonging* with his family and feeling *connected* with them. This moment showed Ricardo what life could be like if he were able to be fully *present* with his family all the time, and allowed him to feel that he was being the best father and husband he could be in that moment. Ricardo mentioned that he had left his work phone in the hotel that morning, which was one thing that perhaps had made that moment so special for him. This was something he didn't do often (I doubt he's alone there), so usually when he was with his family, his attention was split between family and his incessantly chirping, ever-present phone.

Ricardo really struggled to focus on one thing at a time in his life, often telling me (or perhaps himself) in our sessions that, to be successful, he needed to multitask as much as possible. Yet this vacation memory was in sharp contrast to those learned beliefs. In reflecting further, Ricardo realized that by *being present* that day, he was happier and less anxious, which surprised him. When we further examined the values that really allowed Ricardo to experience sweetness in that moment, he identified *connection* as a core value. Through this exploration, Ricardo realized that for him to live a life with less stress and more meaning, he needed to have real and sustained connection with his family. But in particular, this value needed to be applied when it came to his children. Although Ricardo chose to look at his values through a sweet moment, it was not without sadness, as he had not been living his life in line with his core values. Ricardo realized that one of the reasons his marriage was failing might be his lack of connection with his wife and children. Yes, he deeply valued connection but often ignored this key value when his emotions were high (which was often), and as such he spent most of his waking life living a painfully emotion-driven life instead of one driven by values.

Now it is your turn. Turn to your "Experiencing Sweetness" writing exercise, and contemplate it using the next reflection. The goal here is to get you to use your sweetness reflection to identify the values you care about the most.

From "La Bamba" to Values

For a few weeks, I just could not find time to write this chapter. Specifically, I could not "walk the talk." To be honest with you, I got stuck while trying to write my own sweetness exercise around health. Although I have been struggling with getting my health back on track, I was inspired by Ricardo and wanted to see if I could dig up anything that was sweet related to my health, but I was hitting nothing! (Somehow, "sweating through my clothes in public" didn't really inspire much in the way of joy.)

Eventually, I realized that I was avoiding! Once I was able to identify this, I asked myself, *What is the roadblock here?* That is when I noticed a little voice in my head that was complaining: *But I'm so out of shape! The road back is going to be long and arduous! How can I possibly have anything that is joyful in this domain?* So I asked myself, *What would my best friend say in this case?* (*Shifting*

REFLECTION

Identifying Values: How Sweet It Is

Anchoring on your reflection about a sweet moment, try to identify specific values by asking yourself:

What does this moment suggest about the life I want to live?

____

____

____

What qualities in me does this moment bring out that illustrate the life I want to live?

____

____

____

What matters most to me in this moment?

____

____

____

After reflecting on these questions, try to identify a few values that are important to you. At times, *Naming* values is hard, so if you need help identifying yours, please look back at the list of common values on page 191.

in practice!), and arrived at: "Just because you are out of shape *now*, it doesn't mean that you have never, ever experienced joy when you focused on your health." Saying that to myself eased my discomfort and allowed me to finally complete this exercise. Here is an excerpt:

> It is an early morning in April, Diego rushes into my bedroom after waking up, demanding that we go do the Peloton (not to worry: he doesn't have a Peloton—he has a little stationary bike next to mine). I look at him puzzled. Exercise at 7 a.m., just like that? But he tells me that he and David had been exercising daily while I was in Los Angeles for a business trip, and he wanted me to exercise too. "But wait, I want coffee," I protest, but it is clear that I am losing this battle. So Peloton it is! We walk to the basement where the Peloton is, and he is elated. He goes on to lift weights (he has some toy weights we had given him for Christmas). Looking in the mirror, Diego smiles at himself, saying how he was going to get stronger. His smile brings me joy, I feel alive, like I could just hug him forever in that moment. But he quickly persists, demanding that I exercise with him. So I slowly jump on the Peloton (at first dreading it), but Diego's genuine love for exercise in that moment carries me forward. I put on my favorite Latin ride, the music is loud and alive, and the ride quickly gets to "La Bamba" . . . Diego is now dancing, I am smiling and riding, but actually focused on how the music and my son make me feel . . . alive, present, connected. Diego loves the music, and the songs in this ride

often make him dance. Twenty minutes go by, almost in a blink of an eye. I am sweaty, happy, and feeling amazing.

As I reflected about health, and that morning in particular, I realized that what I really care about in the domain of health is connection with myself and my family, a sense of well-being, and also responsibility as a parent. I realized that by exercising often and demonstrating care for my health, I am also modeling a healthy life for Diego, about whom I obviously care a great deal. It cemented in me that I want to have a life where health is a priority. A life where I give my body the space it needs to ensure I stay strong and remain so for as long as possible. It's one thing to hoard health for its own sake, but quite another to create and maintain health to give more to those around you.

When you're a parent, your life is not your own. You live for the well-being of your children. And I know that I need to be strong to give the most of myself to Diego to keep him safe, make him feel loved, and give him the best chance at thriving in this life. Pausing on that morning also allowed me to realize that perhaps I don't *have to choose* health versus family in the mornings. Perhaps there is a way to integrate them. But most importantly, it brought me back to what it had felt like when *well-being* had been my top priority. And so, if I had to anchor all of this on one value, it would be well-being. By infusing this value with a deeper *why*, it was almost as though I was placing a value within a value. Yes: I want to be healthy, but my well-being isn't just about me. It's about being the *most* me so that I can give more to my family, the same way some people want to earn greater wealth so they can give more of it away to charity.

Using Pain to Light the Way

As human beings, we are wired to minimize pain and do whatever we can to not feel discomfort, which is why avoidance is so prevalent and often wins out when we are trying to change our behaviors. Despite its negative side, pain is also an important indicator in life, both physically and emotionally. Think about it this way: What would happen if you couldn't feel pain? (Actually, there is a woman named Jo Cameron in the UK, whose story is essentially the real-life version of my little *what if*... her story is quite interesting and worth a bit of Googling.) Imagine that you are a chef and you have lost your pain receptors in your hands: What would happen if you grabbed the handle on a scalding-hot cast-iron skillet? Nothing! Well, sorta. While you might not feel anything, you would still be susceptible to terrible burns. So, feeling pain, no matter how unpleasant, actually would play a significant role in such a scenario: the pain exists to protect us.

Emotional pain can have a similar utility (I know, hard to believe when you're lying in bed sobbing over a breakup). Emotional pain signals to us potential danger or hurt, and although we often want to run away from emotional pain, it can be an opportunity to better understand our values. Through the lenses of ACT, there is a question that clinicians often ask their clients to help them identify the value behind the pain: "What would you have to not care about in this situation for you not to feel pain?" Often when we are feeling some degree of emotional pain, one of the reasons might be that something we really care about—one of our values—is being compromised, and as a result we are hurting.

REFLECTION

Sour Patches: From Pain To Values

I want you to focus on a situation that brought you immense pain in the past two months. It could be a moment when you felt pain, sadness, discomfort, or any other unpleasant emotion. Visualize that moment as a movie playing out in front of you, and try to capture its essence. Don't censor your brain or try to interpret this moment with needless concepts. Just try to throw yourself back to that moment as much as possible, using all of your senses to land there.

Once that movie is created in your mind, I want you to take a piece of paper and write about that moment for ten minutes. To make sure you keep yourself accountable, set a timer. Just free-form journaling here, nothing fancy. Write whatever comes to mind about this difficult time in your life. We will use your narrative to help you identify some of your core values in the next exercise. Below are some questions that you can use to create this narrative if you find yourself stuck.

Where are you feeling it in your body?

What does it feel like to allow this pain to come in?

What are you saying to yourself in that moment?

What memories might come up when you allow that pain to surface?

For example, when I asked Ricardo this question, he immediately burst into tears and told me, "For me to not feel pain about the divorce, I would have to not care about my wife and children, which is impossible. I love them and that is why this all hurts too much." Similarly, when I asked myself this question, I would have to *not care at all about my well-being* in order to not feel anything when I fail to act in line with that value. When I allow myself to really look at this question, I immediately get tears in my eyes because I know that if I don't invest today in my physical health, I might be robbing myself of precious time I could have later with Diego.

So the idea of finding the value through pain is based on this notion that we only feel emotional pain when it is related to something we really care about.[14] As such, this reflection will help you get in touch with your pain by taking a look behind its curtain to see what you really care about. Once we have this knowledge, we can then create a plan that realigns your life.

Identifying Compromised Values Through Pain: Stephanie's Values

Stephanie did this exercise focused on the latest fight with her family. To be fully in touch with her own pain, she requested to do it in Mandarin, which was an excellent suggestion given that research suggests that using a less proficient language can actually create emotional distance from the topic.[15] If you doubt this, try to write about a serious or emotional time in your life in a language you barely know! My guess is the results won't be terribly gripping to you or the reader. Stephanie wrote about her latest explosive and damaging conflict regarding her American versus Chinese identities. There was always so much wrapped up in these fights with her family, with both sides feeling they weren't being heard or respected. The clash between generations and cultures was something that was causing Stephanie a lot of pain, and that is why she chose to write about it.

I wish I could share more of her writing with you, but as I've established, translating Mandarin isn't in my professional tool kit. But here is what Stephanie and I uncovered through her reflections: Stephanie realized that every time her parents suggested she needed to conform to Chinese culture, she would get angry, upset, and frustrated and often didn't want to engage with them. But why were those emotions there? What was behind her pain? She shared with me her realization that if she didn't care about her parents and love them so much, their opinions would not matter to her, which means she would just disregard their wishes and move on with her life. In other words, when they were fighting, her love for them was compromised, thus causing her pain. It is important to highlight that Stephanie and I had to do a lot of work in therapy before we got to this exercise. When it comes to acculturation, there are pressures both internal and external, and we had to address those before we could get her to look at the family tension through the lens of values. That being said, by looking at her pain and arriving at *love* as a core value, Stephanie was able to start feeling better and less angry and to begin the work of finding a way to integrate the different parts of her identity while negotiating with her parents.

Now it is your turn. Once you've spent time writing about your sour moment in the previous reflection, ask yourself the following question: *What value of mine would I have to not care about for this pain not to exist?* By pondering this question, you will be able to identify what value of yours is likely being violated in this painful scenario. This is an indication that that value matters a lot to you. Summarize your thoughts using the reflection below.

REFLECTION

Uncovering Values in Sour Patches

Anchoring on your narrative about this painful moment, ask yourself:

What value of mine would I have to not care about for this pain to not exist?

____

____

____

What is it that matters to me that is being compromised?

____

____

____

After reflecting on these questions, try to identify a few values that are important to you. At times, *Naming* values is hard, so if you need help identifying yours, please look back at the list of common values on page 191.

The Pain of Reflecting on Pain

If you are struggling to slow down and quiet your brain to engage in this reflection, you are not alone. I have personally found that looking at pain to identify values is very helpful, yet I often avoid it myself because just like Miriam, a patient of mine, said the other day: "It feels like there is a huge fire in my life right now, and instead of putting it out, you want me to let it burn to see what's behind the pain." I had to agree with her: it is counterintuitive to contemplate pain, both from a cultural and biological standpoint, yet every time a client of mine has allowed themselves to go there, the outcome has been absolute clarity in terms of values.

Before we get to *Set* as the next step to align values with goals, I want to share with you my own painful moment, which in many ways led to this book. In fact, if I hadn't allowed myself to experience that pain, I bet I would still be pursuing goals, lying to myself that it was driven by ambition, but knowing all the while that something was off. As I wrote about earlier in this part of the book, there came a time when I knew that things were not working for me in terms of my career, yet I had refused to really address this until I hit a huge pain point. It came in the form of a clash of values between myself and those who lead the institution where I work. The reality is, there were many moments that could have illustrated why I no longer fit, but I will share one here that I think will illustrate the pattern and how pain can reveal our compromised values.

During my career I had a difficult boss—I'll call him Robert. Robert was a physician and senior leader at the hospital where I work. Basically, he's a big deal in our world, and I had looked up to him for more than a decade. A few years ago, he offered me a challenging but fantastic position to work directly with him, and because I idolized him, I jumped at the opportunity. As time went on, however, I noticed I would feel a pang whenever Robert would make one of his little comments to me. There wasn't any single thing he said that killed my spirit, but it was just a pattern of paper cuts that eventually bled me dry. They were the kinds of statements that people of a certain age make without noticing, full of gender stereotypes and microaggressions—like the time he told me I needed to be "a little softer, more like a woman and less like a man." It was just one after the other, and eventually I had had enough.

This scenario and experience is not unique to me. Many women and men, many of us diverse, have gone through experiences of discrimination, microaggressions, and prejudice in life. For those not engaged in conversations around such cultural flash points, microaggressions are brief verbal, behavioral, or environmental insults and invalidations toward people of marginalized identities.[16] These experiences are painful, real, and can negatively impact the recipient's emotional health.[17] For me, the ongoing remarks from Robert and lack of support led me to eventually quit that job—though, shamefully, I did so without addressing the why. I had decided that I simply needed to cut all ties. I told Robert what I believed he wanted to hear: "You're right, this is too much now that I have a son." I'm embarrassed to share this with you, as the sentiment was the furthest thing from the truth at that time.

I had imagined that quitting this way would be easier and less painful, but before I took the job, I had been warned by a senior psychologist in our department: "Whatever you do, don't make Robert angry." I didn't know what this meant or how I would even make him angry, but it turns out, I did just that.

Quitting was upsetting to him, and the weeks that followed were my own personal hell. The conflict arose around financial matters; specifically, Robert believed that, somehow, I had been paid from the wrong fund and because of this I had drained his bank account. This might be confusing to understand if you're not in academia, but our salaries come from a variety of sources: say, 50 percent from Grant X, 25 percent from Grant Y, and so forth. This system is challenging to manage, and mistakes are often made. Without going into needlessly boring details, the long and short of it was that I had negotiated with Robert that he would pay my full salary from one account—his—while I worked for him.

A few days after I quit, I got an email from Robert suggesting that there was some kind of mistake and that I needed to give a large percentage of the money back—namely, an amount of money that would have been equal to an entire year of my salary! This whole thing spiraled into the predictable quagmire of emails and phone calls and arguments and conflict and became the single worst episode from my long career. The kind of situation that keeps you awake at night, anxious all day, and mentally and emotionally exhausted for weeks on end. A really fun time!

Here is a glimpse of the situation from inside my brain:

It's early January, I wake up at 4 a.m., I cannot sleep—my brain is racing with a million thoughts:

Why is he doing this?

What did I do wrong?

I know I negotiated for my full salary.

This is unfair.

I have worked hard for so long, trusted him for so long: Why would he think I stole from him?

Doesn't he trust me?

What am I going to do if I really end up being asked to pay this back?

I don't have this money!

What does this look like for my family and our finances?

Maybe I will take on more clients in the evenings—but I am so tired, I can't possibly do more.

As I write this and let the pain come in again, tears flow from my eyes. This happened nearly two years ago, and still tears are there. My heart shrinks, my breaths are shallow, and I feel like running away from this memory. . . . But as I stay with this pain, many other memories come up: memories of moments when I felt oppressed, when I was told to defer to the majority, either explicitly or implicitly. The faces of the people involved flash in my mind, and more tears come. In the end, I have a knot in my throat, as if I can't speak.

This experience was really painful for me, and it took me months to be able to sit early in the mornings and work through this reflection and feel the pain. At first it was just raw pain and tears, like the fire that my patient Miriam referenced. Some mornings I would allow myself to cry, and some mornings I would just be angry. But slowly the intensity came down and I could really start to look behind that pain and ask myself: *What value of mine would I have to not care about for this pain not to exist?*

I kept asking myself, *Why is this still hurting so much?* And I finally arrived at my answer: *trust*. Trust is one of my core values, and one that is really challenging for me. As an adult I understand that I was never able to trust my father. He was simply too unreliable. Of course, my wonderful mom was always there, so that has long been my model for trust. But I had also seen early in life how she couldn't trust my father either, so trust has always felt like a precious stone that I only share with those who are closest to me. This is not uncommon for individuals who have had traumatic experiences, especially early on in life.[18] So the experience with Robert hurt so much because I felt I could no longer trust him, and all the memories that are associated with this time in my life are related to a violation of trust in some form or another.

So for me to have been able to say, "To hell with Robert; he's out of line!" without any pain, I would have needed to not care about trust, and that just isn't me. I need to trust those around me to feel safe in the world so I can function, and that is why this experience hurt so much. After identifying the value behind my pain, I was able to start healing and find a way to really consider what I would do today if I hit a similar crossroad.

For some of you reading, if you were to be in my situation with Robert, trust might not have been what impacted you the most. It could have been another value, like integrity, truth, or fairness. The value that was compromised is unique to me and my views of the world, but the underlying principle is universal to all of us. For example, if you really care about growth but find yourself in a job where you are constantly underperforming or being asked to do things that you feel underutilize or stymy you, you will likely feel stress in your work life. Similarly, if you care about justice but find yourself in situations where there is constant injustice, you can expect to feel strong emotions. The emotions here are not the problem, as they are indicating to us that something is not working—in this case, that your value is being compromised. But if you can start to take this pain as a point of reflection, you will see that emotions will tend to come down a bit and you will be able to identify the value behind the painful feelings, just like I did.

But I won't lie to you: probing painful moments can hurt. In a strange way, I think of this as emotional surgery. Yes, we could keep taking a painkiller to make the hurt go away, but is that really addressing the root cause, or just lessening a symptom? Also worth noting is that while these feelings and memories may bring up unpleasant emotions, my clinical training has taught me that, if nothing else, emotions can be viewed with detachment the same way we train ourselves to view thoughts as just passing through. If you can notice it, you can learn to observe it objectively without being hooked by it. I don't say this to minimize what you may feel, only to give you the courage to feel your emotions without hesitation—and by doing so, uncover what matters most to you.

Set a Bold Vision

Now that you have identified your values, the next step is to embrace being guided by them. Being guided by our values is one of the keys to cognitive flexibility.[19] Cognitive flexibility is key to pursuing goals even when challenges arise.[20] In other words, values allow us to keep moving forward toward our goals even when we face obstacles.

Many of my clients look at me skeptically when we discuss setting up these values-driven visions, as though it's all well and good to do this as an academic exercise, but quite another thing to apply this to the real world, where chaos reigns. So, how do you do this in an actionable way outside of these pages? Look at it this way: if values are the compass, then we need a general direction (if not a specific destination) that helps us live a more meaningful life. Central to this is having a *bold vision* that is—and this is the important part—*anchored on a value that is intrinsically motivating.* By "bold visions," I don't mean frivolous achievements that are there to be marked off, noted on social media, and forgotten about. I'm talking about important milestones that are central to who you are, the things that are deeply attached to your values and, when experienced, give you a feeling that, yes, this is what I am on this earth to do. It need not be flashy or impressive to others. It only needs to be meaningful to you.

Is your heart pounding as I ask you this question? Because mine certainly is when I consider this in my own life.

I am often intimidated by these kinds of audacious visions. They scare me! The pain, the process, the likelihood of failing . . . all those fears that I am not being enough. But you are not reading a book on how to avoid: you are here to become bold, which is not painless.

My brain won't go there; it is just too scary. One note of caution before we start: the judgment brain is likely to intervene immediately and to try to put a big ROAD CLOSED sign up to warn us not to dream so big. My brain often has "helpful" things to say about my bold visions when I try to engage with them:

You can't possibly do this.

You've attempted bold visions before, and you never achieve them!

Who are you to dream bigger?

Who are you to think that people will care about what you have to say? (A familiar companion voice as I write this book.)

If your brain starts to spin like mine did, I suggest you pull out your TEB cycle reflection from chapter 2 and write out what is happening in your mind. This way you can create a pause and activate your thinking brain before proceeding.

To *Set* your bold vision, I want you to engage in an exercise that I often use with my clients when I first start to work with them. In our first few meetings, I ask them what success would look like in the context of our work together. Usually, I get answers related to their fever: *less* anxiety, *less* sadness, *less* worry. These outcomes are important indicators that our work is progressing, but what I am really asking is, if we are successful, what does your "new" life really look like? And while "less" suffering is indeed a good goal, framing every answer with "less" isn't quite as useful as picturing a life with "more." More connection? More openness? More . . . ?

And for this reflection, I want to push you even further to consider not just *more* but *most*: *What would your life look like if you did what mattered most to you?* In other words, what would it look like to live out your value fully? To be adventurous or humble? To feel a sense of trust or transparency from everyone around you? What would it look like to live every day prioritizing your core value? I have a hint for you: it might look very similar to your sweetness moment (and very unlike your sour moment). Take a moment to consider these question in your magic wand reflection on the following page.

Ricardo's and Stephanie's and My Bold Visions

Stephanie's bold vision had less to do with love in the relationship with her parents and more to do with her own acculturation process. Stephanie wanted to be able to integrate the different parts of her culture within herself in such a way that she would be able to bring her whole self to the table. When we explored this further, Stephanie's bold vision was related to *authenticity*. When I asked her what it meant to be authentic, Stephanie told me that she would like

REFLECTION

The Magic Wand

Anchor this reflection on the value that you identified in your sour moment reflection. Take a moment to imagine having a magic wand that could remove all the pain related to this value, and consider what it would take to *Align* your life to this value that is so important to you by answering the following questions:

Where would you end up?

What is this life like?

What are you doing?

Who are you with?

What are the key values driving this bold life?

Please don't censor yourself. I am not asking for a practical plan here (we have the next step to do that). I want to urge you to really see yourself accomplishing this bold vision. Again, I don't care about the *how* yet, only the *what*. What does your bold vision look like?

to embrace the East and West within her cultural identity and to not be compromised by the externalities of life. So, if she wanted to watch TV in Mandarin, she would do so—not because her parents would approve, but because she liked it. Alternatively, if she decided to dress more "American," she would. She would have sets of friends that embraced both of her cultures and would mostly get to live according to her own internal compass instead of letting cultural norms tell her what was acceptable.

Acculturation is challenging, but having gone through it myself, I could relate to Stephanie's desire to always show up authentically, without feeling the need to apologize for the different, seemingly contradictory, parts of herself. A little secret: I still wear the corporate gray uniform, but not because I want to fit in. Nowadays, when I wear it, I do so because I feel more like my academic, studious self. Though of course, with the Latin touch of a red scarf!

If I were to wave the magic wand for myself with a focus on well-being, my life would look very different. I would live a more balanced life, with less chaos and more time to actually create the well-being I so desire. I would engage in more physical activities, with and without my family, but I would also add joy to this by incorporating hikes, longer walks, and a deeper connection with nature. Courage would also be a value I would align myself with in this magical life. Courage to help me continue to move toward health, especially in moments of avoidance. With one more wave of my magic wand, there would be another value to guide me professionally: impact. Specifically, impacting individuals in the world by teaching them the techniques in *Bold Move* as a way to do my part in addressing the worldwide mental health crisis.

Match: Transforming Bold Visions into Bold Plans

Identifying a value and envisioning a new reality where that value is fully embraced are the first steps to *Align*, but they do not in and of themselves change the game. To do that, we need to translate values into actions! You might be thinking to yourself, *Okay, I can see this bold vision, but I have no clue how to start moving toward it . . . so why even bother? What are the odds this will work?* Welcome to the dissonance party! As we've established, the brain does not like it when two things don't add up (in this case, our vision and our reality). This happens to all of us, especially when we decide to live a life in which we are pushing back against fear and self-doubt. Because after all, to live a values-driven life, you must get used to being "comfortably uncomfortable." When we feel discomfort, our brains can start to panic and try to steer us into avoidance. But have no fear: we're going to use behavioral science to help us create a clear and actionable plan. By doing so, we will take your inner landscape and make it external.

First, we need to break down your bold vision into small steps. Why? Because if we try to do it all at once, we are more likely to fail. If you'll pardon the cliché, Rome wasn't built in a day, and the same applies to your best life. Let me put it another way: Imagine you're visiting a new town and you get a little lost. You ask someone for directions and they blurt out in an unintelligible, hushed, rapid-fire mumble:

TakethesecondrightonSunsetBoulevardDriveuntilyouseeBob's PizzaandtakealeftwhenyoureachSuzie'shousetakealeftthendrive afewmoreblocksandwhenyouseethe"roadclosed"signdisregarditand takearightandit'llbethefirsthouseontheleft.

Whoa! What the hell was that? Chances are, if you were relying on these instructions, you'd never reach your destination. Now imagine this insurmountably incoherent paragraph was the set of directions to your bold vision: Would you ever get there? Your brain would be asking, *Who is Suzie? How many blocks? What if the road really is closed?* And all of these very reasonable questions might either stop you from going on the journey to begin with or lead you down a path that is completely opposite to your values—and that is not what we want! We want to develop a clear plan that describes *when, where, and how* we will get to the place that matters most to us.

Turning Values into Action

To transform your bold vision into a clear plan, we will rely on one of the most revolutionary frameworks I have seen in recent years: Simon Sinek's Golden Circle. Simon is a world-renowned public speaker, author, and unshakable optimist.[21] In his book, *Start with Why*: *How Great Leaders Inspire Everyone to Take Action*,[22] he describes the utility behind the *why, how, and what* that fuel actions using an image of concentric circles.

Although the book focuses heavily on examples from the business world, he has written extensively about the application of the Golden Circle to many diverse domains in life. I use it to structure a lot of my work, life, and ambitions. In fact: I actually used it to structure this book! I start with the *why* for the entire book (because avoidance sucks!), then each part (e.g., *Shift*, *Approach*, *Align*) dives down into *how* we avoid in that domain (3 Rs of avoidance: react, retreat, remain) and then *what* to do about it (boom: science!).

So it might not surprise you that I use the same framework to help my clients create a plan to achieve their bold vision. I've found that it's most helpful to consider four things when creating the steps of a bold plan: 1) Is it *aligned* (the why)? 2) Is it *specific* (the what)? 3) Is it *doable* (the how)? and 4) Is it *scheduled* (the when)? Asking these questions will help you arrive at a workable step. Workable steps will help you navigate life with a plan that is aligned with your values so you don't stray (like I did) by focusing only on the outcome (goals) and not on why you are doing this in the first place (value).

Ricardo's and Stephanie's Values in Action

Let's revisit the stories of Ricardo and Stephanie to get a feel for what bold plans look like. Ricardo's plans were challenging to work on because they involved his children, which meant that, whatever step he outlined he would need to clear with his wife in the midst of an uncomfortable divorce process. Ricardo explained to me that he felt this would be impossible given how challenging their relationship had been. The reality is, Ricardo was actually avoiding a bit here: as we discussed things further, it became clear that there were in fact times when he was with his children and could focus on his connection (*aligned*). While arranging for these moments might be challenging, it was not some insurmountable impossibility. To achieve this, we worked on exactly what he could do within the context of what he could control (*doable*), and he found a great solution.

He decided that he would spend forty-five minutes without his work cell phone when he was with his children (*specific*) twice a week at dinner time (*scheduled*). Specifically, Tuesdays and Thursdays: this was literally in his calendar (*laser alignment*). To make this doable without adding to his stress, he would put an "out of office" alert on his email for that timeframe so he could curb his desire to check the phone. This is important, because you want to ensure that your workable goal does not add additional stress.

For Stephanie, we struggled to identify workable steps that would *Align* with living an authentic life. Stephanie was stuck on how to come up with a *specific* action when it comes to a broad construct such as authenticity. So I asked her to try to define behaviorally for me what this looked like for her. She said she felt that if she were being authentic, she would not have to *try* to fit in in either the Chinese or American cultures that encircled her life. If she was just being authentic, she could show up and express her opinions as . . . herself. Not her Chinese self or American self. Just Stephanie.

So I pressed further, and she felt that the way she dressed would be one way of manifesting this value. Specifically, she would only wear one piece of clothing (*specific*) that she felt represented her cultural identity (*aligned*) each day of the week (*scheduled*), regardless of where she was going. Stephanie was able to get to a bold plan because she took the time to visualize what being authentic looked like for her. This is a trick I use a lot with people, and one you can use too. When you choose an action, ask yourself, *Is it something I can vividly see in my mind's eye?*

Both Ricardo and Stephanie were able to get to workable steps—though not without some challenges, which is to be expected. The

REFLECTION

Creating a Bold Plan to Realize Your Bold Vision

It's your turn to transform your values into actions by creating workable steps. Use the following questions as a guide:

1. **Why: Is it aligned?**

   What matters most to you in your bold vision?

   ____

   ____

   - Identify the value that matters most to you in your bold vision and design the plan based on this value.

2. **What: Is it specific?**

   What action can you take to reach your bold vision? Include enough specificity that you can actually visualize it happening and know the exact moment when it's been achieved.

   - Action: ______________________________
   - Action: ______________________________
   - Action: ______________________________

3. **How: Is it doable?**

   It's time to create an action plan. What do you need to carry out each of these actions?

   - Action:

     ____

     ____

- Action:

____

____

- Action:

____

____

4. **When: Is it scheduled?**

   Break out your calendar. When will you complete the steps you outlined above?

   ____

   ____

point I want to stress is that even if you don't succeed at first, keep trying. I know I usually have to go back to the drawing board more than once to make sure I've set clear enough steps for myself. But as an architect for a life that you actually want to live, you'll have to get used to revising your blueprints from time to time.

Working and Reworking My Bold Plan

I created two bold plans for myself: one related to well-being and one related to impact. For well-being, I set the goal of exercising twenty minutes a day, five days a week, in the morning before Diego woke up, for one month.

Is this a workable step? Is it aligned with my value of well-being? I thought so, but I failed miserably in the first week, even though I really tried. I hadn't exercised for two years and was carrying forty pounds more than my pre-COVID self, so it turned out not to be achievable. But failure is just good data for the next success, and so I didn't get discouraged.

This is something I often see my clients do: create a plan that might have been doable in the past but is perhaps too ambitious given a current reality (e.g., post-COVID Luana creating steps as if she were still pre-COVID Luana). So, if this is your first attempt at creating workable steps, I would suggest you take whatever you created and break it down in half. The point here is to set yourself up for success instead of sabotaging yourself into failure. This is an arbitrary exercise, so you may as well rig it in your favor! For instance, if I were advising someone on writing a book, I might say, "Make your first step one page per day. Literally one page. Take fifteen minutes, or take two hours, but when you hit the end of that page, you stop. Done for the day. *No más.*" This might seem pathetically easy, but it's also wildly sustainable. And this exercise is all about sustainability.

After bombing in my own attempt, I went back to the drawing board and came up with an even more workable step: exercise ten minutes, three times a week, before lunch, for one week. This was definitely better and I was able to stick to it! It did take major work to open up that ten minutes before lunch three times a week, which is an important point: *if your goals don't make it onto your calendars, they will never happen!* The trick here is to really look at your calendar, put your workable step in the place where you think you will be most likely to succeed, and then go for it. This technique really helps ensure that your goal is sufficiently *scheduled*. I know it might seem like overkill, but I promise you, if you don't schedule these things, life *will* get in the way.

Another trick I often use to help myself honor these steps is to imagine them as a doctor's appointment. How many of you would just not show up at all for an important doctor's appointment, especially if it was potentially lifesaving? I bet only a few of us. So, by making an appointment with yourself, you are more likely to keep it. If you find yourself in a pinch, in which you know you are about to miss your appointment, I urge you to do the same thing you would with a doctor: reschedule it! In my well-being plan, I had to exercise at 9 p.m. one night because I just could not get it done during the day. Before lunchtime, I looked at the rest of my day and moved the appointment to the only time that was free: 9 p.m.

Once I realized that ambition no longer guided me at my work, I arrived at *impact* as my professional core value. Specifically, I wanted to find a way to decrease the mental health crisis and as such impact the world in a positive way. For my value of impact, I focused on creating steps related to this book. After all, I am writing *Bold Move* because I believe that the science and experiences in these pages can help make a real impact out there, but writing on a publisher's deadline is challenging. Given that I'm still relatively new to this whole thing, writing is one of these things that ebbs and flows for me. Sometimes my brain gets locked in negative thoughts and stops me from writing. So I realized that the goal could not be about the practicalities of creating the book, per se. I actually didn't set workable steps around the book until I got to chapter 6 and realized that my first draft was horrible, I was frozen in terror, and I needed a kick in the ass to keep this wagon moving toward its deadline.

Here is what I committed to: writing sessions of thirty minutes, three days a week, for three weeks. I often can write for two hours without noticing, so the time commitment and number of days were definitely measured and achievable, but I still ran into a snag. Can you guess what it was? I couldn't picture it! So, I thought some more and came up with a plan I could actually envision.

It turned out that to be successful, I needed to adjust it to: writing at 9 a.m. (when Diego is off to school), Tuesday, Wednesday, and Thursday, for thirty minutes for three weeks. This is the plan that made its way onto my calendar.

But just because I created this plan, it doesn't mean it was easy. Sure, it was easier than no goal at all, but keeping it up for three weeks was tough, and I wish I had made a commitment for fewer weeks. Why? Because I hadn't accounted for a business trip I had to take, which meant I had to really adjust that week.

Stuff Happens, Values Change, Boldness Continues

There are two points about *Aligning* that I want to highlight. First, life happens! All of us will be thrown curveballs, but it is what we do with them that tends to dictate our success. I adjusted that week for my writing plan, waking up earlier while on the trip to write, thus ensuring my commitment. That was challenging and not really "achievable." So if you hit a major bump in the road—a work trip, your kid gets sick, your loved one needs your attention—go back to the drawing board, check in with your values, envision where you want to end up, and revise your plan.

And that is the second point: sometimes we fail our bold plans because external situations force us to shift the value that we are prioritizing (after all, values do clash). In fact, as I was working on this book, there were two weeks where I just threw these steps out the window because my entire family got COVID. I share this with you to ensure you are kind with yourself as you go about setting these plans in place. Yes, you must be disciplined with yourself, but you also must be realistic. Just be real with yourself and err on the side of making this a reality. Nobody is going to force you to live a more meaningful life, so you have to be your own accountability coach here. (Although, if you do have a friend who is going through a similar process, an accountability buddy is a tremendous resource.)

Now, when I compare how I feel on a day when I live in line with my values and get my ass to the gym to a day where I make another excuse to leave my running shoes in the closet, the difference is stark. Put simply: one of those days is awesome; the other one feels crappy. I'm sure you can guess which is which. If you consider a day in which your actions are more in line with your values and contrast *that* with a day where you don't end up doing any of the things that matter most to you, how do you feel? I think you get the idea of why this is an important skill to learn. It's the difference between going to bed fulfilled versus stressing out because each day just bleeds into the next with nothing meaningful to provide the kind of satisfaction and texture that make a life worth living. Of course, I'm not promising you that learning this skill is the key to feeling amazing 100 percent of the time, but what I am promising you is that if you take the time to really *Align* your values and actions, the journey of your life will be far more rewarding than it would be otherwise.

But before we wrap up this chapter, there is an important caveat:

values can change across our lives. In fact, given that life *is* change, you *should expect* your values to shift throughout the days, weeks, months, and years of your life. As we evolve, situations change, and we can decide to prioritize other values. After all, our values are no more static than our lives are, and depending on what is going on at any given moment, we will have to realign what we are doing so that it matches up with our new true north. Think of it like values-driven compass maintenance.

As I learned in my first yoga class back in 2000, everything is a journey, not a destination. With a good compass on hand, you are equipped for the journey. This journey can be rough at times, gorgeous at others, and sometimes just meh. But it is a journey worth traveling because you have a true north pointing you in the direction of fulfillment. And not just the cheap fulfillment from the material world. I'm talking about the satisfaction that accompanies you to bed and makes you excited to see what happens tomorrow. When the downpours of life occur, and you are jolted off course, don't be discouraged: the compass is still there. I have never met someone who always stays dead straight on the course of their true north—that is just humanly impossible.

To move boldly forward is to give yourself time to pause whenever you find yourself in the wilderness. When this occurs, identify your avoidance pattern and match it with a skill that overcomes it (slay that dragon!). If your thinking is what is setting you off course, it will be *Shift* to the rescue. If your reactivity is robbing the best of you, *Approach* through opposite action will recalibrate your journey. And when you're doing what you have always done, following someone else's GPS, it is time to *Align* with your values. As ex-Navy SEAL, author, and speaker Jocko Willink is fond of saying on his podcast: "When you get off the path, it's alright. Just get back on the path."

There is no single solution that will work for everyone forever because these are skills designed to be matched to your current avoidance pattern. With practice, you will be able to catch your avoidance faster, match the solution skill, and act—but that takes practice! There is only one way to fail here, which is to not do anything. When avoidance knocks, answer the door, identify it, but don't follow it. Instead, interrogate it, uncover its plot to derail you, and make a bold move. The stakes for life are high. We are here for such an impossibly brief amount of time, and so I encourage you to utilize these skills as your sword and shield against an enemy (avoidance) that wants to rob your life of meaning. Hyperbolic, maybe, but not by much.

— PART V —

Conclusion

Chapter Twelve

Becoming Bold by Being the Water, Not the Rock

Often at night, when I read to Diego before bedtime, I think about the privilege of having time to read to him. Although some might not think of reading *I am Albert Einstein* by Brad Meltzer for the thousandth time as a privilege, I can assure you that for families with low resources, this luxury of time is very rare. As a kid, I remember my mom working late most nights. When she got home, she would sit with us to watch some TV, but she always had one eye on the screen and one eye on whatever task she needed to do, whether it be mending a piece of clothing or getting our meals ready for the next day. There was always some task that demanded her attention before she had to get up and start the whole cycle again. It wasn't easy keeping food on the table, and part of the difficulty was that there was never enough time. Never enough time to lounge around in the morning, never enough time to just sit and chat, never enough time to appreciate how amazing she was when it came to keeping the house running with so few resources. I imagine that many families around the world are in the same boat, where simply slowing down and spending time reading to their children is just not possible. As a consequence, reading was not something I did much growing up. In fact, when I came to the US and learned that some kids actually read over the summer, I was shocked. It wasn't as though our childhood was a horror show: we played outside, met up with friends, and went swimming, but there were no books in sight, at least not in my family.

But this changed when I moved in with my grandmother in 1995. She had a lot of books in her house, read often, and liked to talk about whatever she was reading. As I reflect on this nearly thirty years later, I feel blessed to have spent time with her as it was a golden opportunity to learn about the world through her books. I vividly remember the first book she had me read: *The Alchemist* by Paulo Coelho. Though *The Alchemist* had become a very popular book all over the world, it especially carried a lot of weight (and still does) within the Brazilian community. She had me read it because I was struggling with the usual career choices—what to do with my life, what I could become—and as I struggled with these questions, I often worried a lot about resources, both current and future. I never saw myself as "resource restricted" per se, but the reality was, I knew we had financial limitations, and it worried me to the point that I could only dream within that narrow lane and never outside of it.

Over coffee one afternoon, my grandmother forcefully insisted that I could become anything that I wanted to be, do whatever I wanted to do, and dream as large as life. The only catch was that if I could dream up something big and bold, it would then be my job to make it happen. This magical reality seemed like nonsense to me. At first, I attributed this "crazy talk" to her strong belief in things like crystals and energy fields. Don't get me wrong: I cherish the crystals that she gifted me throughout the years and I still have them, although the scientist in me is not sure how much power they actually have. Though I must say, the crystals do make me feel powerful because they remind me of her. Anyway, when she painted this rosy Disney picture for me, that I could do anything I could dream of, I was not having it and still remember arguing with her about the limitations that would always shape my life. And now we can bring our focus back to *The Alchemist*. She gave the book to me and said, "Read this, and when you finish it, let me know if you still feel the same way." As I write this chapter, I still have my old Portuguese copy right next to me. If you haven't read the book, it is a wonderful story about pursuing your personal legend in the world by listening to your heart and following your dreams. It sounds cheesy when I just blurt it out like that, but believe me when I say that as a Harvard scientist, I am still puzzled about how this fictional novel came to change my life.

After reading and discussing the book with my grandmother, I experienced the first *Shift* in my life. As you have learned throughout this book, our views of the world are based on our context, our history, and the lessons we have learned in life, and other experiences. And once this perspective is formed, we will do anything possible to maintain it. You may recall how our brains are wired to decrease cognitive dissonance by confirming what we already know (or *think* we know) to be true,[1] so if you grow up being told "the world is hard, we have very little, this is as good as it gets," then that is how you will see the world, and this belief will guide a lot of your actions.

Fortunately for us, science has shown that our brains can change through neuroplasticity.[2] With the right kind of exposure, we can alter the story in our head, and that is precisely what *The Alchemist* did for me. My grandmother didn't know about cognitive behavioral therapy, but her wisdom told her that life could change—and that, for this to happen, a person needed to change what they said to themselves. She used to describe our thoughts as tapes playing in our heads all the time, and if the tape played, "You are not enough," how could you ever think of yourself as anything else? (I know this well because I have tried to change the tune in my brain for the past thirty years.)

My grandmother gave me *The Alchemist* because she knew it would help me see the world differently. In other words, that it would shift my perspective from a limited view of the world—through my lenses of constant financial challenges—to a much broader view of an expansive world, where dreams can become reality when we learn to change limiting messages broadcasting in our brains. Decades of neuroscience research now validate my grandmother's folk wisdom, and whether she knew it or not, she was actually helping me train my brain to be more flexible. Studies have pointed out that the ability to flex and alter our thinking (a skill referred to as *cognitive flexibility*) is directly related to greater resilience.[3] And it makes sense, doesn't it? If we can literally change the way we view ourselves and the world around us, it quickly becomes very easy to bend this skill to our advantage. If everything is an arbitrary story to some degree, then why not ensure that these stories help us live a more enjoyable life?

So here I am writing this book because, thirty years ago, an enthusiastic reader gave her grandkid her favorite book, and this book taught that kid to see her world in a totally different way. One of the most famous quotes from the book (and one of my favorites) goes like this: "When you want something, all the universe conspires in helping you to achieve it." Whenever I hit a roadblock on the way to my dreams, or in moments of fear, anxiety, or sadness, I tell myself this quote. Much like I urge you to talk to yourself as if you were talking to your best friend, I also practiced talking to myself like my grandmother was talking to me. Whenever avoidance knocks on my door, I still run this quote through the tape player of my mind.

To truly shift my perspective took many more years, many more books, and a lot of science. But for me, it all started with *The Alchemist*. I share this with you because one of my deepest desires for the book you now hold in your hands is that it can help you to shift from anxiety, burnout, stress, adversity, pain, and avoidance toward a better life, one that is in line with your heart's desire, where anxiety is transformed into power.

Throughout the book I have shared many of my own stories about times when my brain locks up and tells me that I am not enough, or that I'm an impostor waiting to be found out any minute. As I write this, I laugh because if I look at the objective data from my life, this statement is factually inaccurate. Because the brain remains a wonderful but occasionally faulty predictive machine that doesn't like to change its wiring,[4] it often reverts back to the old core beliefs that we created as children. But living a bold life is not about living a life without distorted or negative thoughts! It's about investing time to learn how to change those thoughts and to *Shift* your perspective again and again, to use compassion to talk to yourself as if you were your own best friend. This still might strike some of you as hokey, but why should we only wish good things for other people? Committing to your own bold life means acknowledging that you want yourself to be happy as much as you want your closest friends or family members to be happy.

Although *Shifting* your perspective is very powerful, it is not the only skill. The reality is that life is hard, and extreme challenges do happen. But thankfully there are two other skills you have learned that can make the journey a little easier, and my favorite one is to *Approach*.

Approach is often misunderstood as a skill because most of the time, when you find yourself stuck, you have already tried a million things to get unstuck. However, *Approach* as a skill is designed to exercise your brain, to teach you that you can calm the emotional brain and bring your thinking brain back online by practicing opposite action. By moving toward your discomfort and experiencing it, you begin to slowly fight the real enemy: avoidance.[5] While *Approach* is one of the superpowers derived from dialectical behavior therapy and cognitive behavioral therapy, it is also one of the hardest skills to practice. By definition, you are going to experience some level of discomfort as you *Approach*. It's like forcing yourself to get out of your warm bed and into a cold shower, even though you know that such a morning routine sets you up to kick ass during the day. While that warm bed feels nice in the short term, it is, metaphorically speaking, the real enemy. When you give in to its siren song, your life slowly becomes smaller and smaller.

My grandmother also taught me to *Approach* when she invited me (aka *forced* me) to talk to strangers as a teenager. After moving in with her in a much bigger city, my brain would scream at me, *People are scary, run away!* and I did just that, avoiding them and the resulting discomfort whenever I could. But instead of letting me sulk at home, my grandmother made me do just the opposite of what I wanted: talk to strangers (opposite action). So, just like how you must start exercising slowly to build competence and strength, you need to choose your *Approach* activities thoughtfully to ensure that you start with something realistic. While this process can be as slow as learning any skill, know this: our brain is an organ that can and does change, and with practice our fear and discomfort decrease.

As you begin to practice, I urge you to start slowly so you can identify your own flavor of avoidance. In addition, remind yourself that this will take time. If you find yourself stuck, you might need some extra guidance in the form of a professional. While I think this book provides many of the skills necessary to live that bold life, I also know that at times we need to see a mental health professional, and I often think of them as coaches. So just as a world-class athlete might need a coach from time to time to help refine a skill, you may find yourself looking for a nudge in the right direction as well. Never forget that to be bold when it comes to *Approaching* is to welcome a life that is always "comfortably uncomfortable." In my life, I've found that it is within this tension that the real pleasures of life are to be found.

Finally, we can't forget about our values. When I first started writing this book, I honestly had no idea the extent to which I had been avoiding living a values-driven life. I had totally ignored my own internal compass and was following the path that I felt the world at large had dictated for me. No one in particular was to blame for my blind approach, and no one was forcing me to live a certain way. But when you are consumed by your profession, your culture, and your bubble, it can often feel like there is only one path to success (however you're defining it), and for me, success meant pushing myself harder and harder to follow some vague sense of ambition. For many years, this definition of success worked out for me, but at a certain point it stopped working and I responded by avoiding this new reality. I often share with my clients that facing reality does not mean you have to *like* reality. But no matter how painful it is to face, ignoring reality is just another form of avoidance.

In a strange way, I am thankful for some challenges I faced at work in the past two years, because it was these conflicts that became the wake-up call for me to deeply revisit my own values. If you look behind the pain and interrogate it by asking yourself, *What would I have to not care about for this not to hurt?* you might be able to see the value that is being violated. As I shared with you, trust is something I need if I am to work with someone, and this ended up being the value that was being compromised in my professional life. That was the kiss of death.

As I searched for a more values-driven life, I started paying closer attention to my moments of joy. What was I doing when I felt the best? Who was I with? What brought me to that flow state? One of these joyful experiences was recording a course on managing anxiety with Dan Harris. I had met Dan when I was on his podcast in March 2020. The topic for that episode was anxiety, and if you were to look back at the date of the podcast, you'll recognize it as the beginning of the pandemic in the US. Neither one of us knew that day that the world would effectively shut down mere days after our recording.

Dan was lovely to work with, and about a year later he invited me to record a course with him for his app *Ten Percent Happier*. The process of developing the course with his team was great, but I especially enjoyed working with Dan. Anyone familiar with his interviews would know that he is an incredible interviewer, and the process of creating the course for him was thoroughly enjoyable. Above all, I noticed how happy I felt throughout this process. It felt as though I was hardly exerting myself, and yet the work was excellent (if I do say so myself). The experience of flow state can be a major indicator in helping you find your true values, because that is when you are acting in line with something that really matters to you, and that is why you may experience less stress during such periods. In fact, next time you come out of a flow state, ask yourself: *Forget about stress. Was I even aware of* myself *during that time?*

When I looked behind the pain at my job versus the contentment I felt when working with Dan, I realized that I needed to do something like that again, and that something became the book you now hold in your hands. Writing this book has been the most transformational piece of my working life, as it allowed me to massively realign my daily actions with my values. While I am not sure how the world will receive it, I am proud to have put down in these pages my own bold journey from poverty to Harvard to striking out on my own to become an author. As you *Align* your life with your values, fear will almost certainly show up. But being bold is not the same as being fearless. Being bold is living a life that is driven by what matters to you the most, no matter what, and doing so becomes one of the most beautiful rewards imaginable.

To bring it all together, I want to close this book with another piece of my grandmother's wisdom, as I think she had the perfect recipe for living a bold life. In one of our many afternoon coffee chats, we were discussing change and how most people go to extreme lengths to avoid it. My grandmother would say that there are two ways people respond to change. Some of us become like a rock, stuck in place and not wanting to move; we hold on to the old, while painfully fighting the new. If you are like the rock, you know what I am talking about. You might stay at a job even though you are miserable (just like I did) because you don't want to stir things up. Or maybe you're in a relationship that is not working, yet the fear of going out there and starting the uncomfortable process of dating again makes you stay put. Or you insist on your point of view in a disagreement, despite reams of evidence to the contrary. In my later years, I have come to understand that what my grandmother called "the rock" is the embodiment of "avoidance." In the end, avoidance is not about what we do or don't do; it is about the *why*. And if your why is to bring your emotional temperature down fast, you are likely avoiding. So, if you think about the description of being like a rock, my grandmother was basically saying that regardless of whether you are reacting, retreating, or remaining, you are simply refusing to change.

On the other hand, my grandmother would say that some of us behave more like water when it comes to dealing with change. When an obstacle is in your way, you become more flexible and adapt to whatever you find in your path. You might choose to go around the rock, underneath it, or over it, or even to shape the rock itself through your actions. Regardless of how you choose to adapt, the water continues to move no matter what. After all, the water in a flowing river is never still and is always changing. My grandmother was not saying that you should jump for joy when confronting change, but that flexibility and adaptability to change tend to have better outcomes.

So how do you become the water instead of the rock? The first step is to always identify avoidance. Though it can be sneaky at times, if you ask yourself whether or not you're doing X to feel better *right now* and the answer is *yes*, there is very likely some level of avoidance going on. Although all of us will avoid in different ways, the fact that you're doing something just to feel better *in the moment* is the key to identifying avoidance. Throughout your life, I can guarantee that you will avoid at times. And when you do, how you respond will determine what happens next. But as my stepdad used to say: you cannot win every battle in life, and you must lose a few to win the war. I think someone more famous actually said this first, but he is the one who taught me how to apply it to my life, so I will credit him. The point being, failure is necessary from time to time.

As a final reminder: we first *Shift* our perspective and look at the world from new angles. Then we *Approach*, moving toward and through the discomfort. Finally, we *Align* each of our actions toward our values. When done repeatedly and in various situations, these three moves will allow us to move like water even in the most challenging moments of our lives.

Being the water and not the rock is an alternative definition of living a bold life. If you look at the most amazing figures in history, like Martin Luther King Jr. or Thomas Edison, you will see individuals who flowed through their times, finding ways to keep going while being driven by a mission and a purpose. For them, being the rock stuck in place while change happened elsewhere was not an option. This water versus rock approach to a bold life can gracefully be summarized in the words of Oprah Winfrey: "When you meet obstacles with gratitude, your perception starts to shift, resistance loses its power, and grace finds a home within you."

So, here we are at the end of our time together. For me, the question remains: Am I enough? And when I ask myself this, I am inspired by Michelle Obama's memoir *Becoming*, in which she writes: "Am I good enough? Yes I am!" And so, even if my brain wants to think otherwise, I end my journey with you by affirming this to myself: YES I AM! As for you, from here on, you are in charge. I hope some of the lessons in this book will remain with you for the rest of your days, giving you guidance and focus when hard times come.

If I may be so bold, I'd like to offer you some final words of wisdom. First: life is hard and challenges are real. I wish I could say that you, dear reader, will be the first in human history to avoid a difficult time or two, but sure as the sun rises, Old Man Trouble has a way of finding us. But to this I say, fantastic. Difficult times shape us, and we can use them to our advantage. Avoidance is the enemy, so keep a close eye out for it. Finally, be bold by following the words from my sage grandmother: be the water, not the rock. Flow past the obstacles you face, and never stop moving toward your values. When in doubt, your values will never fail you. I'd like to thank you for taking this ride with me, and to wish you a bold, beautiful life. Go get it!

Gratitude

Every morning my son, Diego, wakes up and runs to my office. I can hear his little footsteps pounding on the floor as he rushes in to meet the day. He jumps into my arms, gives me a big hug, and then he is off to "work" in my office. Diego, who is five, has just learned what a computer mouse is during his summer camp, and so, every morning, he wants to use it so that he can become a more efficient writer. Yes, you read that right: Diego has informed me that he is writing his own book too. Today's chapter was called "My Mom Loves Me." Because I have been waking up at 3 a.m. to edit this book, by 7 a.m. I am (very) tired, more than a little cranky, and only semi-coherent. Turns out humans actually need sleep! #science! But as soon as my small human wraps his arms around me and I see the excitement on his face that marks the start of his day, all of my discomfort melts away. These morning interactions with Diego are the best distillation of gratitude I could ever share with you. It is almost like Diego knows that I need a little dose of his joy to keep me *Approaching* my discomfort about writing this book. I am so grateful for his love and support, and as I thank many of you here, I want you to know that if I could be with you right now, I would be giving you a "Diego hug" to ensure you too have the support you need during your challenging times.

The home front: Nothing happens in my life that is not accounted for by the fact that right next to me, holding me, assuring me, wiping my tears is my husband, *David*. David, you are my safe haven. I know this book was a lot of work for you too, and I will never be able to thank you enough. *Dieguito*: Your hugs, love, *and* very dramatic meltdowns are the best (and have provided more than a little inspiration for this book). You inspire me to be a better person daily. *Mamãe*: Although our narratives of life are different, our love has never changed. Thank you for standing by me always and for giving me the tools I needed to be who I am. *Juliana*: Your perseverance in the midst of "hell" inspires me! You are one powerful, badass woman! *Donna Maria Helena*, the woman I came to call my grandmother in my life: I wish you could read the Portuguese version of this book. Our years together transformed my journey, and I will continue to do that for those less fortunate in honor of your legacy. And for the rest of the family village behind this book, your love carried me through. Thank you *Familia Elias* and *Familia Zepeda*. And of course, to my stepdad, *Luiz Fernando Esteves Martins,* you have been more of a father to me than any father could ever be. I am very thankful for your eternal support, from the beginning of your relationship with my mom, but even more since you are no longer together. Through the years you have stood by me as a real dad does, and for that I am very grateful.

The life journey front: Although this book is as far from a memoir as it gets, the feeling I had writing it was what I imagine a writer might have at the conclusion of their memoir: a sense of looking over the arc of their life from thirty thousand feet up. With that point of view, I would be remiss if I didn't thank pivotal people who supported my journey. The tribe in Governador Valadares who supported us through the early age when things were challenging, I am very thankful to each of you. My dear friends who were also pivotal in my development, you know who you are, and you are in my heart!

Book front: Although this book is a culmination of many years of research, clinical work, community work, and my own life experience, it would not have been possible without the persuasion of my dear friend and colleague *Anna Bartuska*. Anna, I am so thankful that you saw in me what I had not seen. Thank you for pushing me to *Approach*. I'm so grateful that we made this book together. I can't wait to see how your amazing journey will turn out, and I will be there every step to support you! *Greg White*: Ticking time bombs, iguanas, and the like—your ability to elevate my writing to make it digestible to humans is just incredible. I hope to have you along for every book I ever write (*Bold Move 2: Bold and Furious; Bold Move 3: More Bolder, More Mover*). *Chris West*: The narrative clarity you brought to this book was invaluable. You helped me clarify the shape of this project and guided me toward my own bold move—thank you! *Dan Harris*: Thank you for pushing me to write this book. I know it was only one sentence of encouragement, but you opened doors and supported me through the process with kindness and generosity. *Mel Flashman*: What can I say? You are the best literary agent I could have asked for. Thank you for moving me toward my dreams.

HarperCollins: Thanks to everyone on the publishing team, and most importantly to *Elizabeth (Biz) Mitchell* and *Ghjulia Romiti*. Thanks for believing in *Bold Move* and for providing endless feedback while supporting my journey to the end. Your editorial support was key to ensuring this book is all it can be.

The professional front: First and foremost, I am forever thankful to the clients who have trusted their lives to my care. You have taught me more about the world than you can ever imagine. Your vulnerability and trust during our work together humbles me. Second, although I have shared a lot of challenges about my academic career at MGH/HMS, it is really important to me that I also thank the people who, throughout this process, have stood by me, cheered me on, allowed me to grow into my full "Latina self," and cherished my boldness, even at times when I myself didn't see it. I am thankful to each of you. *Derri Shtasel*: You have been my professional and personal true north for the past thirteen years. I have cried as often as I have laughed with you, and through my own developmental journey as a professional and a human, you have been the anchor that allowed me to always be me. I just love you so much and can't thank you enough for your kindness. *Maurizio Fava*: You have continued to surprise me as our chief. At each of my own crossroads in our department, you have stepped in and fought for fairness and equality whenever you were needed. I am thankful for your support while I wrote this book and also for you encouraging me to use my own voice, without oppression. *Guardia Banister*: What a blessing it was when you came into my life. The best thing you ever asked me was, "Are you being your best self?" I was not, and that was not acceptable for you. I am so glad you created space for me to transform into my full self. I would like to also thank the MGH Research Scholars program, which has recently funded a lot of my work training paraprofessionals in CBT, and especially the Rappaport Foundation for generously funding my MGH scholar work. Your generous support has ensured that hundreds of youth receive mental care aid through our training program. I also want to thank Mrs. Barbara Dalio and the CTOP team, who supported my work in CT, bringing many of these skills to organizations working with inner city youth. Your generosity and mission-driven work is an inspiration to me.

Finally, *the feedback village*: Thank you to all of you who read early chapters, provided feedback, and ensured that we could get to a solid manuscript. Your suggestions, challenges, and edits are why I think this book is great (or may I even say exceptional?): *Derri Shtasel*, *Ludmilla Ferreira*, *Gustavo Ferreira*, *Jennifer Duan*, *Dean Travers*, *and Laurel Zepeda*.

Notes

INTRODUCTION
Am I Enough?

1. J. J. Gross, "Emotion Regulation: Current Status and Future Prospects," *Psychological Inquiry* 26, no. 1 (2015): 1–26.

2. J. S. Beck, *Cognitive Behavior Therapy: Basics and Beyond* (New York: Guilford Publications, 2020); S. G. Hofmann, A. Asnaani, I. J. Vonk, A. T. Sawyer, and A. Fang, "The Efficacy of Cognitive Behavioral Therapy: A Review of Meta-analyses," *Cognitive Therapy and Research* 36, no. 5 (2012): 427–40; and D. David, I. Cristea, and S. G. Hofmann, "Why Cognitive Behavioral Therapy Is the Current Gold Standard of Psychotherapy," *Frontiers in Psychiatry* 4 (2018).

CHAPTER 1
Anxiety Is Painful but It Is *Not* What Is Keeping You Stuck

1. J. D. Power, A. L. Cohen, S. M. Nelson, G. S. Wig, K. A. Barnes, J. A. Church, A. C. Vogel, T. O. Laumann, F. M. Miezin, B. L. Schlaggar, and S. E. Petersen, "Functional Network Organization of the Human Brain," *Neuron* 72, no. 4 (2011): 665–78, https://doi.org/10.1016/j.neuron.2011.09.006.

2. J. B. Hutchinson and L. F. Barrett, "The Power of Predictions: An Emerging Paradigm for Psychological Research," *Current Directions in Psychological Science* 28, no. 3 (2019): 280–91, https://doi.org/10.1177/0963721419831992.

3. K. N. Ochsner and J. J. Gross, "The Neural Bases of Emotion and Emotion Regulation: A Valuation Perspective," in *Handbook of Emotion Regulation*, 2nd ed., ed. J. J. Gross (New York: Guilford Press, 2014).

4. Recent research has identified complex neural networks associated with emotion processing. However, the amygdala remains one of the core regions activated during emotion processing, expression, and regulation. See K. A. Lindquist, T. D. Wager, H. Kober, E. Bliss-Moreau, and L. F. Barrett, "The Brain Basis of Emotion: A Meta-analytic Review," *The Behavioral and Brain Sciences* 35, no. 3 (2012): 121–43, https://doi.org/10.1017/S0140525X11000446.

5. N. P. Friedman and T. W. Robbins, "The Role of Prefrontal Cortex in Cognitive Control and Executive Function," *Neuropsychopharmacology* 47, no. 1 (2022): 72–89; and A. R. Hariri, "The Corticolimbic Circuit for Recognition and Reaction," in *Looking Inside the Disordered Brain: An Introduction to the Functional Neuroanatomy of Psychopathology* (Sunderland, MA: Sinauer Associates, 2015).

6. S. Bishop, J. Duncan, M. Brett, and A. D. Lawrence, "Prefrontal Cortical Function and Anxiety: Controlling Attention to Threat-Related Stimuli," *Nature Neuroscience* 7, no. 2 (2004): 184–88, https://doi.org/10.1038/nn1173; and S. J. Bishop, J. Duncan, and A. D. Lawrence, "State Anxiety Modulation of the Amygdala Response to Unattended Threat-Related Stimuli," *The Journal of Neuroscience: The Official Journal of the Society for Neuroscience* 24, no. 46 (2004): 10364–68, https://doi.org/10.1523/JNEUROSCI.2550-04.2004.

CHAPTER 2
The Superpower You Never Knew You Had

1. David, Cristea, and Hofmann, "Why Cognitive Behavioral Therapy."

2. Hofmann et al., "The Efficacy of Cognitive Behavioral Therapy."

3. S. Joyce, F. Shand, J. Tighe, S. J. Laurent, R. A. Bryant, and S. B. Harvey, "Road to Resilience: A Systematic Review and Meta-analysis of Resilience Training Programmes and Interventions," *BMJ Open* 8, no. 6 (2018): e017858.

4. M. M. Linehan, *Cognitive-Behavioral Treatment of Borderline Personality Disorder* (New York: Guilford Publications, 2018).

5. S. C. Hayes, K. D. Strosahl, and K. G. Wilson, *Acceptance and Commitment Therapy* (Washington, DC: American Psychological Association, 2009).

6. A. T. Beck and M. Weishaar, "Cognitive Therapy," in *Comprehensive Handbook of Cognitive Therapy*, ed. A. Freeman et al. (New York: Springer, 1989), 21–36.

7. P. A. Resick, C. M. Monson, and K. M. Chard, *Cognitive Processing Therapy for PTSD: A Comprehensive Manual* (New York: Guilford Publications, 2016).

8. Beck, *Cognitive Behavior Therapy*.

9. L. Marques, N. J. LeBlanc, A. D. Bartuska, D. Kaysen, and S. Jeong Youn, "TEB Skills: Empower Youth and Build Resilient Communities Through Skills That Impact Thoughts, Emotions, and Behaviors," 2020, https://www.flipsnack.com/655ADEDD75E/teb-skills/full-view.html.

10. H. T. Ghashghaei, C. C. Hilgetag, and H. Barbas, "Sequence of Information Processing for Emotions Based on the Anatomic Dialogue Between Prefrontal Cortex and Amygdala," *Neuroimage* 34, no. 3 (2007): 905–23; and J. C. Motzkin, C. L. Philippi, R. C. Wolf, M. K. Baskaya, and M. Koenigs, "Ventromedial Prefrontal Cortex Is Critical for the Regulation of Amygdala Activity in Humans," *Biological Psychiatry* 77, no. 3 (2007): 276–84.

11. K. N. Ochsner, K. Knierim, D. H. Ludlow, J. Hanelin, T. Ramachandran, G. Glover, and S. C. Mackey, "Reflecting upon Feelings: An fMRI Study of Neural Systems Supporting the Attribution of Emotion to Self and Other," *Journal of Cognitive Neuroscience* 16, no. 10 (2004): 1746–72.

CHAPTER 3
Brain Chatter: Retreating to Avoid

1. M. Leonhardt, "60% of Women Say They've Never Negotiated Their Salary—and Many Quit Their Job Instead," *Make It*, January 31, 2020, https://www.cnbc.com/2020/01/31/women-more-likely-to-change-jobs-to-get-pay-increase.html.

2. B. Artz, A. Goodall, and A. J. Oswald, "Women Ask for Raises as Often as Men, but Are Less Likely to Get Them," *Harvard Business Review*, June 25, 2018, https://hbr.org/2018/06/research-women-ask-for-raises-as-often-as-men-but-are-less-likely-to-get-them.

3. K. G. Kugler, J. A. Reif, T. Kaschner, and F. C. Brodbeck, "Gender Differences in the Initiation of Negotiations: A Meta-analysis," *Psychological Bulletin* 144, no. 2 (2018): 198, https://doi.org/10.1037/bul0000135.

4. A. Barroso and A. Brown, "Gender Pay Gap in US Held Steady in 2020," Pew Research Center, May 25, 2021, https://www.pewresearch.org/fact-tank/2021/05/25/gender-pay-gap-facts.

5. Kugler et al., "Gender Differences in the Initiation of Negotiations"; and R. Kochhar, "Women's Lead in Skills and Education Is Helping Narrow the Gender Wage Gap," Pew Research Center, January 30, 2020, https://www.pewresearch.org/social-trends/2020/01/30/womens-lead-in-skills-and-education-is-helping-narrow-the-gender-wage-gap.

6. D. M. Wegner, D. J. Schneider, S. R. Carter, and T. L. White, "Paradoxical Effects of Thought Suppression," *Journal of Personality and Social Psychology* 53, no. 1 (1987): 5.

7. L. P. Riso, P. L. du Toit, D. J. Stein, and J. E. Young, *Cognitive Schemas and Core Beliefs in Psychological Problems: A Scientist-Practitioner Guide* (Washington, DC: American Psychological Association, 2007), xi–240.

CHAPTER 4
The Brain as a Faulty Predictive Machine

1. J. B. Hutchinson and L. F. Barrett, "The Power of Predictions: An Emerging Paradigm for Psychological Research," *Current Directions in Psychological Science* 28, no. 3 (2019): 280–91, https://doi.org/10.1177/0963721419831992.

2. R. Axelrod, "Schema Theory: An Information Processing Model of Perception and Cognition," *American Political Science Review* 67, no. 4 (1973): 1248–66.

3. E. Harmon-Jones and J. Mills, "An Introduction to Cognitive Dissonance Theory and an Overview of Current Perspectives on the Theory," in *Cognitive Dissonance: Reexamining a Pivotal Theory in Psychology*, ed. E. Harmon-Jones (Washington, DC: American Psychological Association, 2019), https://doi.org/10.1037/0000135-001.

4. M. E. Oswald and S. Grosjean, "Confirmation Bias," *Cognitive Illusions: A Handbook on Fallacies and Biases in Thinking, Judgement and Memory* (August 2004): 79, 83.

5. A. Kappes, A. H. Harvey, T. Lohrenz, P. R. Montague, and T. Sharot, "Confirmation Bias in the Utilization of Others' Opinion Strength," *Nature Neuroscience* 23, no. 1 (2020): 130–37.

6. K. Friston, "The Free-Energy Principle: A Unified Brain Theory?," *Nature Reviews Neuroscience* 11, no. 2 (2010): 127–38, https://doi.org/10.1038/nrn2787; and K. Friston, T. FitzGerald, F. Rigoli, P. Schwartenbeck, and G. Pezzulo, "Active Inference: A Process Theory," *Neural Computation* 29, no. 1 (2017): 1–49, https://doi.org/10.1162/NECO_a_00912.

7. J. T. Kaplan, S. I. Gimbel, and S. Harris, "Neural Correlates of Maintaining One's Political Beliefs in the Face of Counterevidence," *Scientific Reports* 6, no. 1 (2016): 1–11.

8. R. F. West, R. J. Meserve, and K. E. Stanovich, "Cognitive Sophistication Does Not Attenuate the Bias Blind Spot," *Journal of Personality and Social Psychology* 103, no. 3 (2012): 506–19, https://doi.org/10.1037/a0028857.

9. A. Grant, *Think Again: The Power of Knowing What You Don't Know* (New York: Penguin, 2021).

CHAPTER 5
Shifting to Overcome Avoidance

1. D. A. Clark, "Cognitive Restructuring," in *The Wiley Handbook of Cognitive Behavioral Therapy*, ed. D. J. A. Dozois, J. A. J. Smits, S. G. Hofmann, and W. Rief (Hoboken, NJ: Wiley, 2013), 1–22.

2. A. T. Beck, "The Current State of Cognitive Therapy: A 40-Year Retrospective," *Archives of General Psychiatry* 62, no. 9 (2005): 953–59.

3. D. D. van Bergen, B. D. Wilson, S. T. Russell, A. G. Gordon, and E. D. Rothblum, "Parental Responses to Coming Out by Lesbian, Gay, Bisexual, Queer, Pansexual, or Two-Spirited People Across Three Age Cohorts," *Journal of Marriage and Family* 83, no. 4 (2021): 1116–33.

4. W. S. Ryan, N. Legate, and N. Weinstein, "Coming Out as Lesbian, Gay, or Bisexual: The Lasting Impact of Initial Disclosure Experiences," *Self and Identity* 14, no. 5 (2015): 549–69.

5. C. Johnco, V. M. Wuthrich, and R. M. Rapee, "The Role of Cognitive Flexibility in Cognitive Restructuring Skill Acquisition Among Older Adults," *Journal of Anxiety Disorders* 27, no. 6 (2013): 576–84.

6. D. R. Dajani and L. Q. Uddin, "Demystifying Cognitive Flexibility: Implications for Clinical and Developmental Neuroscience," *Trends in Neurosciences* 38, no. 9 (2015): 571–78, https://doi.org/10.1016/j.tins.2015.07.003.

7. P. Colé, L. G. Duncan, and A. Blaye, "Cognitive Flexibility Predicts Early Reading Skills," *Frontiers in Psychology* 5 (2014): 565.

8. J. J. Genet and M. Siemer, "Flexible Control in Processing Affective and Non-affective Material Predicts Individual Differences in Trait Resilience," *Cognition and Emotion* 25, no. 2 (2011): 380–88.

9. W. L. Lin, P. H. Tsai, H. Y. Lin, and H. C. Chen, "How Does Emotion Influence Different Creative Performances? The Mediating Role of Cognitive Flexibility," *Cognition & Emotion* 28, no. 5 (2014): 834–44.

10. J. C. Davis, C. A. Marra, M. Najafzadeh, and T. Liu-Ambrose, "The Independent Contribution of Executive Functions to Health Related Quality of Life in Older Women," *BMC Geriatrics* 10, no. 1 (2010): 1–8.

CHAPTER 6

The Pressure Cooker: Reacting to Avoid

1. J. Perry, "Structured Procrastination," essay, accessed October 19, 2022, structuredprocrastination.com.

2. J. Suls, R. Martin, and L. Wheeler, "Social Comparison: Why, with Whom, and with What Effect?," *Current Directions in Psychological Science* 11, no. 5 (2002): 159–63.

3. A. Robinson, A. Bonnette, K. Howard, N. Ceballos, S. Dailey, Y. Lu, and T. Grimes, "Social Comparisons, Social Media Addiction, and Social Interaction: An Examination of Specific Social Media Behaviors Related to Major Depressive Disorder in a Millennial Population," *Journal of Applied Biobehavioral Research* 24, no. 1 (2019): e12158.

4. C. G. Escobar-Viera, A. Shensa, N. D. Bowman, J. E. Sidani, J. Knight, A. E. James, and B. A. Primack, "Passive and Active Social Media Use and Depressive Symptoms Among United States Adults," *Cyberpsychology, Behavior, and Social Networking* 21, no. 7 (2018): 437–43; and K. Burnell, M. J. George, J. W. Vollet, S. E. Ehrenreich, and M. K. Underwood, "Passive Social Networking Site Use and Well-Being: The Mediating Roles of Social Comparison and the Fear of Missing Out," *Cyberpsychology: Journal of Psychosocial Research on Cyberspace* 13, no. 3 (2019).

5. G. Holland and M. Tiggemann, "A Systematic Review of the Impact of the Use of Social Networking Sites on Body Image and Disordered Eating Outcomes," *Body Image* 17 (2016): 100–110.

6. C. L. Booker, Y. J. Kelly, and A. Sacker, "Gender Differences in the Associations Between Age Trends of Social Media Interaction and Well-Being Among 10–15 Year Olds in the UK," *BMC Public Health* 18, no. 1 (2018): 1–12.

7. J. Kang and L. Wei, "Let Me Be at My Funniest: Instagram Users' Motivations for Using Finsta (aka, Fake Instagram)," *The Social Science Journal* 57, no. 1 (2020): 58–71.

8. L. Silver, "Smartphone Ownership Is Growing Rapidly Around the World, but Not Always Equally," Pew Research Center, February 5, 2019, https://www.pewresearch.org/global/2019/02/05/smartphone-ownership-is-growing-rapidly-around-the-world-but-not-always-equally.

9. J. Turner, "Are There Really More Mobile Phone Owners than Toothbrush Owners?," LinkedIn, April 10, 2016, https://www.linkedin.com/pulse/really-more-mobile-phone-owners-than-toothbrush-jamie-turner.

10. J. D. Elhai, R. D. Dvorak, J. C. Levine, and B. J. Hall, "Problematic Smartphone Use: A Conceptual Overview and Systematic Review of Relations

with Anxiety and Depression Psychopathology," *Journal of Affective Disorders* 207 (2017): 251–59.

11. E. D. Hooker, B. Campos, and S. D. Pressman, "It Just Takes a Text: Partner Text Messages Can Reduce Cardiovascular Responses to Stress in Females," *Computers in Human Behavior* 84 (2018): 485–92.

12. L. Faul, D. Stjepanović, J. M. Stivers, G. W. Stewart, J. L. Graner, R. A. Morey, and K. S. LaBar, "Proximal Threats Promote Enhanced Acquisition and Persistence of Reactive Fear-Learning Circuits," *Proceedings of the National Academy of Sciences* 117, no. 28 (2020): 16678–89.

13. J. Booth, J. L. Ireland, S. Mann, M. Eslea, and L. Holyoak, "Anger Expression and Suppression at Work: Causes, Characteristics and Predictors," *International Journal of Conflict Management* 28, no. 3 (2017): 368–82.

14. D. Abadi, I. Arnaldo, and A. Fischer, "Anxious and Angry: Emotional Responses to the COVID-19 Threat," *Frontiers in Psychology* (2021): 3516.

15. N. G. Bayrak, S. Uzun, and N. Kulakaç, "The Relationship Between Anxiety Levels and Anger Expression Styles of Nurses During COVID-19 Pandemic," *Perspectives in Psychiatric Care* 57, no. 4 (2021): 1829–37.

CHAPTER 7

There's Science Behind Your Inner Hothead

1. S. J. Blakemore, "Imaging Brain Development: The Adolescent Brain," *Neuroimage* 61, no. 2 (2021): 397–406.

2. B. J. Casey, A. S. Heller, D. G. Gee, and A. O. Cohen, "Development of the Emotional Brain," *Neuroscience Letters* 693 (2019): 29–34, https://doi.org/10.1016/j.neulet.2017.11.055.

3. A. O. Cohen, K. Breiner, L. Steinberg, R. J. Bonnie, E. S. Scott, K. Taylor-Thompson, and B. K. Casey, "When Is an Adolescent an Adult? Assessing Cognitive Control in Emotional and Nonemotional Contexts," *Psychological Science* 27, no. 4 (2016): 549–62.

4. J. M. Cisler, B. O. Olatunji, M. T. Feldner, and J. P. Forsyth, "Emotion Regulation and the Anxiety Disorders: An Integrative Review," *Journal of Psychopathology and Behavioral Assessment* 32, no. 1 (2010): 68–82, https://doi.org/10.1007/s10862-009-9161-1.

5. A. S. Morris, M. M. Criss, J. S. Silk, and B. J. Houltberg, "The Impact of Parenting on Emotion Regulation During Childhood and Adolescence," *Child Development Perspectives* 11, no. 4 (2017): 233–38.

6. S. E. Crowell, M. E. Puzia, and M. Yaptangco, "The Ontogeny of Chronic Distress: Emotion Dysregulation Across the Life Span and Its

Implications for Psychological and Physical Health," *Current Opinion in Psychology* 3 (2015): 91–99; and F. Tani, D. Pascuzzi, and R. Raffagnino, "Emotion Regulation and Quality of Close Relationship: The Effects of Emotion Dysregulation Processes on Couple Intimacy," *BPA: Applied Psychology Bulletin (Bollettino di Psicologia Applicata)* 272, no. 63 (2015): 3–15.

7. A. Smyth, M. O'Donnell, G. J. Hankey, S. Rangarajan, P. Lopez-Jaramillo, D. Xavier, H. Zhang, M. Canavan, A. Damasceno, P. Langhorne, A. Avezum, N. Pogosova, A. Oguz, S. Yusuf, and INTERSTROKE Investigators, "Anger or Emotional Upset and Heavy Physical Exertion as Triggers of Stroke: The INTERSTROKE Study," *European Heart Journal* 43, no. 3 (2022): 202–9.

8. Smyth et al., "Anger or Emotional Upset."

9. M. A. Gruhn and B. E. Compas, "Effects of Maltreatment on Coping and Emotion Regulation in Childhood and Adolescence: A Meta-analytic Review," *Child Abuse & Neglect* 103 (2020): 104446.

10. K. A. McLaughlin, M. Peverill, A. L. Gold, S. Alves, and M. A. Sheridan, "Child Maltreatment and Neural Systems Underlying Emotion Regulation," *Journal of the American Academy of Child & Adolescent Psychiatry* 54, no. 9 (2015): 753–62.

11. V. J. Felitti, R. F. Anda, D. Nordenberg, D. F. Williamson, A. M. Spitz, V. Edwards, and J. S. Marks, "Relationship of Childhood Abuse and Household Dysfunction to Many of the Leading Causes of Death in Adults: The Adverse Childhood Experiences (ACE) Study," *American Journal of Preventive Medicine* 14, no. 4 (1998): 245–58.

12. "Fast Facts: Preventing Adverse Childhood Experiences," Centers for Disease Control and Prevention, last reviewed April 6, 2022, https://www.cdc.gov/violenceprevention/aces/fastfact.html.

13. "Adverse Childhood Experiences Resources," Centers for Disease Control and Prevention, last reviewed April 6, 2022, https://www.cdc.gov/violenceprevention/aces/resources.html.

14. S. R. Dube, V. J. Felitti, M. Dong, D. P. Chapman, W. H. Giles, and R. F. Anda, "Childhood Abuse, Neglect, and Household Dysfunction and the Risk of Illicit Drug Use: The Adverse Childhood Experiences Study," *Pediatrics* 111, no. 3 (2003): 564–72.

15. K. Hughes, M. A. Bellis, K. A. Hardcastle, D. Sethi, A. Butchart, C. Mikton, L. Jones, and M. P. Dunne, "The Effect of Multiple Adverse Childhood Experiences on Health: A Systematic Review and Meta-analysis," *The Lancet* 2 (2017): e356–66.

16. J. I. Herzog and C. Schmahl, "Adverse Childhood Experiences and the Consequences on Neurobiological, Psychosocial, and Somatic Conditions Across the Lifespan," *Frontiers in Psychiatry* 9 (2018): 420.

17. D. MacManus, R. Rona, H. Dickson, G. Somaini, N. Fear, and S. Wessely, "Aggressive and Violent Behavior Among Military Personnel Deployed to Iraq and Afghanistan: Prevalence and Link with Deployment and Combat Exposure," *Epidemiologic Reviews* 37, no. 1 (2015): 196–212.

18. Faul et al., "Proximal Threats."

19. J. Meloury and T. Signal, "When the Plate Is Full: Aggression Among Chefs," *International Journal of Hospitality Management* 41 (2014): 97–103.

20. C. Sandi and J. Haller, "Stress and the Social Brain: Behavioural Effects and Neurobiological Mechanisms," *Nature Reviews Neuroscience* 16, no. 5 (2015): 290–304.

21. L. J. Siever, "Neurobiology of Aggression and Violence," *American Journal of Psychiatry* 165, no. 4 (2008): 429–42.

22. Faul et al., "Proximal Threats."

23. R. F. Baumeister and M. R. Leary, "The Need to Belong: Desire for Interpersonal Attachments as a Fundamental Human Motivation," *Psychological Bulletin* 117, no. 3 (1995): 497–529.

24. G. M. Slavich, "Social Safety Theory: A Biologically Based Evolutionary Perspective on Life Stress, Health, and Behavior," *Annual Review of Clinical Psychology* 16 (2020): 265–95, https://doi.org/10.1146/annurev-clinpsy-032816-045159.

25. T. F. Stillman and R. F. Baumeister, "Uncertainty, Belongingness, and Four Needs for Meaning," *Psychological Inquiry* 20, no. 4 (2009): 249–51.

26. R. F. Baumeister, C. N. DeWall, N. J. Ciarocco, and J. M. Twenge, "Social Exclusion Impairs Self-Regulation," *Journal of Personality and Social Psychology* 88, no. 4 (2005): 589–604, https://doi.org/10.1037/0022-3514.88.4.589.

27. F. M. Begen and J. M. Turner-Cobb, "Benefits of Belonging: Experimental Manipulation of Social Inclusion to Enhance Psychological and Physiological Health Parameters," *Psychology & Health* 30, no. 5 (2015): 568–82; R. Renn, D. Allen, and T. Huning, "The Relationship of Social Exclusion at Work with Self-Defeating Behavior and Turnover," *Journal of Social Psychology* 153, no. 2 (2013): 229–49; and L. W. Hayman Jr., R. B. McIntyre, and A. Abbey, "The Bad Taste of Social Ostracism: The Effects of Exclusion on the Eating Behaviors of African-American Women," *Psychology & Health* 30, no. 5 (2015): 518–33.

28. J. Field and R. Pond, "How Adoption Affects the Experience of Adult Intimate Relationships and Parenthood: A Systematic Review," *New Zealand Journal of Counselling* 38, no. 2 (2018); and J. A. Feeney, N. L. Passmore, and C. C. Peterson, "Adoption, Attachment, and Relationship Concerns: A Study of Adult Adoptees," *Personal Relationships* 14, no. 1 (2018): 129–47.

29. K. Beesdo-Baum, E. Jenjahn, M. Höfler, U. Lueken, E. S. Becker, and

J. Hoyer, "Avoidance, Safety Behavior, and Reassurance Seeking in Generalized Anxiety Disorder," *Depression and Anxiety* 29, no. 11 (2012): 948–57.

30. P. R. Shaver, D. A. Schachner, M. Mikulincer, "Attachment Style, Excessive Reassurance Seeking, Relationship Processes, and Depression," *Personality and Social Psychology Bulletin* 31, no. 3 (2005): 343–59.

31. A. Levine and R. Heller, *Attached: The New Science of Adult Attachment and How It Can Help You Find—and Keep—Love* (New York: Penguin, 2012).

32. O. S. Candel and M. N. Turliuc, "Insecure Attachment and Relationship Satisfaction: A Meta-analysis of Actor and Partner Associations," *Personality and Individual Differences* 147 (2019): 190–99.

33. J. D. Power and B. L. Schlaggar, "Neural Plasticity Across the Lifespan," *Wiley Interdisciplinary Reviews: Developmental Biology* 6, no. 1 (2017): e216.

34. B. Brady, I. I. Kneebone, N. Denson, and P. E. Bailey, "Systematic Review and Meta-analysis of Age-Related Differences in Instructed Emotion Regulation Success," *PeerJ* 6 (2018): e6051.

35. S. E. Valentine, E. M. Ahles, L. E. Dixon De Silva, K. A. Patrick, M. Baldwin, A. Chablani-Medley, D. L. Shtasel, and L. Marques, "Community-Based Implementation of a Paraprofessional-Delivered Cognitive Behavioral Therapy Program for Youth Involved with the Criminal Justice System," *Journal of Health Care for the Poor and Underserved* 30, no. 2 (2019): 841–65, https://doi.org/10.1353/hpu.2019.0059.

36. Valentine et al., "Community-Based Implementation."

37. L. Marques, S. J. Youn, E. D. Zepeda, A. Chablani-Medley, A. D. Bartuska, M. Baldwin, and D. L. Shtasel, "Effectiveness of a Modular Cognitive-Behavioral Skills Curriculum in High-Risk Justice-Involved Youth," *The Journal of Nervous and Mental Disease* 208, no. 12 (2020): 925–32.

CHAPTER 8

A Move That Changes the Game

1. Beck, *Cognitive Behavior Therapy*.

2. M. M. Linehan, *Dialectical Behavior Therapy in Clinical Practice* (New York: Guilford Publications, 2020); and C. Dunkley, *Regulating Emotion the DBT Way: A Therapist's Guide to Opposite Action* (New York: Routledge, 2020).

3. Levine and Heller, *Attached*.

4. S. Compernolle, A. DeSmet, L. Poppe, G. Crombez, I. De Bourdeaudhuij, G. Cardon, and D. Van Dyck, "Effectiveness of Interventions Using Self-Monitoring to Reduce Sedentary Behavior in Adults: A Systematic Review and Meta-analysis," *International Journal of Behavioral Nutrition and Physical Activity* 16, no. 1 (2019): 1–16.

5. Linehan, *Dialectical Behavior Therapy.*

6. D. Ben-Porath, F. Duthu, T. Luo, F. Gonidakis, E. J. Compte, and L. Wisniewski, "Dialectical Behavioral Therapy: An Update and Review of the Existing Treatment Models Adapted for Adults with Eating Disorders," *Eating Disorders* 28, no. 2 (2020): 101–21.

7. S. N. Frazier and J. Vela, "Dialectical Behavior Therapy for the Treatment of Anger and Aggressive Behavior: A Review," *Aggression and Violent Behavior* 19, no. 2 (2014): 156–63.

8. N. Warner and M. Murphy, "Dialectical Behaviour Therapy Skills Training for Individuals with Substance Use Disorder: A Systematic Review," *Drug and Alcohol Review* 41, no. 2 (2022): 501–16.

9. E. McCauley, M. S. Berk, J. R. Asarnow, M. Adrian, J. Cohen, K. Korslund, and M. M. Linehan, "Efficacy of Dialectical Behavior Therapy for Adolescents at High Risk for Suicide: A Randomized Clinical Trial," *JAMA Psychiatry* 75, no. 8 (2018): 777–85.

10. T. R. Lynch, J. Q. Morse, T. Mendelson, and C. J. Robins, "Dialectical Behavior Therapy for Depressed Older Adults: A Randomized Pilot Study," *The American Journal of Geriatric Psychiatry* 11, no. 1 (2003): 33–45.

11. S. Dymond, "Overcoming Avoidance in Anxiety Disorders: The Contributions of Pavlovian and Operant Avoidance Extinction Methods," *Neuroscience and Biobehavioral Reviews* 98 (2019): 61–70, https://doi.org/10.1016/J.NEUBIOREV.2019.01.007.

12. P. Ekman, R. J. Davidson, and W. V. Friesen, "The Duchenne Smile: Emotional Expression and Brain Physiology: II," *Journal of Personality and Social Psychology* 58, no. 2 (1990): 342.

13. Ekman, Davidson, and Friesen, "The Duchenne Smile."

14. F. L. Gardner and Z. E. Moore, "Understanding Clinical Anger and Violence: The Anger Avoidance Model," *Behavior Modification* 32, no. 6 (2008): 897–912.

15. M. Jungmann, S. Vencatachellum, D. Van Ryckeghem, and C. Vögele, "Effects of Cold Stimulation on Cardiac-Vagal Activation in Healthy Participants: Randomized Controlled Trial," *JMIR Formative Research* 2, no. 2 (2018): e10257, https://doi.org/10.2196/10257.

CHAPTER 9

Should I Stay or Should I Go? Remaining to Avoid

1. Hayes, Strosahl, and Wilson, *Acceptance and Commitment Therapy.*

2. E. D. Reilly, T. R. Ritzert, A. A. Scoglio, J. Mote, S. D. Fukuda, M. E. Ahern, and M. M. Kelly, "A Systematic Review of Values Measures

in Acceptance and Commitment Therapy Research," *Journal of Contextual Behavioral Science* 12 (2019): 290–304; and K. G. Wilson and A. R. Murrell, "Values Work in Acceptance and Commitment Therapy," *Mindfulness and Acceptance: Expanding the Cognitive-Behavioral Tradition* (2004): 120–51.

3. S. H. Schwartz, J. Cieciuch, M. Vecchione, E. Davidov, R. Fischer, C. Beierlein, A. Ramos, M. Verkasalo, J.-E. Lönnqvist, K. Demirutku, O. Dirilen-Gumus, and M. Konty, "Refining the Theory of Basic Individual Values," *Journal of Personality and Social Psychology* 103, no. 4 (2012): 663–88.

4. A. T. Gloster, N. Walder, M. E. Levin, M. P. Twohig, and M. Karekla, "The Empirical Status of Acceptance and Commitment Therapy: A Review of Meta-analyses," *Journal of Contextual Behavioral Science* 18 (2020): 181–92.

5. "Stress Effects on the Body," American Psychological Association, November 1, 2018, https://www.apa.org/topics/stress/body.

6. T. C. Russ, E. Stamatakis, M. Hamer, J. M. Starr, M. Kivimäki, and G. D. Batty, "Association Between Psychological Distress and Mortality: Individual Participant Pooled Analysis of 10 Prospective Cohort Studies," *BMJ* 345 (2012).

7. I. Guseva Canu, S. C. Marca, F. Dell'Oro, Á. Balázs, E. Bergamaschi, C. Besse, R. Bianchi, J. Bislimovska, A. Koscec Bjelajac, M. Bugge, C. I. Busneag, Ç. Çağlayan, M. Cernițanu, C. Costa Pereira, N. Dernovšček Hafner, N. Droz, M. Eglite, L. Godderis, H. Gündel, J. J. Hakanen, and A. Wahlen, "Harmonized Definition of Occupational Burnout: A Systematic Review, Semantic Analysis, and Delphi Consensus in 29 Countries," *Scandinavian Journal of Work, Environment & Health* 47, no. 2 (2021): 95–107, https://doi.org/10.5271/sjweh.3935.

8. "Burn-out an 'Occupational Phenomenon': International Classification of Diseases," World Health Organization, May 28, 2019, https://www.who.int/news/item/28-05-2019-burn-out-an-occupational-phenomenon-international-classification-of-diseases; and C. Maslach, S. E. Jackson, and M. P. Leiter, "Maslach Burnout Inventory: 3rd ed.," in *Evaluating Stress: A Book of Resources*, ed. C. P. Zalaquett and R. J. Wood (Lanham, MD: Scarecrow Education, 1997), 191–218.

9. "Employee Burnout Is Ubiquitous, Alarming—and Still Underreported," McKinsey & Company, April 16, 2021, https://www.mckinsey.com/featured-insights/coronavirus-leading-through-the-crisis/charting-the-path-to-the-next-normal/employee-burnout-is-ubiquitous-alarming-and-still-underreported.

10. "Workplace Burnout Survey," Deloitte, accessed October 19, 2022, https://www2.deloitte.com/us/en/pages/about-deloitte/articles/burnout-survey.html.

CHAPTER 10
But Why Do I Stay?

1. M. M. Linehan, *Skills Training Manual for Treating Borderline Personality Disorder* (New York: Guilford Press, 1993).

2. S. M. Brown, S. B. Manuck, J. D. Flory, and A. R. Hariri, "Neural Basis of Individual Differences in Impulsivity: Contributions of Corticolimbic Circuits for Behavioral Arousal and Control," *Emotion* (Washington, DC) 6, no. 2 (2006): 239–45, https://doi.org/10.1037/1528-3542.6.2.239.

3. S. Dawe and N. J. Loxton, "The Role of Impulsivity in the Development of Substance Use and Eating Disorders," *Neuroscience & Biobehavioral Reviews* 28, no. 3 (2004): 343–51; and T. M. Pronk, J. C. Karremans, and D. H. J. Wigboldus, "How Can You Resist? Executive Control Helps Romantically Involved Individuals to Stay Faithful," *Journal of Personality and Social Psychology* 100, no. 5 (2011): 827–37, https://doi.org/10.1037/a0021993.

4. A. Wigfield and J. S. Eccles, "The Development of Competence Beliefs, Expectancies for Success, and Achievement Values from Childhood Through Adolescence," *Development of Achievement Motivation* (2022): 91–120.

5. J. M. Dickson, S. Johnson, C. D. Huntley, A. Peckham, and P. J. Taylor, "An Integrative Study of Motivation and Goal Regulation Processes in Subclinical Anxiety, Depression and Hypomania," *Psychiatry Research* 256 (2017): 6–12.

6. A. Winch, N. J. Moberly, and J. M. Dickson, "Unique Associations Between Anxiety, Depression and Motives for Approach and Avoidance Goal Pursuit," *Cognition and Emotion* 29, no. 7 (2015): 1295–305.

7. H. C. Triandis, *Individualism and Collectivism* (New York: Routledge, 2018).

8. J. W. Berry, "Acculturative Stress," in *Handbook of Multicultural Perspectives on Stress and Coping*, ed. P. T. P. Wong and L. C. J. Wong (Boston: Springer, 2006), 287–98.

9. L. G. Castillo, M. P. Zahn, and M. A. Cano, "Predictors of Familial Acculturative Stress in Asian American College Students," *Journal of College Counseling* 15, no. 1 (2012): 52–64.

10. Gloster et al., "The Empirical Status."

CHAPTER 11
Calibrating Your Inner Compass

1. Beck, *Cognitive Behavior Therapy*; and S. Carvalho, C. P. Martins, H. S. Almeida, and F. Silva, "The Evolution of Cognitive Behavioural Therapy: The

Third Generation and Its Effectiveness," *European Psychiatry* 41, no. S1 (2017): s773–74.

2. Hofmann et al., "The Efficacy of Cognitive Behavioral Therapy."

3. A. O'Neil, S. E. Quirk, S. Housden, S. L. Brennan, L. J. Williams, J. A. Pasco, and F. N. Jacka, "Relationship Between Diet and Mental Health in Children and Adolescents: A Systematic Review," *American Journal of Public Health* 104, no. 10 (2014): e31–42; A. J. Scott, T. L. Webb, M. Martyn St. James, G. Rowse, and S. Weich, "Improving Sleep Quality Leads to Better Mental Health: A Meta-analysis of Randomised Controlled Trials," *Sleep Medicine Reviews* 60 (2021): 101556; and A. L. Rebar, R. Stanton, D. Geard, C. Short, M. J. Duncan, and C. Vandelanotte, "A Meta-meta-analysis of the Effect of Physical Activity on Depression and Anxiety in Non-clinical Adult Populations," *Health Psychology Review* 9, no. 3 (2015): 366–78.

14. S. R. Chekroud, R. Gueorguieva, A. B. Zheutlin, M. Paulus, H. M. Krumholz, J. H. Krystal, and A. M. Chekroud, "Association Between Physical Exercise and Mental Health in 1.2 Million Individuals in the USA Between 2011 and 2015: A Cross-sectional Study," *The Lancet Psychiatry* 5, no. 9 (2018): 739–46.

5. J. Kabat-Zinn, "Mindfulness," *Mindfulness* 6, no. 6 (2015): 1481–83.

6. S. B. Goldberg, R. P. Tucker, P. A. Greene, R. J. Davidson, B. E. Wampold, D. J. Kearney, and T. L. Simpson, "Mindfulness-Based Interventions for Psychiatric Disorders: A Systematic Review and Meta-analysis," *Clinical Psychology Review* 59 (2018): 52–60.

7. R. F. Adler and R. Benbunan-Fich, "Juggling on a High Wire: Multitasking Effects on Performance," *International Journal of Human-Computer Studies* 70, no. 2 (2012): 156–68.

8. K. E. May and A. D. Elder, "Efficient, Helpful, or Distracting? A Literature Review of Media Multitasking in Relation to Academic Performance," *International Journal of Educational Technology in Higher Education* 15, no. 1 (2018): 1–17.

9. Hayes, Strosahl, and Wilson, *Acceptance and Commitment Therapy.*

10. Gloster et al., "The Empirical Status."

11. Hayes, Strosahl, and Wilson, *Acceptance and Commitment Therapy.*

12. Hayes, Strosahl, and Wilson, *Acceptance and Commitment Therapy.*

13. S. C. Hayes, *A Liberated Mind: How to Pivot Toward What Matters* (New York: Penguin, 2020); and J. A. Stoddard and N. Afari, *The Big Book of ACT Metaphors: A Practitioner's Guide to Experiential Exercises and Metaphors in Acceptance and Commitment Therapy* (Oakland, CA: New Harbinger Publications, 2014).

14. S. Grégoire, M. Doucerain, L. Morin, and L. Finkelstein-Fox, "The

Relationship Between Value-Based Actions, Psychological Distress and Well-Being: A Multilevel Diary Study," *Journal of Contextual Behavioral Science* 20 (2021): 79–88.

15. C. L. Caldwell-Harris, "Emotionality Differences Between a Native and Foreign Language: Implications for Everyday Life," *Current Directions in Psychological Science* 24, no. 3 (2015): 214–19.

16. D. W. Sue, C. M. Capodilupo, G. C. Torino, J. M. Bucceri, A. Holder, K. L. Nadal, and M. Esquilin, "Racial Microaggressions in Everyday Life: Implications for Clinical Practice," *American Psychologist* 62, no. 4 (2007): 271.

17. P. P. Lui and L. Quezada, "Associations Between Microaggression and Adjustment Outcomes: A Meta-analytic and Narrative Review," *Psychological Bulletin* 145, no. 1 (2019): 45.

18. R. L. Gobin and J. J. Freyd, "The Impact of Betrayal Trauma on the Tendency to Trust," *Psychological Trauma: Theory, Research, Practice, and Policy* 6, no. 5 (2014): 505.

19. M. E. Levin, M. J. Hildebrandt, J. Lillis, and S. C. Hayes, "The Impact of Treatment Components Suggested by the Psychological Flexibility Model: A Meta-analysis of Laboratory-Based Component Studies," *Behavior Therapy* 43, no. 4 (2012): 741–56.

20. J. D. Doorley, F. R. Goodman, K. C. Kelso, and T. B. Kashdan, "Psychological Flexibility: What We Know, What We Do Not Know, and What We Think We Know," *Social and Personality Psychology Compass* 14, no. 12 (2020): 1–11.

21. Simon Sinek's bio, https://simonsinek.com/simons-bio.

22. S. Sinek, *Start with Why: How Great Leaders Inspire Everyone to Take Action* (New York: Penguin, 2009).

CHAPTER 12

Becoming Bold by Being the Water, Not the Rock

1. Harmon-Jones and Mills, "An Introduction to Cognitive Dissonance Theory"; and Oswald and Grosjean, "Confirmation Bias": 83.

2. M. Costandi, *Neuroplasticity* (Cambridge, MA: MIT Press, 2016); and J. Shaffer, "Neuroplasticity and Clinical Practice: Building Brain Power for Health," *Frontiers in Psychology* 7 (2016): 1118. https://doi.org/10.3389/fpsyg.2016.01118.

3. Genet and Siemer, "Flexible Control in Processing."

4. Friston, "The Free-Energy Principle"; and Friston et al., "Active Inference."

5. Dymond, "Overcoming Avoidance in Anxiety Disorders."